Libraries and the Search
for Academic Excellence

Libraries and the Search for Academic Excellence

Edited by

Patricia Senn Breivik
and
Robert Wedgeworth

THE SCARECROW PRESS, INC.
Metuchen, N.J., & London   1988

Library of Congress Cataloging-in-Publication Data

Libraries and the search for academic excellence / edited by Patricia Senn
Breivik, Robert Wedgeworth.
       p.   cm.
   Papers from the National Symposium on Libraries and the Search
for Academic Excellence held March 15-17, 1987 at Columbia University's
Arden House – Pref.
   Includes bibliographies and index.
   ISBN 0-8108-2157-5
   1. Libraries, University and college – United States – Congresses.
2. Libraries and education – United States – Congresses. I. Breivik, Patricia
Senn. II. Wedgeworth, Robert. III. National Symposium on Libraries and
the Search for Academic Excellence (1987 : Columbia University's Arden
House)
Z675.U5L44 1988
027.7'0973 – dc19   88-15855

Table of Contents

Preface   1

1. Connectivity
   by Ernest L. Boyer   3

2. The Academic Library and Education for Leadership
   by Major R. Owens   13

3. Libraries and Learning
   by E. Gordon Gee and Patricia Senn Breivik   25

4. The Academic Library and the Non-Traditional Student
   by Colette A. Wagner in consultation with Augusta S. Kappner   43

5. Excellence in Education: Libraries Facilitating Learning
   for Minority Students
   by James A. Hefner and Lelia G. Rhodes   57

6. Libraries and the Humanities: A Case for Scholarly Activism
   by Charles T. Cullen   75

7. Academic Libraries and Teacher Education Reform:
   The Education of the Professional Teacher
   by Jo Ann Carr and Kenneth Zeichner   83

8. Fostering Research
   by Herbert C. Morton and Sharon J. Rogers   93

9. The Jewel in the Temple: University Library Networks
   as Paradigms for Universities
   by Louis Vagianos and Barry Lesser   105

10. Academic Libraries and Regional Economic Development
    by Joan B. Fiscella and Joan D. Ringel   127

11. Technology and Transformation in Academic Libraries
    by Ward Shaw   137

12. It's Academic: The Politics of the Curriculum
    in American Higher Education
    by Irving J. Spitzberg, Jr.   145

13. Learning Technologies: Problems and Opportunities –
    Summary of Panel Discussion   165

14. Strategies for Improved Use of Libraries in Support of Academic
    Excellence – Summary of Panel Discussion   169

15. Academic Libraries and the American Resurgence
    by Frank Newman   173

16. Discussion Outcomes and Action Recommendations   187

17. Symposium Participants   195

    Index
    Compiled by Bettie Jane Third   197

Preface

Libraries may be poetically referred to as the heart of the university, but like the physical heart, they are largely ignored unless there is a major problem. Despite the realities of the Information Age in which the current and all future generations must exist, it seemed likely that education's current reform cycle would be completed without a serious examination of the role of libraries in the search for high quality education. Two events changed this situation. The Carnegie Foundation's report, *College*, released late in 1986, stated that the way to measure the quality of a college is "by the resources for learning on the campus and the extent to which students become independent, self-directed learners." The second event was the holding of the first higher education conference on academic libraries on March 15-17 at Columbia University's Arden House.

The national Symposium on Libraries and the Search for Academic Excellence was a joint effort of the University of Colorado and Columbia University. Columbia's involvement was the first in a series of activities to honor the hundredth anniversary of library education in the United States, which began at its institution. The Symposium marked the first time these two institutions had worked together on an academic issue. The Symposium convened seventy-two persons, including higher education faculty and administrators, librarians and library educators plus a scattering of representatives from business, government, and educational institutions.

Ten papers were commissioned to address the overriding themes of the educational reform reports and to explore how institutions were using or could use their libraries to achieve related campus objectives. These papers, which were not formally presented but were used as background for the discussions held at the Symposium, are included in this volume along with the speeches made at the Symposium by Ernest Boyer on "Connectivity," and by U.S. Representative Major R. Owens on "The Academic Library and Education for Leadership." Also included are Frank Newman's summary of the Symposium, recommended action items and discussion highlights – all of which reflect the high quality of the participants and their ability to make their own connections on this important topic in a most expeditious manner. This book is dedicated to those leaders who attended the Symposium, and in particular to University of Colorado President, E. Gordon Gee, who was the driving force behind the effort.

While the Symposium was useful in terms of the experience of the participants, its ultimate success will have to be judged by whether an impetus is created for thoughtful educators across the country to take a new look at their academic libraries. Until libraries are assessed and then empowered in terms of achieving the educational goals of their institutions, the primary source of information on campuses, the library, will continue to be "on the bench" while higher education seeks to provide high-quality education for the Information Society. Moreover, the nation will lose a valuable asset in its struggle to improve education.

Patricia Senn Breivik
Robert Wedgeworth

September 1987

Connectivity

by Ernest L. Boyer

In 1871, a relatively unkown Republican politician addressed the alumni at a
dinner at Williams College. "The ideal college," he said, "is Mark Hopkins at
one end of the log and the student at the other." The speaker was James A.
Garfield, who became the 20th President of the United States. But nothing
Garfield said during his tragically short term in office was to be as well remembered as his romanticized view of the American College.

Today, no one even remotely familiar with the modern college or university with its classrooms and stadiums and its student unions would compare
the campus to a log – a jungle perhaps – but surely not a single log. Still,
President Garfield's touching image of Williams College reminds us that
Americans have a love affair with collegiate education.

During the past three years, we at the Carnegie Foundation have been
looking at undergraduate education in the United States, and we conclude
that America's higher learning institutions are the envy of the world. We have
over 3,200 colleges and universities and over 12,000,000 students, and college remains, in this nation, the ladder to success. Indeed, while about 56
percent of today's high school graduates are going on to college, 96 percent
of all the parents we surveyed said they hoped their children would go on to
college someday.

I do not mean to suggest that all young people should attend college. I
only say that the genius of our system is the inspiration that education offers.
The nation's mood was captured by a student who said to one of our researchers, "I want a better life for myself; that means college."

During our recent study of the undergraduate college, we found great
achievements, but we found challenge as well. And this evening I should like
to focus on four issues that connect the future of the college to the theme of
this conference – excellence through the library resources on the campus. In
fact, everything that I shall say this evening can be summarized in the simple
word "connections."

I. The first issue we address in our report has to do with the connections
between the schools and higher education.

During our study we repeatedly heard faculty complain about the academic quality of their students. In our national survey of 5,000 faculty we
found that more than half of them rated the academic preparation of their
students as only "fair" or "poor." Incidentally, this negative rating has increased eight percentage points since the Carnegie Foundation last conducted a survey in 1976. Eighty-three percent of the faculty said that today's

high school students should be academically better prepared. And two-thirds agreed that their institution spends too much time and money teaching students what they should have learned in school.

There is, to put it simply, a dramatic distance between the expectations of faculty and the academic preparation of their students. And the failure, in large measure, has to do with the students' capacity to read and write.

The use of symbols is the condition that sets human beings apart from all other forms of life. I am convinced that if colleges and schools could empower students in the use of language that effort would bring excellence to education. And libraries and learning resources have an absolutely central role to play in affirming the dignity and the majesty and the sacredness of language. I'll reverse the proposition: if we do *not* have a culture that affirms the centrality of language, there is no possibility that the role of the library and learning symbols can be central on the campus or even strategic in the learning patterns of the student.

We found during our study that some colleges are giving English proficiency examinations to their students. But many of these tests focus far too much on the *mechanics* of language rather than on its *meaning*. The head of the English Department at one university in our study said: "in this state we have now imposed a state-wide English test. And yet, the test devastates the content of our composition program." He said, "Our teaching tends to focus on the minimum, not the maximum; a circumstance that guarantees mediocrity in the end."

Last year, the National Assessment for Educational Progress released a significant report on adult literacy in the United States. The report concludes that – based on UNESCO standards of literacy – almost all Americans are literate; that is, they can read and write and recognize words in isolation. But a large percentage of the Americans could not comprehend even simple passages. To put it another way, there was recognition of the words but there was no insight and understanding as to content.

I am suggesting that this conference on libraries and the information revolution address itself first to this issue: Are we educating our students to be proficient in the written and the spoken word? Are we preparing graduates who are able not only to read and write, but also to think critically, draw inferences, and convey subtle shades of meaning?

Here I should make an essential point: language begins long before the student marches off to college. Indeed, I suspect that language begins in utero as the unborn child monitors the mother's voice. My wife, who is a certified nurse/midwife, insists that, at birth, the child turns almost instinctively to identify the mother, having monitored that voice for some weeks prior to the birth.

We do know that during pregnancy the young child responds with a startle reflex to noises outside the mother's body. We know that if you hold your ears and speak, you can monitor your own voice through the vibrating tissue of your body. We also know that the three middle ear bones – the hammer, the anvil, and the stirrup – are the only bones that are fully formed at birth.

Certainly the young child extends this majestic and miraculous process we call language, first through guttural utterances and then through phonemes, simple words, and finally through complex sentence structures that convey subtle shades of meaning. And now that I am a grandfather, and can observe this process unencumbered by dirty diapers and burpings late at night, I am absolutely in awe of the majesty and the miracle of the symbol system.

Lewis Thomas wrote that "childhood is for language," and it is my belief that our search for excellence in education should begin with the conviction that nothing is more powerful than a spoken message; both as an expression of joy and as a weapon, as well.

When I was a boy we used to say "sticks and stones will break my bones but names will never hurt me." What nonsense! I used to say it with tears running down my cheeks. Hit me if you must but for goodness sake stop those painful words.

For several years I have paid tribute to my first grade teacher, who on the first day of school, said, "Good morning class, today we learn to read." Those were the first words I ever heard in school, and no one said, "No, not today. Let's string beads." If Miss Rice said today we learn to read, we learn to read. I really did think that you went to school to learn to read; that schooling was synonymous with the empowerment of the symbol system. And on that first day we spent all day on four words, "I go to school." We traced them, we sang them, and God forgive her, we even prayed them. (Incidentally, on that delicate subject, I heard recently that there is one school prayer which is acceptable to all: "Dear God, don't let her call on me today.")

I find it mystical that when we at the Foundation got around to writing our report *High Schools*, and then *College*, I had a chapter in each of those books on the centrality of language. And if I write a report on graduate school, I guarantee you there will be a chapter on the essentialness of language. All of this because an unheralded first grade teacher taught me that language is not just another subject. It's the means by which all other subjects are pursued.

In the Carnegie *College* report, we say that colleges can be no stronger than the nation's schools, and one of the major points that connects them is the urgent need to develop writing skills and speaking skills in the early years. If students do not have a good foundation, remediation will never do the job and the libraries will remain as under-used as they are today.

Another point. In the Carnegie report we do not only stress reading – we give priority to *writing*, too, because it's through writing that clear thinking can be taught. You hear a lot of talk these days about teaching critical thinking. I do not know how you teach students to think critically unless they are asked to write and then have those thoughts carefully critiqued.

Oral communication should be emphasized as well. I was at a distinguished university about a month ago and one of the professors asked a group of seniors, "How many of you could go through four years of this college and never say one word in class?" Seventy-five percent of the students raised their hands.

I am talking about the empowerment of language. It starts before children go to school. It is enhanced by teachers in the early grades who either stir or diminish a love of language, and I believe that if we give as much status to first grade teachers as we do to full professors, that one act alone would enormously strengthen education. Can students, at an early age, become proficient in the written and the spoken word? If we can achieve that goal, much of the concern about books and the effective use of learning resources on the campus will be dramatically reduced.

While talking about the connectiveness of education, there is a related issue to be faced. The sad fact is that parents do not read aloud to children, and high school seniors actually spend less time reading books than do fourth graders in this culture. Indeed, the budget for books in preschools is disgraceful. In 1983, the minimum rate of expenditure for books for high school libraries was $3.71 per pupil. And while the price of children's books has risen 30 percent since 1970, the average per pupil expenditure for books in the schools has increased about 7 percent. It's especially alarming that in many high schools the library has become little more than a study hall, or, worse still, a detention center. It is where custodial activities are carried on for children who are misbehaving in the classroom.

To put it bluntly, most students during twelve years of formal learning are given no training as to how to use the library nor do they discover the richness it contains. Again, we cannot provide an enriching climate on the campus, without asking what is going on before in the twelve years of study and the home environment.

I would also like to suggest that, in the end, language has to do, not just with clear thinking, but with integrity as well. Several centuries ago the Quakers would risk prison and even death because in court they would refuse to swear to tell the truth, the whole truth, and nothing but the truth, so help me God. The problem was not just that they were against swearing, although they were. The larger problem was their unwillingness to swear to tell the truth in *court*, suggesting that *outside* the courtroom truth might be an option. After all, wasn't truthfulness something that one should just assume, not something that one would swear to only under oath? And so, in the court of law they would look to the judge and say in their quiet way, "Your Honor, I speak the truth."

Well, that perhaps is too fine a point to draw, especially if your head is on the block. But there is a larger issue at stake. The use of symbols is not simply a mechanism to complete an academic exercise. It is in fact a sacred trust; and as individuals refine their linguistic skills, there emerges a whole new quality of thinking, and they become intellectually and socially empowered. This vision is transcendentally important, and to achieve this end, colleges must work closely with the public schools.

II. This leads to priority number two. Not only do we need to strengthen connections between colleges and the schools, we also must find ways to strengthen the connections between the classroom and other learning resources on the campus. The truth is that students spend only 12 to 14 hours every week in class and they spend over 150 hours doing other things. We know they sleep and eat occasionally. But students should also become self-directed learners. The classroom, we say in our report, should be a place where learning just begins. Yet we found that life outside the classroom does not stir a vigorous intellectual quest and faculty often do not see a connection between classroom learning and other resources on the campus.

Especially disturbing is the neglect of libraries. In our survey of 5,000 undergraduates we found that 65 percent of them use the library four hours or less each week. One out of four undergraduates we surveyed said that they never go into the library. This means that of 5,000 undergraduates we surveyed from coast to coast, about half spent no more than two hours a week in the library.

Further, most students said they came to the library because they needed a quiet place to study. One freshman put it this way: "there is no other good place to study on this campus. In the dorm, something is going on around the clock: My roommates play records all the time and so I go to the library to get some peace and quiet. I do not check out books, but at least I can concentrate on what I am doing."

I am all for finding quietness for study, but the library should be viewed as something other than a retreat from chaos in the dorm. And yet, also through our survey, we discovered that over half the students never use the library to consult specialized bibliographies or to read a basic document. Forty percent never use the library to run down leads or to look for further references.

Harvey Branscomb, in a 1940 study of college libraries, concluded that some of the blame for the underuse of the libraries might be assigned to librarians themselves. He said that "librarians are placing more and more emphasis on acquisition and preservation than on use." There may be some truth to this conclusion but the responsibility for disconnectedness must also be shared by the professsors. We found that textbooks dominate the teaching, and only occasionally during our campus visits was the library mentioned; and even then the reference was to put books on reserve. Here was a typical comment from the professor: "I put several books on the reserve shelf you should read this term." Then he added almost glibly, "But you'd better grab them early because they usually disappear or get cut up." There was a chuckle in the nervous class. All this seems to trivialize the view of the student as an independent self-directed learner.

In our report, *College: The Undergraduate Experience in America*, we conclude that the library must be viewed as a vital part of the undergraduate experience. We suggest that the college has an obligation to support the library adequately and to sustain the culture of the book.

For five years I have served with Daniel Boorstin on the Board of the Center for the Book at the Library of Congress. I am mindful of the new sources of knowledge. But there is something special about the printed page, and unless students have a love for books, unless the habit of reading is firmly established by the time the students graduate from college, there is little chance that it will develop once occupational and family cares take over. On the other hand, if students discover the joy of reading independently, colleges may not need to worry about covering all education before graduation.

Learning will be life-long.

In our report on *College* we say that for the library to become a central learning resource on the campus, we need liberally educated librarians – professionals who understand and are interested in undergraduate education, who themselves are involved in educational matters, and who can build connections between the classroom and the rest of campus life.

III. This leads to priority number three. To achieve excellence in undergraduate experience there also should be a connectedness between general and specialized education on the campus. During our study we were struck that the baccalaureate experience is divided between general education and the academic major. It's the 2+2 arrangement which encourages students to divide study between the liberal and the useful arts. In the ideal world, specialists would be joined by the generalists, and students would combine their work with the values of a liberal education.

During my days in government I would often be seated at a table where experts were trying to prove their competence as specialists. But as I look back, almost all the really tough questions that we studied had less to do with specialized knowledge than with insights, wisdom, even compassion. The kinds of questions we talked about were these: Should HEW fund gene splicing research that might introduce new mutations on the planet Earth? How could we keep human subjects from being harmed during experiments in the lab? And how could the city of Chicago desegregate its public schools in a way that would serve all children in the face of the flight to the suburbs?

One of the urgent challenges of the undergraduate college is to break down the artificial division between generalized and specialized education and to put the major in historical, ethical and social perspective. Students must find ways to blend the liberal and the useful arts. Eric Ashby wrote on one occasion that the path to culture should be through a man and woman's specialization, not by bypassing it. "A student who can weave his technology into the fabric of society can claim to have a liberal education," Ashby said. But a student who cannot weave his technology into the fabric of society "cannot claim even to be a good technologist."

IV. This brings me back to the learning resource centers on the campus. It is my own opinion that students as they move from the freshman to the senior year should become increasingly self-sufficient. They should move into the library and the learning resource centers and become self-directed. By the time they are seniors, is it too much to expect that they will begin to integrate the larger fields of study and create interdisciplinary perspectives in order to put their own learning in a larger context? In the end, the librarian should be a guide and mentor to the students. Those in charge of information services on the campus should be renaissance people who guide students and help them discover relationships that no single department and no single professor can provide.

The model of the undergraduate experience we propose would be one in which students become increasingly independent, increasingly creative, increasingly able to integrate knowledge across the disciplines. As they advance toward their senior year, students would spend less time in the classroom, and more time consulting other information sources. The library would serve as the coordination center on the campus. This, to me, is the vision of the ideal collegiate education.

V. One final point. As I look toward the year 2000, I am convinced that there must be a connection between the formal and informal teachers in the culture. When I grew up in southern Ohio, half a century ago, we had a Silver-Tone radio at home, a little Sears and Roebuck model, which introduced me to the outside world. We received only one magazine, the *National Geographic*, and I learned my geography and my anatomy from that source. We had a Ford that, with luck, would take us 50 or 100 miles from home. I did not see television until our high school graduating class traveled to Radio City in New York where there was a demonstration model, a little 10-inch screen. I stood there with my girl friend and the guide said that the signal we were all viewing on the screen was the image of someone six floors below. I was skeptical and said to my girl friend "nothing will ever come of this." She thought I meant our romance, and walked off in a huff.

Today, children view 5,000 hours of television before they even go to school. They spend 15,000 hours in front of the television before they graduate from high school and spend only 11,000 hours with teachers. Today students are, through the "informal teachers," extending their knowledge at exponential rates and the teacher in a formal structure of learning is viewed by some as obsolete.

When I marched off to school I viewed my teacher reverentially. I believed everything she said. She was almost saint-like. Today children are no longer in awe of teachers. With the explosion of sources of information available to children, there are no secrets left. Childhood is disappearing. We have created an awesome extension of the channels of knowledge and yet we pretend that teachers are the only sources when, in fact, our children and our students know otherwise. They come to school with a certain skepticism. When teenagers were asked in 1960 "What influences you the most?" they listed teachers and parents first. When the same question was asked in 1980, peers and television had moved close to the top. I am convinced that if schools and colleges could use technology – television, computers, video cassettes, for example – more effectively, we could have in this country the best educated generation in many decades. It's scandalous that with so many sources of knowledge available, we talk about adult illiteracy and ignorance among our children!

I leave you with this question: How can we, in the years ahead, bring together the formal and informal teachers in our nation? How can we create networks of learning in which teachers become the guides? How can we help students become empowered to study on their own? I am convinced that unless we achieve these goals teachers will go through classroom rituals while the informal teachers will dominate and powerfully influence the coming generation.

If those assembled in this room encourage colleges and schools increasingly to use learning centers on the campus, our students will become increasingly empowered, truly educated human beings. If they fail to use the full range of learning opportunities available, the potential of our students will be enormously diminished.

Conclusion

Here then is my conclusion: To strengthen collegiate education, we must strengthen the connections between the colleges and schools, between the classroom and the other resources of learning on the campus, between general and specialized education, and, in the end, between formal and informal teachers in our culture. And in all of this the librarian has a crucial role to play. As we depend increasingly on your vision and your knowledge, the student will become empowered and the search for academic excellence will be enormously enhanced.

The Academic Library and Education for Leadership

by Major R. Owens

"*Human history* becomes more and more a race between education and catastrophe." This quotation from H.G. Wells' *Outline of History* is well-known, but familiarity does not increase its compact profundity. It is a basic truth, a warning which, when not heeded, causes massive dislocation and suffering. It is a living prophecy that foreshadows the decline and fall of societies, nations, world religions, and political ideologies. And as human history progresses, education becomes more and more a matter of education for leadership.

In the global village which we now inhabit, numerous nations are losing the education race. They do not have a large enough group of leaders able to manage the complexities of their national situations, and they are not capable of educating enough leaders to meet their needs. But we do not need to go to other nations to see the failure of education to keep pace in this escalating race. In the United States, numerous industries and neighborhoods are suffering their own small catastrophes as they find their workers and leaders inadequately trained, prepared, and educated for the tasks they face.

Throughout human history, the survival of the group has always depended on the fitness of its leaders. As civilization has evolved, the only change in this rule has been in the definition of and the requirements for "fitness." Fitness is no longer defined by the brute strength to wield a club or throw a spear, or by the skill to use a sword effectively. Even the strategic and tactical genius employed by the best World War II military commanders is now obsolete. For centuries, diplomatic and negotiating skills have been as important as military combat skills; today, they have been elevated far higher.

The primary mission of any college or university is the training of leaders. Colleges and universities have an obligation to produce leaders, leaders with the skills and qualifications needed to ensure their societies' survival and fitness. The primary skills our leaders need today are those of research, writing, rhetoric, statistical calculation, computer conceptualization, and media manipulation. No set of institutions other than colleges and universities has the ability or the capacity to develop these skills in large numbers of people.

The people who are fortunate enough to receive college training automatically become members of the elite group. All college students anywhere in the world belong to an elite. The overwhelming majority of the people of the world never graduate from high school; mere admission to a college places one in a special class. Even in America, all students who receive higher education belong to a select body, whether they attend an Ivy League school or a recently established public community college.

Education produces leaders; it brings privileges and honors; but along with these privileges and honors come the obligations of leadership. Society has a right to expect that the graduates of higher education institutions will be capable of assuming leadership and will be willing to exercise that leadership for the good of all members of society. Society has a right to expect that college graduates will be better prepared than non-graduates to lead in their area of expertise, in their neighborhoods, their cities, their states, their nations, and their world. Society has a right to insist that the small minority that has been provided with higher education must strive to understand the complexities of the world, must act as a resource when their leadership is needed.

When the development of leadership is seen as a primary concern of higher education, the role of the academic library assumes new dimensions. In addition to its traditional supportive role, the university library should also be a major vehicle for leadership education. To make its unique contribution to the mission of leadership development, the academic library must strive to establish and maintain the highest common denominator on campus.

If the library is to fulfill its potential it must be a salon for the setting of universal aesthetic standards and intellectual values, a permanent exhibit of the powers and benefits of information literacy, a general information smorgasbord where specialists may diversify their diets; a window on local events; a well-placed watch-tower overlooking our global village; and a multi-media kiosk continually highlighting leadership data. No other campus component or department has the resources or the capacity to present these personal development opportunities to the total university community.

A more specific exposition of the role of the academic library in citizenship and leadership education could begin with the four library-related recommendations in the recently released report of the Carnegie Foundation for the Advancement of Teaching, *College: The Undergraduate Experience in America.*

Recommendation #1: That all undergraduates should be given bibliographic instruction and be encouraged to spend as much time in the library as they spend in class. This call for more bibliographic instruction is an ancient wail. But while the higher education community repeatedly and accurately identifies this priority need, there is little evidence of any widespread resolve to take a few simple steps to remedy the problem.

College students often receive a negative and ridiculous introduction to the campus library through a unit of their freshman composition class on "bibliographic instruction." One weekend assignment requiring the "treasure hunt" style pursuit of a set of standard questions via certain standard library tools is the total mandated bibliographic study for most of the nation's entering classes. After that introduction, as noted in the Carnegie Report, for all except a small percentage, the library becomes a trysting place or the quietiest place to study when cramming for an examination.

Campus administrators sincerely seeking to close this long-standing shortcoming might begin by integrating the libraries more thoroughly with the general academic program. While physical education is often a required course with at least one unit of credit, very seldom is credit given for a library sponsored bibliographic instruction course. Perhaps the neanderthal notions which still exist to deny faculty status to librarians are a part of this problem. Or, perhaps, except for a few unusual campuses, librarians have never made a convincing case for their mainstream involvement in the training of leaders. In this fundamental area – bibliographic instruction – most academic libraries lose their first opportunity to become the highest common denominator on the campus.

In addition to bibliographic instruction taught by librarians, colleges should also consider offering as an elective a general research and methods course taught by librarians. Students should not be compelled to wait until graduate school before they are allowed to upgrade their general information literacy. The ability to apply information to whatever tasks are encountered is one definition of information literacy. Or, stated in another manner, it may be deemed the ability to maximize the utilization of information in problem-solving. One synonym for information literacy might be "information engineering."

Students gain information literacy or learn information engineering in their own areas of specialization. Colleges go out of business when they are not able to adequately train specialists. The campus library and its librarians may serve as a major resource in completing the education of all students by increasing their competency as generalists. *To be capable of assuming responsibilites as a leader, each college graduate must possess competency as a generalist as well as competence as a specialist.* There is no automatic or inevitable contradiction or collision between these two goals. An assumption that this is another way of making the argument for a liberal arts core program on every campus would be a correct assumption. Unfortunately, liberal arts advocates are seldom creative enough to include the campus library or the disciplines of library science in their programs. This blind spot has hurt the much-needed liberal arts efforts a great deal.

Consider the fact that the "survey" courses which most liberal arts programs endorse have for a long time been the victim of almost as much misguided undergraduate contempt as the campus library. Only the most creative teachers have been able to inspire respect for a given field through survey courses mandated for students who are specialists in some other field. The pre-law students ridicule the required science survey courses as much as the chemistry majors ridicule the required literature courses. Meanwhile, on very few campuses have there been experiments designed to achieve the broadening of each student's education by requiring courses similar to the "literature" courses offered in library schools.

Why not have specialists approach the study of areas where they are not seeking in-depth specialized knowledge in order to prepare for the next higher step in the learning chain by studying the "literature" or "materials" or "information" environment for that discipline? The courses that librarians have traditionally called literature of the social sciences, sciences, fine arts, technology, business and commerce, etc. are courses which cover the videotapes, microfilms, computer programs, films, audiotapes and electronic databases, as well as print items. Students exposed to an examination of the total information environment of an unfamiliar discipline would probably complete the course with an abiding respect for that field. At the same time a framework would be established for the lifetime pursuit of any facet of the subject which may have aroused an unusual interest.

Needless to say, students thus exposed would view the campus library with a light that fosters greater comprehension of the total potential of the library to enhance their intellectual growth and development. Exposure to the library science brand of "literature" courses would develop an understanding of how and where to find information relevant to a particular field; how to compare sources; how to check for accuracy, validity and timeliness; and how to search fruitfully within the full universe of available information.

Recommendation #2: That colleges should "sustain the culture of the book" through such activities as author visits and faculty seminars on influential works. An extension of the commentary offered above on Recommendation #1 quickly reveals the gross inadequacy and outdated conceptualization underlying this second recommendation. Attempting to "sustain the culture of the book" is a rather precious and quaint way to approach today's college students. A more creative attempt to develop an appreciation for the "information culture" with a bold assumption that the book, that is, the printed word, remains as the foundation for all information and communication would be more timely and more likely to achieve the desired objectives. A wide range of library activities designed to promote and illuminate the information culture is needed and also doable within the milieu of present day campus life.

Making the kind of "bibliographic instruction" breakthrough into the mainstream of the academic program advocated in the above response to the first recommendation of the Carnegie Report may prove to be exceedingly difficult. Moving back to the supplementary or enrichment posture which is more traditional for libraries places the campus library and librarians on more practical ground. Exhibits and library programs are routine enterprises. Whether such exhibits and programs are supervised by the library professional with the least seniority (as is too often the case) or by a specialist in public relations, such tasks would prove to be easy ones if done in the usual mode with the usual spirit and attitude.

But in order for the library to fulfill its function in the overall process of educating leaders by becoming the place of the highest common denominator on campus, the usual mode, spirit and attitude must be discarded. Instead of viewing the the exhibit and programming component of the library's mission as a window dressing operation – the parsley sprinkled over the main course; instead of assuming a museum-like posture, these activites should be infused with new energy and creativity.

Why not begin on every campus with at least one central and permanent library-based or library-supervised exhibit designed to demonstrate the vital role of information in the local, national and global decision-making environment? Why not a facility patterned after the "Situation Room" of the U.S. State Department? Such an exhibit must have certain permanent features such as a set of clocks which tell the time in five to ten major cities in the world; globes and maps which cover the entire world; more detailed map renditions of the campus locale, the city and the state; and an information resource map showing library and information facilities throughout the city and the state.

Among the free-standing items there should be a demonstration computer solely for the purpose of illustrating the role of the computer in data gathering and information dissemination. In some highly visible spot there should be a simple, old-fashioned, brightly-colored kiosk where any person may post items. In addition to microfilm and micro-card readers containing the most needed campus life and local information (as determined by campus librarians), there should be an accessible set of videotape players with a supply of video cassettes for review by individual students on general matters ranging from the campus library processes of acquisition, classification, processing and dissemination of learning materials to a history and structure of the faculty and student governing bodies. Video cassettes evaluating the best available materials on marriage and parenting should be included, since the majority of the students will ultimately get married and become parents. Similar material on how to build a personal and family library with an extensive section on children's books and materials is an absolute necessity.

Several electronic screens must be placed on highly visible walls to provide ongoing updates of rapidly changing information of importance to all of the university community. Included there must be a screen for world, national and local economic data. Students who will become leaders, regardless of their areas of specialization, must learn that the gyrations of the stock market, the changes in the national unemployment rate, budget deficit, and other similar indices are matters which will have an impact on their lives and the lives of those they will lead. Also, the changing prices of gold, oil, cotton and other commodities as well as the balance of payments for international trade, the number of new housing starts, the consumer price index: all are examples of what must be made familiar to future leaders.

Another electronic screen should feature important developments in the scientific, technological and medical world which are likely to impact on the general populace. General education and cultural developments which are not likely to be covered in other available media should be featured on another screen. Included here would be listings and annotations of significant current books, video cassettes, television documentaries, etc. In addition to providing current information, the contents of such electronic screens, as well as the other items in the "Situation Room" type exhibit, would display to the students a great deal about the ability of librarians to select relevant items from among the vast global sea of information being generated each month, week and day.

In addition to the awareness and information gained from the subject contents, students would learn a great deal about the essence of librarianship from such an exhibit. Every educated person should learn how to better extract information of value from the total universe of information. All educated persons should develop skills which enable them to take a chaotic batch of information and impose some system which creates order. In these areas librarians are the experts. Librarians dare to select from that complex flood of information materials being generated. And librarians dare to impose order, not by "shushing" people in a room, but by carving a niche for any fragment of information that appears and by facilitating the retrieval of that fragment of information when it is needed.

Of course the "Situation Room" permanent exhibit must contain books and other printed materials. A wide range of significant types and prototypes of materials must be available for hands-on examination. Needless to say there should be a sampling of reference tools for each major discipline. The spirit of the "literature course" approach outlined above must be kept alive. But there should also be a section for children's books and a section for foreign books and periodicals. The complete English language translation of *Pravda* must be made available. The exhibit which starts with the "Situation Room" motif thus will be enlarged into an "Information Amphitheater."

Programs to promote and illuminate the "culture of information" should be conducted in a spirit which parallels the thrust of the "Information Amphitheater." Entrepreneurs from the information industry should be invited in addition to book authors and editors. Nothing would enhance the "culture of the book" more than expositions by the producers of outstanding television documentaries. Such lectures would dramatically illustrate the role of the printed word in the monumental tasks of researching and pre-shooting preparation for the film medium. And likewise, computers never get programmed without extensive advance print work. Speakers who reveal and review the volumes of instructional materials that must be prepared to facilitate the operation of computers and other technological wonders would generate greater respect for the book.

In addition to persons knowledgeable about micro segments of the information culture, the campus library programs would seek to expose students to the experts who have key roles in the macro information world. The Librarian of Congress; the Chief Librarian of the CIA; the manager of the New York Times information service; the Army Colonel in charge of U.S. Army information systems; the publisher of *World Book Encyclopedia;* top agents and editors who have produced several best-selling novels within the last decade; the Chief of Communications for the White House; all of these are persons who conduct information engineering on a high level or a mass level. These and other similar persons possess the capacity to impressively promote and illuminate the "culture of information" as well as "enhance the culture of the book."

Recommendation #3: That support for the purchase of books should be increased, with a minimum of five percent of the college's operating budget going to libraries. And now the neanderthal limitations of the best available conventional thinking are shamefully exposed. Is the five percent recommended here for the purchase of books or is this five percent for the total expenditures for libraries? If the five percent is for books, then there should be another five percent for the more expensive non-print materials and services.

Without unduly belaboring the point, there is at least one compelling question to be asked. How does the five percent figure compare to the expenditure of colleges for athletics? If per capita formulas were used, would the amount spent per school on each athlete be greater or less than the per capita amount expended for library materials? Should the great universities strive to spend at least twice as much per student on library materials as they spend per athlete on the sports program?

One can readily see that while the recommendation that support for the purchase of books should be increased is a welcome statement, the failure to recognize the need for the more expensive learning materials inhibits any move to make the library a more active and relevant component of the mission to train leaders. The kind of mind-expanding "Information Amphitheater" approach discussed above requires not only an extensive initial capital outlay for equipment and facilities alterations, it also necessitates a significant additional expenditure for non-print materials.

Most higher education faculty members would argue that the books must come first. But this conventional assumption is no longer a self-evident one. If teaching is the prime concern of the college professor, then it would be negligent to ignore the contributions which non-print materials make to the process of learning. More than fifty years ago the United States armed forces learned that one visual image is worth a thousand words in the teaching process. As the items to be learned grow more complex, visual images do not become less effective. Indeed the geniuses who may become pioneers on the abstract scientific and technological frontiers of tomorrow have often decided to pursue the subject only after having their imaginations fired up by some specific film, video or television presentation. Even still photographs from outer space have recruited far more promising young physicists, astronomers and geologists than the printed theories and predictions could ever inspire.

In literature and the social sciences, visual images are equally as potent. Certainly a more thorough preparation of competent generalists can be achieved through non-print media. To understand this assertion, consider the "trigger principle" in communication. At one end of the spectrum non-print media is not at all concerned about clarifying and highlighting what appears in print. Bits of data fed into computers or electronic transmission devices are examples of this kind of raw information. At the other extreme, beginning with charts, graphs and photographs and moving to video and film, non-print is usually seeking to summarize, clarify and highlight information that already exists in print and could be thoroughly explained when committed to print. These non-print items, in reality, are nothing more than "triggers" in the learning process. The "triggers" on the movie screen, the video or audio cassette, or the television screen set off a search for more information.

When handled properly, a documentary on Halley's Comet can "trigger" a search for hundreds of books and articles. *Eyes on the Prize,* a documentary about the American Civil Rights Movement currently being aired on public television throughout the nation, is a magnificent work of art which may stand alone without the embellishment of other materials. However, each episode about this recent controversial and dramatic chapter in American history stimulates a desire to go search out the answers to certain questions that are raised. Or, in some cases, a need is generated to close the gap or complete an outline of events or a sketch of a key personality. In most of these instances the search for more information can be satisfied only with print materials. The end of the information-seeking chain reaction "triggered" by television is usually a book.

Which is most important and which must be purchased first, print or non-print materials? The question is an obsolete one when you are concerned with training students to be competent generalists as well as competent specialists.

Recommendation #4: That colleges should work with local schools and community libraries to help strengthen library holdings. Strengthening information systems for both its students and the general populace should be a concern of the university library. Certainly, the preparation of students for leadership is enhanced through the interaction between the campus and the community. Although the campus is not an ivory tower, it is a place where students and faculty are freed from the pressures of day to day reality in order to pursue more long-term goals. Some degree of involvement with the community is highly desirable to prevent campus inhabitants from acquiring a distorted view of reality.

Institutional interaction is highly desirable. In too many instances individual students and faculty members have used community groups for their own research purposes and then disappeared, leaving a bitter remembrance. Both the college and the community would benefit from a more formal set of cooperative agreements. The campus library would obviously be compatible with local public libraries, special libraries, school and other university libraries. Already libraries are ahead of many other institutions or campus departments in achieving a high degree of resource sharing with surrounding communities.

But the sharing is usually among professionals and scholars. And the sharing is usually an activity which involves the movement of materials from collections to persons with the capacity to identify their own needs. New York City is second to none in achieving this kind of cooperation. Columbia University has contributed greatly to this effort. But in very few places in the nation is there a joint effort among libraries to promote and illuminate the "culture of information."

The "Information Amphitheater" approach described above looms as a monumental undertaking; however, for a consortium of libraries, the project would be far less awesome. Why not have the college, neighborhood and municipality collaborate on a project which all students and all citizens may utilize? Average citizens need to undergo certain mind-expanding experiences which heighten their awareness of the information environment around them and nurture insights as to how they may use that environment.

In other words, part of the campus library's effort to contribute toward the development of students capable of serving as leaders would also be useful in encouraging citizens to function better or inspiring more self-education utilizing all available media.

To use a hypothetical but not far-fetched example: If a great university like Columbia University decided to construct an "Information Amphitheater" of the kind enumerated above, it would be wise to make the facility available to the general public. Such a gesture might encourage immediate municipal participation in the funding. Of still greater importance is the fact that great corporations like IBM, Xerox and Lockheed would probably be willing to donate the entire facility and thus reap the benefits of the public appreciation which would be engendered. A state of the art, technologically exciting illumnination of the role of the "culture of information" in today's world and in the next century would represent a monumental achievement.

In addition to serving as a magnificent training laboratory for Columbia students, the exhibit would be one of Emerson's "better mousetraps" encouraging ordinary citizens to "beat a path" to its door.

Columbia University would be an ideal sponsor for such an undertaking. The School of Library Service would be the most appropriate "lead" department for the development of such a facility. The entire national community of academic librarians and schools of library science should be called upon to help meet the challenge of designing a facility that would serve the basic purpose and at the same time be exciting. Technological freakishness would not be allowed to take over if librarians remain in control and retain a clear vision of the results being sought.

The "Information Amphitheater" must impact on individuals at several levels. First, it must be capable of creating a kind of positive "information shock" for the student or citizen on tour for the first time. Second, the experience must be a seductive one which brings each initial visitor back for subsequent visits and more detailed exploration of the "Information Amphitheater." And finally, the amphitheater exposure must be a "trigger" experience which stimulates life-long exploration and utilization of libraries, other information facilities and a wide variety of information materials and products.

This unusual or even extreme example of a state of the art "Information Amphitheater" at Columbia with joint government and corporate participation is not a recommendation for a standard or usual procedure. Academic libraries across the country are not expected to emulate such a model. The expectation is that the principle of the core "Situation Room" supplemented with more immediately utilitarian information equipment and library tools to make an "Information Amphitheater" will be implemented on some scale in any college or university library concerned with making a more profound and lasting contribution to the process of better educating students to be leaders.

In summary and conclusion, it should be noted that the proposition is a simple one. Academic libraries can play a major role assisting with education for leadership. To serve as leaders, college graduates must be competent generalists as well as competent specialists. The notion that one can be a competent generalist is not widely understood or accepted. But it is a concept at the very heart of the library profession. There is also a critical need in our society for more competent generalists, since competent specialists are able to lead only in their chosen field of specialization. College graduates will be called upon to provide leadership of many kinds at many levels. A thorough immersion in the "culture of information" contributes greatly to the achievement of competence as a generalist.

Emphasis on a "culture of information" is very much in harmony with the liberal arts program advocated by the leadership of most college administrations. The failure to more fully involve the campus library and campus librarians has contributed greatly to the difficulties experienced by core liberal arts programs. Instead of being stimulated by the generalist component of their education, most students develop contempt for those courses required to "round off" their education.

Academic librarians can make a vital contribution by pressing for greater involvement in bibliographic instruction and by promoting the format utilized in graduate library school "literature" courses. The greatest innovation, however, which academic libraries may accomplish could be implemented within the context of current academic library functions. Combining its obligation to provide a library orientation for all students with its obligation to "sustain the culture of the book" and its obligation to promote and illuminate the "culture of information," the academic library should develop an "Information Amphitheater" as a major vehicle for contributing to the education of leaders.

Such an "Information Amphitheater" could simply be fashioned out of a more imaginative use of space in rotundas and hallways. Or it could be achieved via the conversion of an existing "exhibition" room within the campus library. Or it would be possible to convert or build a facility outside of the library building but operated under supervision of campus librarians.

The recommendations contained in this discussion are generally in harmony with the recommendations concerning libraries contained in the recently released Carnegie Foundation report on U.S. colleges. In every instance, however, the Carnegie report has been deemed to be too conventional and too limited. The report is another example of major policy-makers failing to rise above that traditional thinking about libraries and librarians.

History is a race between education and catastrophe. One vital purpose of education is to develop leaders who will steer society away from the quicksand pits of catastrophe. There is a danger that for lack of imagination educators will fail to develop a sufficient number of leaders and thus lose the race. Librarians are among the educators who must apply more imagination, and librarians must be bold in the practical implementation of new ideas and concepts.

Libraries and Learning

by E. Gordon Gee and Patricia Senn Breivik

Since *November of 1983* and the publication of *A Nation at Risk*,[1] there has been a steady stream of reports issued on the condition of education in the United States. The issues raised in this current reform movement are not new,[2] but what is significantly different from earlier reform efforts is the omnipresence of the Information Age. Yet, although academic libraries constitute the point of access to most information on campuses, they have been largely ignored.

One exception was Frank Newman's 1985 report for the Carnegie Foundation for the Advancement of Teaching.[3] This effort does not address the instructional potential of libraries beyond the suggestion that not all learning need take place in classrooms but that "more imaginative use of the library, laboratories and other learning opportunities can contribute greatly" (p. 64). The report, however, does not deal with concerns regarding gaining access to materials within the information explosion.

It was not until November of 1986 with the reporting of the Carnegie Foundation Report on *Colleges* in the *Chronicle of Higher Education*[4] that there was any acknowledgement of a direct relationship between libraries and quality undergraduate education. The Report stated:

- The quality of a college is measured by the resources for learning on the campus and the extent to which students become independent, self-directed learners. And yet we found that today, about one out of every four undergraduates spends no time in the library during a normal week, and 65 percent use the library four hours or less each week.
- The gap between the classroom and the library, reported on almost a half-century ago, still exists today.
- The college library must be viewed as a vital part of the undergraduate experience. Every college should establish a basic books library to serve the specific needs of the undergraduate program.
- All undergraduates should be introduced carefully to the full range of resources for learning on a campus. They should be given bibliographic instruction and be encouraged to spend at least as much time in the library – using its wide range of resources – as they spend in classes.

The education imperatives, which are addressed here in terms of library use, have been largely the same throughout the reform reports. People need to be prepared for lifelong learning and involved citizenship, which in turn equates with a more active learning process. On an intellectual level faculty and academic officers accept the fact that lectures, textbooks, materials put on reserve, and tests which ask students to regurgitate information from these sources do not make for an active, much less a high-quality, learning experience. To this intuitive base must also come the acknowledgement that:

> ...the curve for forgetting course content is fairly steep: a generous estimate is that students forget 50% of the content within a few months.... A more devastating finding comes from a study that concluded that even under the most favorable conditions, "students carry away in their heads and in their notebooks not more than 42% of the lecture content..." Those were the results when students were told that they would be tested immediately following the lecture; they were permitted to use their notes; and they were given a prepared summary of the lecture. These results were bad enough, but when students were tested a week later, without the use of their notes, they could recall only 17% of the lecture material.[5]

Given the rapidly shrinking half-life of information, even the value of that 17% which is remembered must be questioned. To any thoughtful educator it must be clear that now and forevermore teaching facts will be a poor substitute for teaching people how to learn, *i.e.,* giving them the skills to be able to locate, evaluate and effectively use information for any given need. Yet change is always slow in coming; and the centers for information on campuses, the academic libraries, are largely ignored in addressing this challenge.

The response of the University of Colorado (CU) to the recognition of the Information Society which occurred in the late 70's was very much like other institutions across the country. It quickly, for an academic institution, established computer literacy course requirements on its campuses which, to a large extent, emphasized computer programming. At the time this was occurring, librarians on the three general campuses produced a thought paper raising the broader issue of information literacy, but their effort was ignored. Libraries were passé; computers were "sexy." Now the combination of the current concern for reform in undergraduate education and our knowledge that computer literacy, as initially defined, has proven inadequate is causing a fresh look at information literacy at the University of Colorado.

How can higher education effectively address the challenges of the Information Society? Can higher education, which is only now beginning to use television effectively, incorporate the implications of this Age of Information into its operations and instruction? If computer programming is not an appropriate much less an adequate response to the challenges of the Information Society, what is?

College catalogs have alluded to an obvious answer for years. Regularly, academic institutions cite the importance of students learning how to think effectively and have guaranteed that their graduates will be able to analyze and synthesize well as part of effective problem solving. But seldom has anyone questioned the value of people being able to analyze and synthesize well if they cannot discern whether or not they are starting with an accurate or adequate information base. High-quality education in an Information Society must include skills related to the accessing and evaluating of pertinent information for problem solving. "Garbage in – garbage out" does apply as well for human thinking as for use of computers, and for human thinking the concerns are even broader, since they must encompass quality issues such as propaganda and cultural biases.

Underlying the new challenges of the Information Society then is the need to foster the development of information-literate people; and, one would hope, in more prestigious institutions the commitment would go beyond competency levels to graduating effective information consumers. So essential is the ability to gather information independently and appropriately that a case could be made for expanding the definition of literacy to include accessing, retrieving, and evaluating of information. In an era when today's "truths" become tomorrow's outdated concepts, individuals who are unable to gather pertinent information are equally as illiterate as those who are unable to read or write. The college- educated person can no longer rely on previous knowledge, textbooks and faculty to provide the information necessary to make informed judgments; no one person or even group of individuals is capable of keeping abreast with new information as it is created. Instead, the ability to gather information independently and appropriately will determine mobility, and ultimately, the upper range of the continuum of literacy itself; and the provision of the opportunity to master this aspect of literacy, rather than computer programming, must be central to higher education's response to the challenges of the Information Age.

Why has higher education limited itself to computer rather than information literacy? Why are not libraries used more effectively? At the heart of the problem seems to be a reluctance for change and the lack of a philosophy for education that effectively incorporates library resources and personnel.

Before articulating the necessary ingredients for such a philosophy, time will be well spent in exploring some of the old teaching patterns and why they are so difficult to overcome.

The Reserve System, Lectures and Textbooks

President Henry Wriston (Lawrence and Brown), who fought a lifelong battle against the reserve system, believed that the library should reflect a campus' educational philosophy; which in his mind included major curtailment of the use of libraries by faculty for placing materials on reserve. The following excerpts are taken from his autobiography:[6]

> From first-hand contact I found out that the contents of the reserve shelf supplied a fairly accurate index of diminishing expectations on the part of the professor, and concrete evidence that the student was being short-changed in his education. The professors who were most successful induced students to buy books as well as to read widely from the library collections. They required writing which involved bibliographical work. Their list of reserved books was short or non-existent (p. 133).
> The books put on the "reserve shelf" were studied with extreme care. It became manifest, after long scrutiny, that more than a quarter were never called for at all. Another fifty percent were used five times or less during an entire year. The bulk of the use was concentrated in less than a quarter of the whole number. Moreover, the active service of a "reserve book" usually occupied a relatively short time. Thus even those volumes which were "statistically active" were idle most of the months they were kept on reserve. This led to an astonishing discovery: many books actually circulated more often when not on reserve – a fact which astounded professors who had assumed the contrary to be true. Subsequently I tested the conclusion again and again, and always with the same result.
> For thirty years, therefore, I waged war on the reserve shelf – not to abolish it completely, but to keep it in scale and reduce its adverse effect upon the broader use of the library. The campaign had various degrees of success and failure. But if I were to begin all over again I should fight even harder. In "real life," as the commencement orators so often refer to the years after graduation, there is no reserve shelf. If we seek to make students into intellectual self-start-

ers, we should inculcate, during college, the habits which will be useful thereafter (pp. 136-137).

Although Wriston's autobiography was published in 1959, it is difficult to improve upon his assessment today. The results of a 1968-69 study of the use of reserves on the city campus of the University of Nebraska at Lincoln[7] can help, however, to underscore Wriston's conclusions. The results showed that the percentage of titles never circulated rises sharply for lists longer than 20 titles. On the average, of a list with one to 20 titles, 33 percent never circulated. Of lists with 21 or more titles, 42 percent never circulated. Experiences of library staffs across the nation would support the tentative conclusion offered by the Nebraska study "that there is a rather substantial gap between the teaching methods of the professor and what the student reveals to be his study habits."

There are alternatives. For example, the Nebraska study suggested heavy use of paperback books which could be purchased by the students. Such use of paperbacks would allow acquisitions money to be used more effectively in collection building as well as freeing a great many hours of library staff time for other educational duties. More importantly it would be a way of having students gain experience in using one of the sources of information which will be available to them throughout their lives, i.e., paperback books. It is also worth noting that surrounding students with quantitites of paperback books, newspapers and magazines has been documented as having significant influence in motivating young people to read and learn.[8]

Reserves, lectures and textbooks constitute the heart of most college teaching today. An article in *Improving College and University Teaching* highlights some of the main limitations of this approach:

- adjusting lecture notes or assembling a few ideas from a reserve list into a "research paper" does not lead to critical thought;
- lectures usually present a one-sided view of a subject;
- textbooks do not compensate for the inadequacy of the lecture hall. They may provide a useful outline of a particular subject but are not a substitute for the primary literature;
- the effect of lecture-textbook teaching is to divide knowledge artificially into unrelated bits.[9]

These conclusions are not new. In 1937 the Association of American Colleges commissioned a study of libraries and their role in high-quality undergraduate learning. The study resulted in a publication entitled *Teaching with Books* which similarly articulates the limitations of the lecture/textbook approach and concludes

> ...these criticisms of the traditional form of American college teaching are now generally recognized. The conventional method tends to make the student responsible to the course rather than to the subject matter of the field, to separate him from the literature of the subject, and to inculcate a deference to the authorities which have been set up, rather than to develop critical discernment and independent judgment. Modification of the system, designed to secure a greater measure of responsibility and independence on the student's part and an adjustment of the program to the differences which exist between individuals, are being effected in many places. These newer educational devices are familiar enough and need not be detailed. They give the student more freedom, make him more responsible for his own education, and endeavor to test more adequately the progress he makes. This means that in place of specific assignments and set lectures, the student is directed to the literature of the subject, and the instructor becomes an aid in acquiring and understanding this knowledge rather than its source and final end.
> The trend is plainly toward a greater use of books and related materials, rather than less.[10]

While the conclusion that a trend away from the reserves-lecture-textbook approach was underway did not prove accurate at that point in time, it is to be hoped that the current focus on improvement of undergraduate education will result in a fulfillment of that prophecy.

To progress, however, one needs to address the question of why professors are so wedded to reserves, lectures and textbooks. The answer is threefold: it is what they experienced themselves as students, fear, and the fact that on most four-year and university campuses the institutional climate continues to favor research as opposed to improving teaching. The faculty perspective in this area is perhaps best presented by writings of a professor. The following is quoted from a speech made by Paul A. Lacey, professor of English and former provost at Earlham College.

What has been our experience as professors, after all? We have been accustomed to having the toughest courses we took and the toughest we teach introduce the longest list of books on reserve. Our professors gave us fine annotated bibliographies and we may do the same for our students. Often it has been our experience that the most challenging graduate seminars we took specified both the paper topics and the works we were to consult for all but the final paper; and frequently the final paper was an outgrowth of one of the shorter papers we did under instruction. That is to say, our best graduate courses in our discipline, like the best undergraduate courses we expected to teach, gave exclusive attention to mastering the content of major works in our field. Except in the rarest cases we were taught to regard the library solely as the place where all those things should be waiting for us.

I think of my very good experiences with reference services in college and graduate school, but I recall that I, and everyone else I knew, tended to go to the reference desk as a last resort and that I asked questions with no notion that I might learn a generalizable method of research which could help me become more expert in research and conceive of more interesting questions to pursue, either on my own or with the help of a reference librarian. And, I would add, I do not believe I ever thought of a librarian as a teacher until I began to work at Earlham. Except for the most obvious things, such as using the card catalogue and bibliography if I came across one, each piece of study I did through college and graduate school, if it had a research dimension to it, was essentially another hit or miss, hunt and peck activity. I might become more at home in my area, such as the Romantic Period, which is one of my areas of specialization, so I could cover more material in each subsequent piece of study, but I did not know much if anything about how to branch out efficiently into a new area. My independence as a student and as a thinker was consequently very limited, and I didn't even recognize the fact....

I suggest that my experience is not untypical of both undergraduate and graduate use of the library even now. If I am right in this, it would follow that many of us who are now teaching in colleges and universities are only slightly at home in libraries; and, that being the case, we do not know how to set our students off on interesting and do-able topics which we haven't done a dozen times before in our course.[11]

Faculty, who are "only slightly at home in libraries," will have little inclination to encourage students to venture into areas where they feel less than secure. The reserves-lecture-textbook approach to teaching offers a far safer way to proceed in that faculty can limit the information studied to that which they have mastered. There is no danger in this approach to students' being exposed to ideas of other scholars who differ in viewpoint from their own; nor is there quite the same imperative to keep class lectures so up-to-date if students are not being encouraged to familiarize themselves with currently emerging research.

If the desired outcome is independent learners rather than comfortable professors, such faculty need to be encouraged to move beyond the reserves-lecture-textbook approach to becoming facilitators of learning, assisting students to make use of the wide range of materials available in and through campus libraries. The challenge is for institutions to ensure that a climate exists on their campuses that encourages such learning and offers incentives for faculty to develop such capabilities.[12]

An Educational Philosophy for the Information Age

The underlying problem confronting education in today's Age of Information is that, given the ever-expanding information explosion, to become an expert in an area requires an increasingly narrow focus to allow subject mastery, while the generalist's knowledge must become increasingly superficial to allow broad coverage. The dilemma is real. The dilemma is known. Yet no articulated educational philosophy currently exists which effectively addresses the realities of the problem. Three elements are essential to an adequate philosophy:

- the half-life of information keeps shrinking; therefore, learning strategies rather than facts should be mastered during the college years.
- effective problem-solving is dependent upon an adequate and accurate information base; therefore, learning in college should be structured around information resources that will continue to be available after graduation, *e.g.*, books, magazines, television, and online databases.
- the information basis is constantly expanding in all formats; therefore, students need to develop skills to access, evaluate and judge format suita-

bility of information resources.

The importance of some written campus statements of educational philosophy addressing the above cannot be over-estimated, as it should set the stage for academic planning. For over twenty years the serious projects, which have been undertaken on campuses to create an opportunity for students to develop sophisticated understanding of the library and to develop information skills, have met with minimal success at best because of the difficulty in obtaining the commitment of classroom faculty.[13] Campus statements of educational philosophy for high-quality learning in an Information Age can provide a focus for discussion and curricular change. However, until strong leadership emerges to effect such change – to bridge the gap between the classroom and the library and to have the library viewed as a vital part of the undergraduate experience – it is unlikely that the next twenty years will produce any significant progress from the reserves-lecture-textbook approach.

President Richard Van Horn of the University of Houston, for example, advocates that the kind of learning that takes place in the library should be replicated across the curriculum in order that students gain experience in problem-solving within an unstructured universe such as they will encounter after graduation.[14] Such an approach clearly builds on the philosophical issues that have been raised and addresses the concern that many educators have for the need to see issues in a larger context. The ability to move beyond competence in a very narrow field to being competent within a meaningful perspective, for example, is underscored in the 1986 Carnegie Foundation Report on *Colleges* and in a speech given at the October 1986 American Council on Education Conference by Ernest Boyer in which he raised the question as to whether the "future of liberal learning now lies not in separating it from the major but better integrating it within the major so that through their specialties, students will start to ask fundamental questions."[15]

Assuming that these opinions reflect a consensus of what the focus should be for high-quality undergraduate education in an Information Age, then the expanding educational role for libraries would seem unavoidable. If the challenge is to learn how to learn and how to place one's learning within a broader societal and information environment, then libraries and their resources become the logical center for such learning.

Yet it is likely that integration of library-based learning into campus curricula will only take place when testing and credit-giving procedures change. If, for example, Ernest Boyer's suggested outcomes measurements that focus on integrating learning beyond individual classes are adopted, then the need for students to develop into sophisticated library users or effective information consumers would be essential. In his American Council on Education speech quoted earlier Boyer called for testing students' capacity "to integrate knowledge, to analyze what they have learned and to apply knowledge creatively to contemporary problems."[16] His specific recommendations include: a senior thesis requirement that focuses on some aspect of their major but places it within the larger historical, social and ethical contexts, seminars in which their theses would be orally presented and critiqued and/or senior colloquium series where the theses would be presented in a public forum and discussed with faculty and students. Where this sort of evaluation system is adopted, for the first time a campus-wide imperative would be created for the type of integrated learning experience that would require effective use of the wide variety of information resources available in or through libraries. With such an imperative, motivation would exist for faculty to explore seriously the integration of library-based learning into the curriculum.

Introduction of Library-Based Learning Into the Curriculum
An examination of the generally accepted characteristics of high-quality learning/teaching experiences within the framework of closing "the gap between the classroom and the library" would indicate that the potential value of library-based instruction may be unusually high.

First, a good learning experience imitates reality. Once students graduate, no one is going to stop work to lecture them each time they need to learn something new for their jobs. No one is going to hand them a textbook or reading list. No one is going to put books on reserve for them in the public library. Traditional teaching methods no longer apply.

If, however, while in school, people have gained an awareness of the information resources in their fields, learned how to access them, to evaluate them, and to use them effectively, they will be well prepared for the post-graduation, real-life situations they encounter. Library-based instruction can prepare people to cope with the multimedia and computer information that is so much a part of society today. It can prepare them to screen and employ effectively the mass media that bombards them everywhere they go. Faculty and librarians working together can help students learn how to deal with the realities of the world's vast, multitudinous store of information.

Second, a good learning experience is active not passive. The lecture method, even if it allows time for questions and answers, does not meet this criterion. It is the essence of passivity. Educators have said for years and continue to say that students should be provided with opportunities to learn by discovery – by developing concepts from specific incidences in varying contexts, by starting with an initial problem and thinking it through to some conclusion. Library or research skills obviously have a part to play in this process. Once students have acquired basic information-handling skills, they can begin to frame questions, to find the information that relates to these questions, and then to decide what is important or what needs to be done with the information they have uncovered.

Third, a good learning experience is individualized. Young people reach college campuses with a wide range of academic abilitites. Open-admission policies, as well as the large numbers of students who have learned English as a second language, have exacerbated the problem. While some differential placement is generally the rule in freshman English and math courses, in other subject areas classes may well contain both academically well-prepared students and those who are almost illiterate in English.

No one instructional approach can be effective with such a wide range of needs. No one textbook or single reading assignment can be effective with thirty students of widely ranging abilitites. One way to individualize the learning process is to have students learn from information in libraries and other resources in the wider community. In that way students can deal directly with topics close to their special areas of interest, and materials can be varied to accommodate individual reading levels. By concentrating on magazine articles, for example, a student with a reading deficiency can find time to go over the material repeatedly until it is mastered.

Fourth, a good learning experience makes provision for a variety of learning styles. Some students learn best by listening, some by seeing, some in lab situations; some work better in groups and some individually. Once faculty free themselves from the lecture, the textbook, and the reading or reserve lists, and start looking for alternate approaches that utilize multimedia resources, multiple opportunities to learning in a particular area can become a reality.

Fifth, a good learning experience is up-to-date. The rapid obsolescence of most information is well documented. To address this issue, almost every school and college pays at least lip service to preparing people for lifelong learning. Education for lifelong learning begins to become a reality when people acquire an appreciation for the richness and variety of the information base of a discipline and develop basic search strategies for locating and evaluating needed information. Such learning goes a long way toward ensuring that education will not stop once students receive their diplomas, for they will have the skills for accessing and monitoring the changing information base in fields of concern to them. Moreover, such individuals will be far more likely to be active users of public libraries, which have long been responding to non-school learning needs by providing adult independent-learning programs, reader advisors, reference and online searching services.

Sixth, psychologists tell us that students learn best when the environment is least threatening. Once teachers adopt learning/teaching approaches in which students learn by discovery, by working through a problem, students are relieved of the pressure and fear (real or imagined) of trying to guess what their teachers "really" want. Moreover, allowing students to learn by exploring a variety of resources can further enhance motivation to learn, because students can perceive (particularly if it is pointed out to them) the relationship between the learning process in which they are engaged and what will face them once they leave school, i.e., the relevance of the learning process to "real life" is greater than in traditional teaching situations.

These six elements of high-quality learning provide a strong rationale for library-based learning, but only when classroom instructors and librarians cooperate in this endeavor can such learning experiences be structured and implemented so as to achieve the best results. To promote such cooperation, a shared campus vision of the implications of the Information Age and a corresponding statement of educational philosophy is important, but even more so is institutional leadership.

Given many professors' predilection for reserves, lectures and textbooks, the initiation of campus-wide information literacy programs and how they are offered depend on the importance academic leaders place on the mastery of such skills and how other basic skills are acquired through the curriculum. The foregoing pages make a strong case for information management learning across the curriculum. For campuses or programs with a commitment to writing across the curriculum, this approach makes a great deal of sense, because information becomes important in relation to a particular need.

Where other approaches to writing competency exist, a parallel for information literacy should be found. For example, at the University of Wisconsin at Parkside, competency requirements must be met in four areas before the junior year, one of which is a requirement in library skills and writing research papers. When students cannot pass the competency test, they may take prescribed courses to meet the requirements. Other campuses such as California State University at Long Beach and Wayne State University have built introductions to libraries and information literacy into university-wide for-credit courses which also include introductions to the university, higher education and other learning skills. While not providing enough exposure to ensure information literacy, such an approach does indicate the importance placed on the skills by the university, and it does provide a campus-wide foundation for further learning experiences. Whatever the approach, library learning experiences should always be structured so as to infuse the methodology, perspectives, and substance of the curriculum with immediacy and reality. Ideally, cooperation between classroom instructors and librarians plus some good imagination will endow such learning experiences with all the excitement of the detective or trial lawyer seeking the very information needed to solve a front-page case.

Moreover, students need to understand throughout these learning experiences how the skills they are learning can be applied to home and work situations. If they finish their education thinking that libraries are only useful for classroom assignments and recreational reading they are not information literate. Indeed, it is this transferability that is the essence of information literacy. If college graduates working in credit departments of a bank do not know to consult library resources when seeking information related to a loan recommendation, those people are information illiterate whether or not they hold a Phi Beta Kappa key.

William H. Harvey, a biology professor also from Earlham College, in a speech underscored the importance of faculty commitment.

> ...the library, through the use of library-related assignments, becomes heavily integrated into the fabric of all the courses in our department. We are a faculty enthusiastic about the value of the library as a focus in our courses and are committed to the needs of students in library usage. Enthusiasm is a highly contagious disease and it appears that our enthusiasm has paid off; for our students are not only motivated to use our libraries, which of course is the key to it all, but they do so with enthusiasm and skills that I certainly never acquired at the same educational level. It goes without saying that the faculty member is also learning a great deal in the process. For these reasons, I favor course-related library instruction over a separate library instruction course. I believe that the student is more

successfully motivated to use the library when library skills are integrated into the curriculum as a fundamental component of the learning process or philosophy of a course. Skills become real for students when relevant examples presented as a demonstration by the librarian can focus reference sources and devices on a specific library assignment. The students' efforts can then result in a definite expansion of the classroom experience that is faculty reinforced.[17]

Because of Earlham College's long-term commitment to library-based learning, the campus offers a particularly rich environment for observing such activities and practice. However, examples of discipline-specific models can be found at many other institutions. Two University of Colorado faculty members, for example, have spoken at both the state and national levels[18] on their long-term commitments to library-based instruction. CU-Denver chemistry faculty member John Lanning is a proponent of both writing and information management skills across the curriculum and has team-taught chemical literature courses with librarians.[19] CU-Boulder theater arts faculty member Richard Knaub has the same commitment, but the type of research his students need to do is far removed from that of chemistry journals:

In an area like theater, much is audio-visual. What does a Greek chorus sound like? How does the meaning in Shakespeare come through the iambic pentameter when spoken by a master actor? What was the stage set like in the Broadway production of Mr. Roberts? Who played with Henry Fonda in that show and what did they all look like?...[20]

To cite another example from Colorado, the Department of History at the U.S. Air Force Academy has as a major goal "to develop and to enhance student abilities to use sources of both information and data." At a 1983 conference entitled "A Colorado Response to the Information Society: The Changing Academic Library," Colonel Carl W. Reddel explained how this goal is achieved particularly in the more specialized courses required of the history major where "the link between the history instructor, the student, and the library staff and resources, becomes more explicit and developed."[21]

The purpose of this symposium paper is not to provide a comprehensive list of discipline-related efforts in library-based instruction. The staff of any academic library could locate models in any subject area of interest to faculty. Chances are also good that, on any particular campus, some classroom faculty are already cooperating with librarians in such undertakings so that local models would exist for other departments on campus. The hope is that these few examples will serve to document that faculty, who become comfortable enough with libraries and librarians to venture beyond the reserves-lecture-textbook approach of instruction to become facilitators of learning through more extensive use of libraries, are enthusiasts for this more active approach to learning and consider both themselves and their students winners in the educational process. Working with librarians, these faculty, and others like them across the country have more than met the educational challenge put forth in the Carnegie Foundation Report on *Colleges*. They have closed the gap between the classroom and the library. They have made the library a vital part of the undergraduate experience. They have carefully introduced students to the full range of resources for learning. They have given students bibliographic instruction. They have encouraged students to spend significant amounts of time in the library – using its wide range of resources. When one measures the quality of their programs according to the ability of their students' becoming independent self-directed learners, they merit a four-star rating. These faculty and the library-based teaching they represent provide higher education with the needed models for high-quality undergraduate education in an Information Society.

A version of this paper will constitute part of a monograph to be published under the auspices of the American Council on Education by Macmillan in the fall of 1988.

References

1. The National Commission on Excellence in Education, *A Nation at Risk: The Imperative for Education Reform*, (Washington, D.C.: National Commission on Excellence in Education, April, 1983).
2. Arthur Levine, *Change* 18 (January/February 1986): 50-52.
3. Frank Newman, *Higher Education and the American Resurgence: A Carnegie Foundation Special Report*. The Carnegie Foundation for the Advancement of Teaching, 1985, 64.
4. "Prologue and Recommendation of Carnegie Foundation's Report on Colleges," *Chronicle of Higher Education*, 33 (November 5, 1986): 16.
5. K. Patricia Cross, "A Proposal to Improve Teaching or What 'Taking Teaching Seriously' Should Mean," *AAHE Bulletin*, 39 (September 1986): 10-11.
6. Henry M. Wriston, *Academic Procession: Reflections of a College President* (New York: Columbia University Press, 1959).
7. Bob Carmack and Trudi Loeber, "The Library Reserve System - Another Look," *College & Research Libraries* 32 (March, 1971), 105-109.
8. Daniel Fader, *The New Hooked on Books* (New York: Berkley Books, 1982). Original edition published by Berkley in 1976.
9. Bruce E. Fleury, "Lectures, Textbooks, and the College Library," *Improving College and University Teaching* 32 (Spring, 1984), 103-106.
10. Harvie Branscomb, *Teaching with Books: A Study of College Libraries* (Chicago: Association of American Colleges and the American Library Association, 1940), 62-63.
11. Paul A. Lacey, "The Role of the Librarian in Faculty Development; Professor's Point of View," in *Library Instruction and Faculty Development: Growth Opportunities in the Academic Community*, ed. Nyal Z. Williams and Jack T. Tsimako (Ann Arbor: Pierian Press, 1980), 20-21.
12. Jerome F. Wartgow, "Implementing Nonclassroom Learning: Management Considerations," in *Managing Programs for Learning Outside the Classroom*, ed. Patricia Senn Breivik. *New Directions for Higher Education*, vol. 56 (San Francisco: Jossey-Bass, Winter 1986), 7-15.
    Wartgow's case for the importance of symbolism, institutional climate and leadership for the effective incorporation of nonclassroom learning on campuses well applies to the incorporation of library-based learning.
13. Richard M. Dougherty, "Stemming the Tide of Mediocrity: The Academic Library Response," in *Libraries and the Learning Society: Papers in Re-*

sponse to A Nation at Risk (Chicago: American Library Association: 1984), 6-9.

14. Richard L. Van Horn, "Technology Needs in a University Sysytem," speech presented at the SHEEO/WICHE Conference on Higher Education and the New Technologies: A Focus on State Policy, September 25, 1986, Denver, Colorado.

15. Ernest L. Boyer, "Renewal of the Undergraduate College," speech presented at the American Council on Education Conference, San Francisco, October 7, 1986.

16. Boyer, *ibid.*

17. William H. Harvey, "A Biology Professor Looks At Library Instruction," in *Faculty Involvement in Library Instruction*, ed. Hannelore B. Rader (Ann Arbor: Pierian Press, 1976), 30-31.

18. CU President E. Gordon Gee, Director Patricia Senn Breivik, Professor Richard Knaub and Professor John Lanning presented a program, "Information Literacy: The New Imperative," at the American Association of Higher Education Conference, March 2, 1987, Chicago, Illinois.

19. Betsy Porter, John Lanning and Beth Forrest Warner, "Team Teaching the Chemical Literature" in *Preparing for the 21st Century: Proceedings of the Mountain Plains Library Association Academic Library Section Research Forum* (Emporia, Kansas: Emporia State University Press, 1986), 55-61.

20. Richard Knaub, "Confessions of a Former Scenic Designer," paper presented at the Colorado Response to the Information Society: The Changing Academic Library Conference, (Denver, CO: ERIC Document Reproductions Service, ED-269 017, 1983).

21. Carl W. Reddel, "Using the Library to Teach History at the United States Air Force Academy," paper presented at the Colorado Response to the Information Society: The Changing Academic Library Conference. (Denver, CO: ERIC Document Reproductions Service, ED-269-017, 1983).

The Academic Library
and the Non-Traditional Student

by Colette A. Wagner in consultation with Augusta S. Kappner

"*I told the Englishman* that my alma mater was books, a good library."[1] Thus, Malcolm X, one of the most influential non-traditional students of our times, provided the secret of his "home-made education" – a relentless course of self-study begun in the library of the Norfolk (Massachusetts) Prison Colony as a young adult, and avidly pursued until his death. Unconcerned with whether social status may be conferred along with a formal degree, Malcolm X defined his freedom through the exercise of his rights to read and acquire information, and the right to proclaim what he had learned. A fiercely dedicated adult independent learner, Malcolm X designed his own curriculum using a prison library collection which was uneven in coverage and scope and administered by prison authorities who were clearly not in the business of assisting adult learners.[2] Without the benefit of a traditional college experience, he intuitively recognized the paramount importance of that library in his life, and made it his primary instructional resource.

In some ways Malcolm X was a precursor of the non-traditional college student of today. Older than the typical college freshman, poor, academically unprepared for college level work, a member of a minority group, he was a man whose life experience brought him to the realization that he needed new skills and new knowledge in order to pursue his goals. Although the circumstances in which the imprisoned Malcolm X embarked upon his education differ vastly from the learning environments experienced by non-traditional college students, today's students, like Malcolm X, must contend with the presence of libraries in their lives, and must establish a working relationship with libraries and the information which they contain in order to survive.

Using Malcolm X's intimate relationship with libraries as a yardstick against which to measure success, what can be said about the relationship between academic libraries and today's non-traditional students?

Non-Traditional Students/Non-Traditional Library Users
Malcolm X is by no means the only precursor of the culturally and ethnically diverse group of individuals known as non-traditional or "new students" who have enrolled in American colleges and universities as the result of the sweeping social changes of the 1960's. There are many examples of today's non-traditional college student in the popular consciousness. One of the most entertaining early indicators of these so-called "new students" can be found

in the 1948 George Seaton film entitled "An Apartment for Peggy." In the film, William Holden is a World War II veteran attending college full-time under the provisions of the G.I. Bill, and Jeanne Crain is his intelligent, wise, and somewhat off-beat wife. As the plot unfolds, we learn that Holden and his fellow students, having been accustomed to making command decisions that affected the lives of other men, are finding it difficult to adjust to student life; while their wives, war-time single parents and members of the work force, both fear and resent being left behind in peacetime by their college educated husbands. While the men struggle with traditional courses, a special non-credit lecture series is designed for the wives as a means of "catching up" with their husbands, and, as a result of the dedication and eager class participation of the women, at least one senior faculty member is rescued from an extreme case of faculty burnout. In essence, these characters were the proto-types of the non-traditional college students of today – mature, goal-oriented, and highly motivated. At the heart of their struggles was the need to gain power or control over their interrupted lives, and education was their chosen path to power.

In the decades that have intervened between the classroom of that 1948 movie set and the very real college classrooms of the late 1980's, non-traditional students have changed considerably – in terms of socio-economic status; country of origin, race and ethnicity; dominant language, and competency in the basic skills of mathematics, reading, writing and speaking English – but their dreams have remained unchanged. Today, more than ever, they are conducting delicately balanced lives as husbands and wives, wage earners, parents (often single parents) and college students.

Within the cohort of today's non-traditional college students, women predominate (*e.g.*, at the City University of New York, which is largely composed of non-traditional students, 64% of the student enrollment is female), although individuals of both sexes represent various age, racial and ethnic groups. Based on the landmark definition of "new students" advanced by K. Patricia Cross in 1971[3] and the subsequent study of Open Admissions students at the City University of New York by Lavin, Alba and Silberstein (1981),[4] today's non-traditional college students can be characterized by the following combination of facts and attitudes:

- *academically*, they are at high risk in the traditional college classroom due to insufficient preparation at lower levels of the educational system;
- *economically*, they are struggling for survival and require financial

assistance in order to undertake college study;

- *socially*, they are predominantly members of minority groups and first generation college students. In urban centers, they are also likely to be first generation Americans as well. As first time college students, they share the expectation that the college experience will provide them with a means to occupational success;
- *experientially*, they are likely to be older and more accustomed to bearing the wage-earning, child-rearing, and other responsibilities of a mature adult;
- *attitudinally*, they are less likely to take college for granted, skeptical of authority, interested in exerting some "ownership" rights over their own education, and highly motivated.

It has been observed that non-traditional college students pay for their success with their struggles.[5] Having passed the first point of access – *i.e.*, college admission – they constantly re-qualify for their place in college through a complex interplay of academic standards, financial concerns and personal responsibilitites.

Along the way, among the many obstacles these non-traditional college students encounter is the academic library. Expected to condense so much learning into a very short time-frame, many non-traditional students seem to miss the connection between libraries and learning that Malcolm X perceived as the source of his freedom. Whereas traditional college students have experienced the library as the centerpiece of their curriculum as much as the architectural center of their campus, the typical non-traditional student seems to approach the academic library as if it were a dangerous pit of intellectual quicksand. Viewed from the vantage point of the reference desk, these seekers of power are intimidated by the power center. There can be no doubt that the library-related behavior of these students is a function of their previous library history. Perhaps there were only small reading collections, or no libraries at all in their earlier experience; perhaps the libraries which they used collected only materials that validated the existence of a prevailing political philosophy; perhaps their experience of learning has been limited to unquestioned acceptance of the information imparted by a single textbook, or a single teacher. Whatever the reasons, unschooled in the logic of library organization yet cognizant of their dependence on the library for success, non-traditional students come to the academic library and play a dangerous survival game in which time is the critical factor.

In their lives, time is one of their most precious commodities, and they are impatient and frustrated to learn that the library reference desk is not a McDonald's service counter where quick stops yield fast information in neat, take-out containers. Unwilling to waste time learning how to find the required information because every second must be spent mastering the subject at hand, non-traditional collegs students will frequently reject what appears to be time-consuming and arcane research methodology in favor of clutching a few comfortable sources which can be located by fast-paced browsing. It seems that they will settle for anything as long as they escape without being ensnared by learning a complicated new research process which will interfere with their primary studies.

For example, it is a rare hour at the reference desk in a community college library in which a student assigned to read three recent periodical articles on a "Fortune 500" company (or a similar topic) does not elect the security of literally paging through the last year's issues of *Business Week* over the complication of learning how to use the *Readers' Guide to Periodical Literature* in combination with the library's unique list of periodical holdings. In their system of logic, it is faster and easier to go to the magazine itself where the information will eventually turn up than it is to deal with the unknown time factor of learning how to use an intermediate reference tool. For the student trapped in such a faulty definition of library-related time management, information is important only insofar as it is quantifiable *and* portable. Asked to find a book or three articles, the non-traditional student stops as soon as the magic quota is reached, without regard for the quality or authority of the works he has found.

Thus content to limit their knowledge base, non-traditional students gather and process only limited amounts of information and isolate themselves from the power they seek. The bitter irony of their success in the library survival game, as they have invented it, is the fact that these dedicated power seekers are ill prepared to function in the intensely competitive arena of the information marketplace where they eventually hope to establish successful careers. By functioning at the lowest possible load limit for the handling of information, they seal their fate as the "information poor" in a society dominated by the information rich.

Tactics and the Teaching Library

Faced with this dramatic shift in their constituent user population, how have academic libraries responded? What intervention strategies have been attempted? What new patterns or instructional designs might be considered for non-traditional library users?

At the outset, it must be acknowledged that the influx of "new students" is not the only variable which has affected academic libraries in recent years. Over the past three decades, the library world has been buffeted by gale force winds of change. In the face of these challenges, the boundaries of the field have been extended, and new frontiers of activity have been opened. No segment of library service has remained static; automation has changed the ways in which libraries are managed, the ways in which they organize their collections and make them intellectually accessible, and, indeed, the ways in which information itself is stored. Thus, the entire library world has been plunged into a frenzy of activity as the impetus for change has been continually accommodated, and change after major change has been assimilated into the business of delivering library service.

Unaccompanied by the growing numbers of non-traditional students who now populate our college classrooms, these sweeping innovations in library service would have been sufficient cause for academic libraries to launch a massive library user education program. In combination, these two factors constituted compelling reasons for the re-definition of the teaching responsibilities of academic libraries nationwide.

Traditionally, the teaching function of the academic library has been carried out at the reference desk in the classic library learning situation known as the reference interview. Each reference interview unfolds in a time-tested pattern – *i.e.*, the librarian works with students to ascertain the nature of their information needs, instructs them in the preparation of a viable search strategy, and introduces them to new, specialized sources which (hopefully) satisfy the stated information need. In the process, it is expected that students will also acquire secondary learning as they are exposed to the pattern of logic which guides the development of the subject being researched, and are indoctrinated into some of the subtleties of scholarly communication in that field.

While the depth and breadth of the library's collection and the expertise of the reference librarian are important elements of the reference scenario, it is the student who initiates the action and dominates the drama. Thus, to a great degree, the success of the reference interview is dependent upon the skills and attitudes of the student – *i.e.*, the student who is articulate, at ease in the library environment, and self-confident enough to approach a librarian to ask questions, reveal needs, listen and follow directions is more likely to benefit from the reference encounter. The non-traditional student – the hit-and-run library user previously described – typically possesses very few of the prerequisites for success in the library research game as played by the traditional rules of reference. By re-inventing the research game, defining the librarian as enemy rather than ally, and waging a campaign of blitzkrieg attacks on the academic library, the non-traditional student has tossed the gauntlet of challenge onto the reference desk. In response to such desperate action, academic libraries have hastened to undertake special instructional initiatives which reach beyond the physical limits of the reference desk and, indeed, beyond the walls of the library itself.

The most radical revision of the architecture of the academic library's instructional activities has emerged from the community colleges (where the impact of non-traditional students has been felt for the greatest length of time), and, specifically, on community college campuses where firm organizational links have been established between the library's traditional printed resources and non-print instructional support services. In the process of building collections to support the basic skills curricula of their developmental studies programs, and in embracing new instructional technologies (such as videotaping and computer-assisted instruction techniques), these community college libraries became not only depositories of published information, but also creators and providers of information through the activities of their new and sophisticated production units. Having undertaken the production effort, it became a logical extension to incorporate individualized learning services and, in some cases, the operation of full-scale tutorial services under the auspices of the library. Through this enlightened extension of the library's influence into the design and delivery of instruction, and through the symbolic designation of these community college libraries as the Learning Resource Centers, the stage was set for other academic libraries to follow.

Inspired by these developments and the successes of model college library programs directed at more traditional, research-oriented students (such as those of the library-college and Earlham College), other academic libraries began to design and implement bibliographic instruction programs. In formulating these new instructional models, most academic libraries defined the reference interview as the basic unit of instruction and predicated their activities on the "point of need" teaching philosophy which underlies the reference interview – *i.e.*, the conviction that the best time to teach the student literary research skills is the moment at which the student absolutely must use the library in order to complete a required assignment of sizable proportions such as a research paper.

While there are many excellent examples of credit-bearing library instruction courses offered under the auspices of the academic library as a teaching department, the typical library instruction program has evolved into a highly developed series of non-credit activities which involve the library in some form of partnership with faculty from other disciplines. Within the context of these partnerships, the library assumes an active instructional role at the point in the semester when the students are initiating their research projects – the point of need. These instruction sessions are tightly organized, and arranged in the same format as the reference interview – identification of information need, formulation of initial search strategy, and instruction in the use of particular library tools (generally the library's catalog, one or more periodical indexes, and a selection of specialized reference materials). Utilizing the best pedagogical techniques of remedial instruction, the concept of learning reinforcement is prominently featured in the design of the library instruction session – specially tailored printed guides to research on the assigned topic are distributed as reinforcements of the students' note-taking activities, specially produced video-tapes and computer-assisted instruction materials are used as primary modes of instruction or assigned as review materials, and special efforts are made (generally via follow-up class sessions in the library) to link the classroom-based library instruction activity with the actual practice of newly acquired research skills in the academic library.

Thus, the academic libraries have pursued their retreating non-traditional students and waged an aggressive counter-attack against their fears and trepidations on a battleground where students are more confident of their footing – the classroom. While this bold frontal attack has sparked the creative energy of the library faculty to produce many excellent instructional materials, and has achieved the desirable result of enabling more non-traditional students to approach the library, several inherent problems remain to be addressed.

Non-credit, "point of need" library instruction programs are essentially reactive enterprises which rely on forces outside of the library (*i.e.,* other academic departments) to create the pressure points that drive reluctant students to the library instruction session, and, subsequently, to the reference desk. In this configuration, the library is literally teaching on borrowed time, and surrendering its instructional prerogatives in the realm of teaching the complexities of information retrieval to colleagues whose instructional priorities are directed at mastery of content.

Furthermore, in the non-credit scenario, there is the overriding force of bureaucratic inertia which stifles the creativity of classroom faculty member and librarian alike. On those campuses where non-credit classroom-based bibliographic instruction is mandatory (*e.g.*, one or two required library sessions in the freshman composition course), such requirements were undoubtedly negotiated years ago, and the channels of communication between the two sponsoring departments on a program level may have clogged over time. In the interim, the emphasis on instruction in the course in question may have shifted without the library's knowledge, and the old library instruction session may no longer be relevant from the content instructor's point of view. On the other side, after years of working with an unchanging course assignment, the library may envision a more effective design for the research assignment. While it is true that individual librarians and departmental faculty find it easy to negotiate such changes for specific class sessions, it is generally not the custom for the two sponsoring departments to review and refine a mandatory bibliographic instruction component within the context of a given course once it has been established.

Finally, there is the inherent danger that the non-credit format constitutes a pressure tactic that alienates non-traditional students, turns them away from the library, and forces them into an empty research exercise, grudgingly performed and quickly forgotten. One need only review the findings of Patricia Senn Breivik's study of open enrollment students at Brooklyn College in 1972 to confirm the devastating effect of library orientations (*i.e.*, the library tour/introduction to card catalog and *Readers' Guide*) on non-traditional students. Breivik divided her freshman cohort into three groups based on degree of exposure to library programs – one received weekly library instruction specially integrated into regular coursework; another received the usual library orientation tour, and a third received no formal introduction to the library. At the conclusion of her study, Dr. Breivik discovered that the students exposed only to the library tour experienced the most negative effects of all three groups in terms of library use and academic success.[6]

On the other hand, the considerably smaller number of academic libraries which have taken the credit-bearing route to the development of a library instruction program have also encountered problems in reaching the non-traditional student. While the credit-bearing activity guarantees the library's authority in the design of its own instructional program, and also offers the library an opportunity to improve its librarian-to-student ratio through funds generated by course enrollment, there is an inherent problem of isolation associated with this approach. Unless the course is a graduation requirement or an acceptable elective within a major sequence, it will never reach its intended audience, because non-traditional students are supremely conscious of their progress toward the degree, and assiduously avoid any course which they perceive as an empty, unrestricted elective. In this scenario, no amount of pre-registration promotion will secure the required enrollment for the course, and a pattern of course cancellations begins to emerge. Once students – even those individuals who want to take the course because they recognize an advantage to the acquisition of library research skills – perceive this cancellation pattern, they will not risk enrolling in the course when it is listed out of fear that the course will be cancelled (since it usually is) and they will be closed out of another course which is a graduation requirement.

In their recent study of the success of developmental studies programs, Kulik, Kulik, and Schwalb noted that the structure and content of instructional designs in remedial subjects was not a major factor in student success. Rather, the determinant of student success was the fact that these programs are constantly being revised and changed, with the least successful programs being those which have been least reviewed.[7] In view of these findings and the limitations of both approaches to the design and delivery of a library instruction program which have evolved and been most widely replicated to date, the pattern of bibliographic instruction in academic libraries has remained static for too long. It is time to re-assess the teaching efforts of the academic library, and design a new library instruction curriculum which takes into account not only the characteristics of non-traditional students, but their library behavior as well, and builds research skills in an incremental fashion – establishing comfort levels, not pressure points, as they attempt to master the use of the academic library. It might accommodate both credit and noncredit offerings, but it should be predicated on the tenet that library skills are basic skills which are most effectively taught and reinforced across the curriculum.

Further, the new instructional design should be conceived along the practical distinctions which are used in the teaching of athletic skills – *i.e.,* establishing minimum competencies or fitness skills at developmental levels (such that basic library survival techniques are mastered early and become part of non-traditional students' set of operational skills regardless of whether they stop out, drop out, or graduate), and advanced level, competitive information retrieval skills for those who aim to complete their degrees and establish careers in the information marketplace. In drafting this new blueprint for library instruction, the critical factor of defining the relationship between library faculty members and their classroom colleagues must be addressed in a new fashion. Through the traditional structure of the library committee, or by creating a new library instruction advisory body, or opening a discussion at the campus curriculum committee, a comprehensive library instruction plan can be designed that will demolish the confrontational relationship which non-traditional students have been driven to establish with the library. Inherent in this new initiative is the concept of a faculty development program which provides teams of library and classroom faculty with the opportunity (possibly through a creatively conceived release time arrangement) to re-define their relationship such that the classroom faculty member retains authority over the content learning but the librarian is admitted more directly as a partner in the instructional design of research assignments. As Dougherty indicates, it is this recognition of the librarian's partnership in the teaching/learning process that will be the most difficult barrier to overcome.[8] Yet tackle it we must.

For example, a recently submitted proposal to improve student retention in the Accounting/Managerial Studies Department at LaGuardia Community College (CUNY) requested that two faculty members (one from the Library and one from the Managerial Studies program) receive released time to review the syllabi for all courses required in the Managerial Studies concentration. For each course, the partners were to identify a required set of library competencies specific to the subject matter, and develop a set of library related assignments for Managerial Studies faculty to use in each required course. The program was intended to enable students to constantly develop and apply research skills which would help them progress smoothly and efficiently within the discipline; to create an opportunity for librarians and Managerial Studies faculty to work more closely together toward the improvement of both the collection and the curriculum; to enable the Managerial Studies program to easily communicate its research standards within the context of the campus library collection to a growing number of adjunct faculty in the department, and, finally, to test a new model for faculty-library interaction on the campus.[9]

An assessment of the librarian/student ratio, and a careful analysis of the best use of the limited resources of the library instruction staff are key elements of the proposal for library instruction across the curriculum. In the new model, once the classroom faculty and the library faculty have clearly defined library research competencies for the basic skills "fitness" level and within each major curriculum, decisions about the placement of the librarian in the classroom can be made. Strategically speaking, it would be best to place library faculty members in the classroom where their presence is most critical – at the two extremes of the curriculum (*i.e.*, the earliest "fitness" level where the developmental studies student is literally oriented to the logic of library orientation, and the advanced "competitive skills" level where the student might be taught how to conduct a bibliographic database search) – while the classroom faculty member handles the integration of library competencies in the usual course of instruction as it is defined by the research priorities and patterns of the discipline.

In attempting to implement such a program, there can be no doubt that the most essential component to be developed is the fitness level of library skills for non-traditional students. As Dr. Breivik demonstrated in her study of Brooklyn College students, it is at this level that library skills have proved to be a factor in improved student retention,[10] and it is at this level that the students themselves are closest to their support network on campus. It is also at this level that academic libraries have consistently failed to provide adequate support services.[11] In order to reach their new students, academic libraries need to study the program structures which serve them – the counseling components, the English as a Second Language departments, the remedial reading and writing programs – and make the initial breakthrough in the programs where student self-image is bolstered and the course of their academic success is charted. Thus, it behooves the academic librarian to become a "significant other" in the College's efforts to retain and graduate non-traditional students.[12]

Instruction at this fitness level must be defined not only in terms of teaching the basic logic of library use and research strategy; it must be defined in terms of intellectual access to the collection. For example, a careful examination of the library's materials selection policy might reveal that the library collects only materials in foreign languages taught on campus. If the curriculum is limited to the teaching of romance languages, how can Japanese, Korean, Greek or Chinese students in the English as a Second Language (ESL) program experience an early library success by finding a major newspaper or magazine in their native language or from their homeland? Furthermore, since collection development priorities of traditional academic libraries are research-oriented, remedial students (whether they are native speakers of English or ESL students) may be thwarted in their earliest attempts to use the academic library for their remedial studies assignments because they cannot sift through the complexities of the research collection. As E.J. Josey suggested in 1971, where developmental studies programs exist on campus, library collection development priorities must be assigned to them in order to provide non-traditional students with access to information in a format which is compatible with their developing skills and divergent learning styles.[13] Typically, this implies the development of a mini-collection of "high [interest]-low [vocabulary]" reading materials and non-print programs. Where there are ESL programs on campus, the library collection should include the best available translations of the native folklore and literature of the students enrolled in these programs as a means of welcoming them to the learning environment while providing familiar constructs and contexts in which to practice their newly acquired language skills.

Once a specialized collection has been developed for the use of high risk students in a required sequence of remedial courses, new finding tools should be designed which will enable these students to successfully locate materials targeted at their course assignments without having to wade through the main catalog, and becoming intimidated by the entire range of sophisticated resources in the collection. One possibility might be the creation of a teaching catalog – a subset or extract of the library's main catalog – which would lead remedial students to appropriate materials. In the proper context, such a teaching catalog would be analogous to the existence of the undergraduate library in a library system – it would lead non-traditional students to effective use of the library's research collection, yet insure that their initial library experience would neither intimidate nor overwhelm them, and it would provide a bridge to the larger collection at a point of need which would be more correctly described as a point of readiness. Having established such a program, it is imperative that the academic library measure and report results in terms of the effect of the program on student success.

Clearly, the design for a program of library skills across the curriculum which has been offered here is only one approach to the problem of the reformation of bibliographic instruction as it has evolved for non-traditional students in most academic libraries. It, and all the other programs which will be proposed and piloted in the future, will work only on one condition – *i.e.,* the re-definition of "point of need" library instruction as it relates to the non-traditional college student population. There can be no doubt that non-traditional college students' point of need for library skills is not a singular locus in their academic careers; it is a linear progression which originates with their admission to college and extends through the course of their formal higher education.

Re-Affirming the Power-Base

At the outset, it was suggested that Malcolm X's deeply felt appreciation of the role of libraries in his life might be a standard for determining the impact of academic libraries on the lives of non-traditional college students. On reflection, it is not only academic libraries which should be judged against this standard, since these libraries are merely creatures of the campus which they serve. At the heart of the relationship between the non-traditional college student and the academic library is the question of whether the library still constitutes the center of the college's curriculum.

Over the past few decades, the academic library and its relatively quiet evolution within the broader context of the Information Age has been overshadowed on the higher education scene by concerns over shrinking budgets, growing student needs, changing modes of instruction, shifting curricular emphases, and a host of other important issues. Currently, the major challenge to the instructional resourcefulness of any post-secondary institution is the growing problem of student retention. A palpable, measurable piece of the solution of this problem is a campus-wide program of clearly defined information retrieval skills which are incrementally acquired over the course of a student's career, and which clearly re-affirm the "new" academic library as the staple of the teaching/learning process as it relates to "new students," indeed, to all students. The result of such an information skills curriculum will be a more independent, more academically capable student, who will presumably be able to engage more readily in the dialogue of learning with the faculty. While it is improbable that the information retrieval skills alone will stem the tide of student attrition, there is every reason to anticipate that a newly designed program of library or information retrieval skills across the curriculum will contribute to the success of some students.

In the context of the national movement to return to basic educational values, and in light of the potential for empowering students to complete their degrees and broaden their participation in the learning process, it is clear that academic libraries – the new, technologically advanced teaching libraries that have been developing over the last decades – have a considerable contribution to make. It only remains for the libraries to be empowered within the context of their respective institutions to participate more fully in the instructional process.

References

1. Malcolm X, with Alex Haley. *The Autobiography of Malcolm X.* (New York: Grove Press, 1964), 179.
2. Malcolm X, 173-4.
3. K. Patricia Cross, *Beyond the Open Door* (San Francisco: Jossey-Bass, 1971).
4. David E. Lavin, Richard D. Alba, and Richard A. Silberstein. *Right versus Privilege; the Open Admissions Experiment at The City University of New York.* (New York: The Free Press, 1981).
5. City University of New York. *Report of the University Task Force on Student Retention and Academic Peformance.* (New York: The City University of New York, Spring 1984), 34.
6. Patricia S. Breivik. *Open Admissions and the Academic Library* (Chicago: American Library Association, 1977), 61.
7. Chen-Lin Kulik, James A. Kulik, and Barbara J. Schwalb, "College Programs for High Risk and Disadvantaged Students: a Metanalysis of Findings." *Review of Educational Research,* 53 (Fall 1983), 397-414.
8. Richard M. Dougherty, *Stemming the Tide of Mediocrity: the Academic Library Response [to] "A Nation at Risk."* (Washington, D.C.: Center for Libraries and Education Improvement, ED243 888, 1983), 19.
9. Colette A. Wagner and Jeffrey Davis, "Proposal for a Pilot Retention Project to Reinforce Information Gathering Skills in the Managerial Studies Curricuum [at LaGuardia Community College]" (New York, Spring 1986).
10. Breivik, 67.
11. Carol Truett, "Services to Developmental Education Students in the Community College: Does the Library Have a Role?" *College and Research Libraries,* 44 (January 1983), 27.
12. Joe Jackson, "Significant Others: Necessary Components in the Academic Development of Non-Traditional Students," *Linkages,* 4 (Spring 1986), 123-4.
13. E.J. Josey, "The Role of the Academic Library in Serving the Disadvantaged Student," *Library Trends,* 20 (October 1971), 437.

Excellence in Education: Libraries Facilitating Learning for Minority Students

by James A. Hefner and Lelia G. Rhodes

An alarm has been sounded across the country, warning of the impending crisis that will confront the American educational system. At the outset that alarm emanated from a single source – *A Nation at Risk: The Imperative for Educational Reform.*[1] At the center of this report was the conclusion that American education has been permeated by mediocrity, thus permitting an educational system that had served as a model for the world to become severely diminished. Indeed, as the report states, "We have, in effect, been committing an act of unthinking, unilateral educational disarmament."[2]

It would be difficult to imagine a single report that has generated the degree of commentary prompted by *A Nation at Risk*. Over seven hundred newspaper articles pertaining to the report were published in the four months after its release. Education in general and the report in particular were reviewed by virtually every major magazine in the country, while most news and public affairs programs on television, local as well as national, devoted special segments to the report and the state of education.[3] The education reform movement had captured the attention and conscience of the American public and had provoked not mere discussion, but subsequent investigations, research and reports. *A Nation at Risk* focused primarily on the perceived weaknesses in the secondary educational system, but following that report, other commissions and research groups released their findings and evaluations of American education from the preschool to the college level. Chief among the studies that have concentrated on higher education are: 1) *Involvement in Learning: Realizing the Potential of American Higher Education,*[4] 2) *To Reclaim a Legacy: A Report on the Humanities in Higher Education,*[5] 3) *Integrity in the College Curriculum: A Report to the Academic Community,*[6] 4) *Higher Education and the American Resurgence,*[7] and 5) "To Secure the Blessings of Liberty."[8] While each of the above reports was prepared from slightly different perspectives, there is a similarity of thought pervading each. The basic assumption of each report is that American higher education is failing in its effort to educate the public. In failing to educate its constituents, higher education will effectively prohibit an unacceptably large percentage of Americans from full participation in society.

All of the major education reform reports cited previously have called for various remedies to reverse the condition of education, and in so doing have identified corrective measures that call upon the combined skill, imagination, and energy of parents, teachers, counselors, administrators, authors of textbooks, government officials and legislators. Noticeably lacking in all of the reports, save one, is the role that the librarian will play in education reform. It is not, however, the purpose of this paper to belabor the issue of why the library was excluded from the majority of these reports. Rather, this paper proposes to explore how academic libraries can facilitate excellence in education for the minority student, and how one academic library in particular, Jackson State University's H.T. Sampson Library, contributes to and enhances the learning environment of a historically black institution of higher learning.

What the Reports Say

Paralleling *A Nation at Risk*, the reports exploring higher education detail some alarming trends – decreases in the scores of Scholastic Aptitude Tests and American College Testing; the numbers of college graduates who lack basic communications skills and the proliferation of remedial programs provided by business and industry to rectify those deficiencies;[9] a high school dropout rate that is approaching twenty-five percent; at least fifty million households in which no member of the family has a bachelors degree, with that number increasing yearly;[10] and a functional illiteracy rate among adult citizens that stands at twenty-three million.[11]

While such reports portend calamity for the entire spectrum of American youth, minority youth are identified as facing even greater consequences due to deficiencies in the educational system. At least thirteen percent of American youth have been judged to be functionally illiterate, but among minority teenagers the functional illiteracy rate rises to forty percent.[12] Indeed, in a study conducted in 1985 it was determined that the average reading proficiency of seventeen-year-old black students was just slightly higher than the proficiencies of thirteen-year-old white students. Moreover, it was also indicated by this study that only twenty percent of black seventeen-year-olds had sufficient reading proficiencies to engage in college level work. For black seventeen-year-olds in the South, that percentage dropped to seventeen percent.[13] Nationwide, high school dropout rates exceed twenty-five percent of the student population. In disadvantaged urban settings, the dropout rate for minority students may approach forty to fifty percent.[14] Since the decade of the sixties, during which black enrollments at colleges and universities increased eighty-five percent, the percentage of black youth attending college has steadily declined.[15]

To complicate matters further, not only are blacks entering college in decreasing numbers, but sufficient numbers of blacks and other minorities are not entering college programs that would lead to degrees in engineering, business, law and medicine. The vast majority of students pursuing professional degrees have, in the past, been middle class whites. Estimates indicate that this same group of students will decline by thirty-five percent during the next ten years, while the numbers of minority youth will increase. Thus, if minority enrollments in professional degree programs do not increase, minorities will be prevented from securing top level jobs. Whites (and Asian-Americans as well) will control an even greater disproportionate share of the professions, while minorities will be relegated to lower level, menial employment. As the Carnegie Foundation states, "such a society will not work."[16]

Factors Influencing the Decline in Black Education
Some thirty years have elapsed since the Supreme Court rendered the decision in *Brown v. the Board of Education* (1954)[17] that put an end to segregated education, and yet the scholastic attainments of black students have not reached parity with their white counterparts. Historical antecedents, as well as several contemporary social and cultural factors, have been identified as the impediment confronting the black student's quest for exellence in education.

Separate But Equal Doctrine
Until 1954, *Plessy v. Ferguson* (1896)[18] was the law of the land, and blacks were entitled to receive an education that was indeed separate, but hardly equal to education being afforded white students. Black public schools were universally underfunded, underequipped, and understaffed. A review of education statistics for Mississippi graphically illustrates the inequities that were perpetrated upon black school children. In 1916 the per capita cost of educating white children in Mississippi was $10.60 per pupil, while the per capita cost for each black student was $2.26. Twenty-three years later, for every $9.88 spent on education for whites, only $1.00 was expended on education for blacks. For that same academic year (1939) Mississippi had 379,303 white school-age children; a white enrollment of 308,883; 9,575 white teachers; and a school year that lasted from eight to nine months. Black school-age children in 1939 numbered 464,387; had an enrollment of 299,847; were taught by 5,930 teachers; and attended school for six months.[19] Federal funds provided for education in Mississippi followed similar patterns of disbursement.

During 1935 and 1937, the PWA and WPA distributed monies for the construction of school buildings, with $8,000,000 being used for white schools, and $400,000 expended upon black schools.[20] Funding for higher education in Mississippi showed even greater degrees of mal-apportionment among black and white schools. In 1941, state funding for white schools was $1,500,000, while black schools were allocated $50,000. Thus, for every $30.00 spent on post-secondary education for whites, Mississippi chose to invest only $1.00 on the higher education of its black citizens.[21]

Vocationalism
A massive debate as to the proper course of study that blacks should pursue was waged during the early decades of the twentieth century. Southern states overwhelmingly endorsed the position taken by Booker T. Washington that blacks were best suited to vocational endeavors, and as a result the great number of black colleges became, in essence, "nonintellectual institutions."[22] The forces that were opposed to the vocationalization of black education were led by W.E.B. DuBois. College was viewed by DuBois as "the true founding stone of all education,"[23] and throughout his long career he advocated that blacks would be best served in pursuing a liberal arts education. Paradoxically, contemporary education reforms are echoing the contention of DuBois that "the education that trains men simply for earning a living is not education."[24] To many, the college undergraduate curriculum has become so muddled, so lacking in definition that it is not clear if the curriculum is "an invitation to philosophic and intellectual growth or a quick exposure to the skills of a particular vocation."[25]

In spite of the obstacles to education just enumerated, blacks did, however, make significant scholastic advances. In the thirty-five years separating 1895 and 1930, the illiteracy rate among blacks was reduced from sixty percent to twenty-five percent, while enrollments in colleges had increased by 18,000 students.[26] Why then has black education failed to meet the progress that was anticipated in the wake of *Brown v. the Board of Education* (1954)?[27]

Financial Assistance
The need for financial assistance exists among black students. It is estimated that minority students require financial aid to cover at least eighty percent of their educational expenses.[28] While the numbers of college age black youth have increased, monies available for student aid have decreased. When this decrease in financial aid is coupled with inflation and the increase in the cost

of education, the purchasing power of student aid has been reduced by twenty-five percent within the past five years.[29]

Academic Preparation

Frequently cited among the factors influencing black success in higher education is the degree to which the student is academically prepared to enter college. Far too often black students are scholastically ill-equipped to embark upon a college career. Statistically a greater number of black students in secondary schools pursue a vocational/technical program rather than an academic curriculum.[30] To assess competencies in reading, science and mathematics, the National Center for Educational Statistics administered tests to high school students in their sophomore year (1980) and their senior year (1982). Black students scored consistently lower on all tests as well as exhibiting the least improvement when re-tested in the senior year. Not surprisingly, test results indicated that students enrolled in academic curricula had the highest test scores and made greater improvement by the time the second test was administered.[31]

Family Support and Academic Rewards

Aside from the various degrees of racism encountered by all blacks in this country, part of the problems facing black students stems from a lack of motivation and the absence of an active support group. While failure to be motivated by the educational process is hardly a phenomenon reserved exclusively for black students, this group's lack of motivation is, however, engendered by unique circumstances.

Although deplorable, it has nevertheless been proven "that whites get greater rewards for any given amount of schooling than non-whites."[32] Might this, in part, explain the high dropout rates of minority students? Further, many blacks believe that society has lost interest in securing educational opportunities for minorities, and that the recent calls for excellence in education are not too thinly disguised means of keeping greater numbers of black students outside the educational system.[33]

The contention is made that white students persist in academic endeavors because they, unlike their black counterparts, have access to a large network within their communities. "The banker, business owner, lawyer, doctor and government official all live in the white student's neighborhood" and "provide a network of assisting, informing, advising and motivating."[34] One might ask, what proof exists to support the theory that motivation and psychological support have a positive influence upon a student's academic accomplishments? Recently a new ethnic group began immigrating to America. Although encumbered by poverty, racism, minimal prior education and a language barrier, Asian-American students have outdistanced their white and other ethnic peers in class standings, scores on nationally administered tests, and academic honors. These educational successes have been achieved, it is believed, because Asian-American students receive strong support from their families and ethnic group, possess self-confidence in succeeding, and are sufficiently motivated to devote the time required to attain excellence in education.[35] It must be concluded, therefore, that psychological factors exert a potent influence on the outcome of a student's education.

Academic Library Services and the Minority Student

Until the late 1960's, institutions of higher learning served a very homogeneous clientele – a cadre of students who came from similar cultural and social backgrounds, had similar academic preparation, and possessed similar scholastic abilities and skills. As a result of national legislation, higher education became accessible to a more diverse and greater proportion of the American public. Schools, and all their ancillary agencies including the library, conducted a major re-orientation as they geared themselves to serve the students of "open admissions." In this respect, the historically black institutions had a head start on their academic colleagues, as the black schools have always practiced an open admissions policy of sorts. Indeed, since their inception, the historically black colleges have existed to provide a high-quality education to those who have been excluded from the educational mainstream.

The function and purpose of the historically black academic library parallels its white counterpart; however, "over the century of their existence, black institutions have added to their traditional functions the responsibility of educating a race long deprived of excellence in educational pursuits. Perhaps the major contribution of black academic librarianship is in this area of 'making do' and pursuing excellence."[36] Now that the focus of academia is to re-capture "excellence in education," while simultaneously struggling against severe budgetary declines, the libraries of the historically black institutions may perhaps serve as role models.

Goals and Objectives of the Academic Library

It is possibly a case of stating the obvious, but any program developed by an academic library must advance and implement the goals and objectives of the parent institution. Truly, all segments of the university must follow a common course of action that will advance the mission of the school. Furthermore, it is believed that the academic library has an opportunity, unrivaled by even the academic departments, to clarify and implement the goals and objectives of the institution.[57] Therefore, serving as the framework and foundation of every program developed by the H.T. Sampson Library is the commitment:

> to provide for the needs of the students in aspects of education: general, liberal, professional...to guide students in developing the knowledge, skills, appreciation and attitudes which are essential to an education...with a special mission to provide educational opportunities for needy and disadvantaged students from both urban and rural environments.[58]

E.J. Josey admonishes that if the academic library is to have a favorable impact upon the minority student, "it must become a teaching agency offering aid to the disadvantaged with action oriented programs."[39] It is teaching, research and service that transform and expand the role of the library into one of a teaching library.[40] As a teaching library, the H.T. Sampson Library has exerted its influence in promoting excellence with the following "action oriented programs."

Bibliographic Instruction
Of the options available to the library for implementing the above mission, bibliographic instruction dominates the greater proportion of the library's activities. That teaching occupies the major focus of the professional staff of the H.T. Sampson Library is only natural and lends credence to the assertion that "the librarian must be considered an educator as well as a librarian."[41] The concept of bibliographic instruction is not new nor is it an innovation designed to respond to the educational reform movement. Various theories of library instruction have existed since the nineteenth century.[42] Since the 1970's, the term bibliographic instruction has been used to describe methods to increase students' competencies in conducting library research. This library's support of bibliographic instruction can perhaps be explained by two factors: 1) the information explosion and 2) minority students frequently lack the library skills required to succeed in higher education.

Statistics corroborate the assertion that we are in the midst of an information explosion. In the United States, annual scholarly book publications have risen by 12,000 volumes within the past twenty years, while for that same period in worldwide publishing, the number of new books appearing annually has been increased by over 30,000 new titles. By sheer volume alone, accessing information is, at times, a challenge for even the experienced researcher. When combined with the diverse and still developing formats from which information may be retrieved, access to information can become a frustrating exercise in futility for the unskilled library user. The only solution to this problem, as one educator recommends, is a "systematic and sustained" bibliographic instruction program. Moreover, this educator believes that successful information manipulation and retrieval will be "high level technical skills" that students will have to master in order to do well in college. In addition, it is believed that the next century will see library skills courses becoming a part of the required curriculum and library tutorial programs being developed for faculty.[44]

Gaining mastery over information is essential for success in contemporary society, and it is the minority student who is most often the "information poor."[45] Most often the minority student is the individual who encounters the greatest difficulty in handling information, and yet it is the minority student who has the most to gain from information. Frequently, detractors claim that library instruction programs do not work, that students' library skills are not improved, nor are their academic standings raised as a result of bibliographic instruction. Studies have been conducted and have validated the contention that bibliographic instruction programs do have a positive influence on students' educational pursuits. Moreover, both Breivik[46] and Suarez[47] report the success of bibliographic instruction programs within minority student populations.

Thus, the H.T. Sampson Library is dedicated to a strong bibliographic instruction program and has long advocated the concept of the teaching library, believing as does Wedgeworth that "the library could again play an important role in the lives of our minority population, applying what James Baldwin so aptly called the 'lever' into a world of hope and accomplishment."[48] In addition to pursuing "standard" models of bibliographic instruction, *i.e.*, general library orientation, basic skills courses and advanced discipline-oriented skills courses, the Library has also initiated several unique programs to advance library competency and fulfill the objectives of a teaching library.

Great Books Reading Forum. One of the earliest of the teaching library programs, the Great Books Reading Forum, was a collaboration between the Library and two humanities scholars. The basic premise of this program was to expose the student to the works of the great writers and thinkers and in the process increase the students' involvement in library use and develop their ability to analyze and assimilate knowledge.

Project LAMP. With funding provided by the National Endowment for the Humanities and the Council on Library Resources, Project LAMP was a six-year, innovative library-oriented teaching program in the humanities. Cited by Marshall as a model library instruction program,[49] the Project endeavored to widen the learning experiences of the student through a greater use of library resources; to stimulate creative and independent learning; and to make students and teachers more cognizant and reliant on library resources.[50] Among the devices employed to accomplish the above goals were bibliographic instruction and counseling; the creation of pathfinders, handbooks and bibliographies; book reviews; lecture/demonstrations; and various symposia. Guest lecturers for the Project included CBS correspondent Ed Bradley, renowned artist Elton Fax, and librarian Virginia Lacy Jones.

Wonderful Wednesday. One component of Project LAMP, Wonderful Wednesday, closely resembled the type of Library Arts College envisioned by Louis Shores. With administrative approval classes were suspended or limited on Wednesday for one semester. On this day, the library became the classroom, and librarians were the teachers as students conducted research, completed class assignments, or pursued recreational reading.

FIPSE Pilot Project. The Atlanta University School of Library and Information Studies instituted a pilot project to enhance the bibliographic instruction expertise of librarians at seventeen historically black institutions. This project, supported by the Department of Education's Fund for the Improvement of Post-Secondary Education (FIPSE), is being conducted over a three year period and is designed to optimize bibliographic instruction through the application of computerized modules. Jackson State University students and personnel are indeed fortunate that one of the H.T. Sampson Library's professional staff was selected to participate in this program and further refine reference assistance skills.

Science Technology Students Workshop. The students pursuing degrees within the science and technology disciplines have far less exposure to the library than do their peers majoring in the social sciences and humanities. As a result, the library skills of science and technology students are often poorly developed. One professional staff member has served internships at the

Lawrence Livermore Laboratory, Berkeley, California, and at the Los Alamos National Research Laboratory, New Mexico. Contacts made by this librarian during the internships led to the creation of the Science Technology Students Seminar. To date, two seminars have been held that have employed the expertise of consultants on loan from each of the research facilities. Typically, the seminars include an overview of subject resources and online database searching capabilities. The chief focus of the seminars has been to impress upon the students the necessity of being able to conduct independent research, not only in the laboratory, but in the literature of the discipline as well.

Resources

Any high-quality academic library program designed for the minority student must include resources that support the general curriculum as well as resources that are relevant to and reflective of that student's cultural background.[51] Again in this respect, the historically black institutions have been pathfinders and have amassed a wealth of information by and about the Afro-American. Both Smith[52] and Jordan[53] cite the immeasurable contributions made by the historically black academic libraries in preserving the heritage of black Americans.

The H.T. Sampson Library has long subscribed to an active collection development program of Afro-Americana. The major impetus for this library's Afro-American collection was provided by its immediate past director, who in 1947 expanded and refined the collection with the expertise gained while a member of the famed Schomburg Collection staff. Currently the Afro-American holdings of Jackson State University include many first editions, original manuscripts, art works, oral history recordings and transcripts, as well as other audio and video recordings. The Library has created a total learning environment for the minority student by providing access to a wide and varied general collection, and a collection that is of special significance to the black student. Josey perhaps states it best when advising that:

> an important source of self-confidence and racial pride will be found in books and resources which will give ethnic disadvantaged students an appreciation of their own and other ethnic and cultural heritages.[54]

Outreach Programs

One vital component of the teaching library involves a commitment to dynamic outreach programs.[55] Former Secretary of Education Bell stresses the importance of lifelong learning.[56] For this reason, programs aimed at the adult non-student population serve to strengthen the learning environment of which the University is a part. Similarly, *Higher Education and the American Resurgence* advises that universities should form stronger links to the secondary schools as a means of improving minority education.[57] To these ends, the H.T. Sampson Library has been involved in sponsoring various outreach programs that include the following:

The Afro-American Heritage: Viewing the Past from Mississippi. Funded by the National Endowment for the Humanities, this recently concluded eighteen-month program was developed to promote a greater awareness of and appreciation for the many contributions made by black Americans to the disciplines of art, music, literature and the social sciences. As it was a learning library project for the adult out-of-school population, study guides and subject bibliographies figured prominently. The opening program was devoted to the musical heritage of black Americans and was successful to the extent of inspiring the local educational television network to produce a program devoted to black and white gospel music in Mississippi. Preeminent scholars/artists presented under the auspices of the project included: Lerone Bennett, Elizabeth Catlett, Margaret Walker Alexander, Joyce Ladner, Lawrence D. Reddick, Jessie Carney Smith, Robert Wedgeworth and Edward Holley.

Gowdy - Cherishing the Heritage. In an effort to capture the history of a disappearing black community, this project was developed as a direct response to assist a history class' assignment to conduct research on Gowdy. With funding provided by the Mississippi Endowment for the Humanities and the institution's Department of Development and Research, four librarians conducted oral history interviews with elderly and middle aged residents of Gowdy to discover the development and unique qualities of the community. The project culminated in a public forum in which humanities scholars and life-long Gowdy residents explained the lessons to be learned from the past, as well as the contributions to society of one cohesive, educationally progressive black Mississippi community.

Library Program for Upward Bound Students. Jackson State University has participated for several years in the Upward Bound Program and has contributed significantly in the academic preparation of college-bound minority students. These special summer programs have frequently incorporated a library component into the curriculum, thus enhancing further the academic foundation of the student.

Pre-Science Major Enhancement Program. Another of Jackson State University's summer programs aimed at the secondary school student is the Pre-Science Majors Enhancement Program. In this program the library was extensively involved in the academic preparation of future science majors. One librarian met with two groups of students, twice weekly for the duration of the program, and taught an intensive library skills course in the science disciplines.

Special Services
Online database searching is recognized as the research mode of the future, and yet its cost makes it prohibitive to a great number of students, particularly those students from disadvantaged backgrounds. The H.T. Sampson Library has sought out means to provide a more equitable access to online databases by means of securing free searching time. One librarian participated in the previously mentioned FIPSE Pilot Project. A component of this training project provides for a certain number of free database searches. Another librarian was able to provide free online searches for students as a part of the previously discussed Science Technology Students Workshop. Still one other librarian secured a grant from AT&T. In addition to receiving training in online database searching, the librarian also obtained funds to finance searches for students enrolled in computer science programs. With some imagination and perseverance it is possible to extend special services, even those that are fee-based, to a much broader segment of students.

Future Areas of Concern
The above discussion has highlighted some of the activities and services that the H.T. Sampson Library has employed to facilitate excellence in education. Clearly, however, there is more that this Library can do to increase the quality of the learning environment at Jackson State University. Some of the areas in which the teaching role of the Library should be expanded include:

Freshman Orientation. Part of the undergraduate curriculum requires that each freshman take an orientation class. Under the direction of the Department of Guidance and Counseling, orientation classes include such segments as an introduction to college life, the history and traditions of the school, career education and library orientation component. While it is laudable that library instruction is part of this program, it is less than desirable that (in most instances) non-librarians are responsible for teaching library skills. Certainly the administration and faculty would not permit personnel to teach in an area without the proper training and credentials, and yet untrained faculty are being called upon to teach library skills. The library faculty should, therefore, exert the position that all library instruction be taught by those who possess the recognized expertise and credentials.

Honors Program. An honors program lends prestige to any institution, and Jackson State University has one that is flourishing and marked by quality. The institution's Honors Program operates under the leadership of a capable director and a designated honors faculty. It is commonly agreed that libraries and honors programs are ideally suited to one another. Therefore, it is obvious that an already excellent program could be strengthened further if an honors librarian were added to its distinguished faculty.

Continuing Education. In an era of lifelong learning, this urban university's Department of Continuing Education plays a role of increasing importance. The adult student who possesses only vague remnants of once pertinent library skills and who is unaware of or untrained in new information technologies will utilize the services and teaching of the library faculty to an unprecedented degree. Therefore, it is imperative that the Library forge stronger ties with the Department of Continuing Education to prepare in meeting the information needs of this expanding segment of the university population.

Conclusion

The world has embarked upon a new era, one that will be dominated by information. As one of the first to identify this period as being one of information, Naisbitt observes that "the United States is rapidly shifting from a mass industrial society to an information society, and the final shift will be more profound than the nineteenth-century shift from an agricultural to an industry society." More importantly, he continues, there is "a powerful anomaly developing: as we move into a more and more literacy-intensive society, our schools are giving us an increasingly inferior product."[58] Mere literacy, however, will not be enough to ensure one's success in the decades ahead, for effective utilization of information will be realized only when one garners and develops the skills necessary to access and retrieve information. Indeed, information will exert such a tremendous force on society that the ability to access, extract and otherwise manipulate information will not remain the exclusive domain of the information professional, but will, by necessity, be prerequisite skills of the participants of this new age. Typically, minority students are seen as the information poor and are identified as the group who would benefit most from information management skills. If not the librarian, who is better to empower this group of students to gain mastery of information? The library facilitates educational excellence in many ways, but particularly through teaching students that one's knowledge is limited only by the ability to gain access to information. Thus, the librarian will equip the student to navigate the labyrinths of the information maze and, in the process, will unlatch the door to knowledge.

References

1. D. P. Gardner *et al. A Nation at Risk: The Imperative for Educational Reform.* National Commission on Excellence in Education, Department of Education, Washington, D.C. (ERIC Document Reproduction Service, ED 226 006, 1983).

2. *Ibid.*, 5.

3. U.S. Department of Education, *A Nation Responds: Recent Efforts to Improve Education.* (Washington, D.C.: U.S. Government Printing Office, 1984), 13-14.

4. Study Group on the Condition of Excellence in American Higher Education, National Institute of Education. *Involvement in Learning: Realizing the Potential of American Higher Education.* (Washington, D.C.: U.S. Government Printing Office, 1984).

5. W. J. Bennett, *To Reclaim a Legacy: A Report on the Humanities in Higher Education.* (Washington, D.C.: National Endowment for the Humanities, 1984).

6. Project on Redefining the Meaning and Purpose of Baccalaureate Degrees, *Integrity in the College Curriculum: A Report to the Academic Community.* (Washington, D.C.: Association of American Colleges, 1985). (ERIC Document Reproduction Service, ED 251 059).

7. Frank Newman, *Higher Education and the American Resurgence.* (Princeton, N.J.: The Carnegie Foundation for the Advancement of Teaching, 1985). (ERIC Document Reproduction Service, ED-265-759).

8. Terrell H. Bell, *et al.,* "To Secure the Blessings of Liberty," *The Chronicle of Higher Education* 33 (November 12, 1986): 29-36. (Reprint of text of report isued by the National Commission on the Role and Future of State Colleges and Universities, American Association of State Colleges and Universities).

9. Project on Redefining, 1985, 11.

10. Bell, 1986, 29.

11. Gardner, *et al.,* 1983, 8.

12. *Ibid.,* 8.

13. J. L. Marks, *The Enrollment of Black Students in Higher Education - Can the Decline Be Prevented?* (Atlanta, GA: Southern Regional Education Board, 1985). (ERIC Document reproduction Service, ED 264-817).

14. Bell, 1986, 29.

15. R. F. Lassiter, *Minority Access to Excellence in Higher Education.* (Santa Fe, NM:

Governor's Commission on Higher Education, 1983). (ERIC Document Reproduction Service, ED 251 059)

16. Newman, 1985, 5.

17. *Brown v. Board of Education of Topeka,* 347 U.S. 482, 1954.

18. *Plessy v. Ferguson,* 153 U.S. 537, 1896.

19. C. A. Wilson, *Education for Negroes in Mississippi Since 1910.* (Newton, MA: Crofton Publishing Corporation, 1947), 51.

20. *Ibid.,* 55.

21. *Ibid.,* 592.

22. J. Fleming, *Blacks in College.* (San Francisco: Jossey-Bass Publishers,1985), 6.

23. W. E. B. DuBois, *The Education of Black People: Ten Critiques 1906-1960.* (Amherst, MA: The University of Massachusetts Press, 1973), 3.

24. *Ibid.,* 115.

25. Project on Redefining, 1985, 2.

26. DuBois, 1973, 65.

27. *Brown v. Board of Education,* 1954.

28. Lassiter, 1983, 4.

29. Bell, 1986, 33.

30. Marks, 1985, 16.

31. National Center for Education Statistics, *The Condition of Education.* (Washington, D.C.: U.S. Government Printing Office, 1985).

32. L. Weiss, *Between Two Worlds: Black Students in an Urban Community College.* (Boston, MA: Routledge & Kegan Paul, 1985).

33. Marks, 1985, 2.

34. Lassiter, 1983, 6.

35. B.H. Alexander & P.M. Royster, "Issues in the Educational Progress of Black People," in *A Blueprint for Reform,* ed. C. Marshner. (ERIC Document Reproduction Service, ED 250-775), 200.

36. C. L. Jordan, "The Black College Library in a Changing Academic Environment," in *New Dimensions for Academic Library Service,* ed. E.J. Josey. (Metuchen, N.J.: The Scarecrow Press, 1975), 142-151.

37. K. H. Jordan, "The Community College Librarian as a Catalyst for Curriculum Change," in *Reform and Renewal in Higher Education: Implications for Library Instruction,* ed. C. A. Kirkendall. (Ann Arbor, MI: Pierian Press, 1980), 9-19.

38. Jackson State University, *Graduate Catalog,* 1985-87. (Jackson, MS: Jackson State University, 1985), 28.

39. E. J. Josey, "The Role of the Academic Library in Serving the Disadvan-

taged Student," *Library Trends*, 20:2 (1971), 432-444.

40. C. J. Stoffle, A. E. Guskin, and J. A. Boisse, "Teaching, Research, and Service: The Academic Library's Role," in *Increasing the Teaching Role of Academic Libraries*, ed. T. G. Kirk. (San Francisco: Jossey-Bass, 1984), 5.

41. Libraries and a Learning Society, U.S. Department of Education, *Alliance for Excellence: Librarians Respond to "A Nation at Risk"*. (Washington, D.C.: U.S. Government Printing Office, 1984), 4.

42. B. P. Lynch and K. S. Seibert, "The Involvement of the Librarian in the Total Educational Process," *Library Trends*, 29:1 (1980), 127.

43. C. C. Walton, "The Role of the Academic Library Within the Institution," in *Academic Librarianship: Yesterday, Today and Tomorrow*, ed. R. Stueart. (New York: Neal-Schuman Publishers, 1982), 184.

44. C. Hendrick, "The University Library in the Twenty-First Century," in *College and Research Libraries*, 47:2 (1986), 128.

45. K. H. Jordan, 1980, 18.

46. P. S. Breivik, *Open Admissions and the Academic Library*. (Chicago: American Library Association, 1977).

47. C. C. Suarez, "The Library and Remedial/Developmental Compensatory Education: A Case Study," *Library Trends*, 33:4 (1985), 487-499.

48. R. Wedgeworth, "A Library Agenda for the 1980s," in *An Information Agenda for the 1980s*, ed. C. C. Rochell. (Chicago: American Library Association, 1981), 96.

49. A. P. Marshall, "This Teaching/Learning Thing: Librarians as Educators," in *Academic Libraries by the Year 2000*, ed. H. Poole. (New York: R.R. Bowker Company, 1977), 54.

50. Jackson State University. H.T. Sampson Library. *Summary Report of Project LAMP for 1970-1975*. Unpublished report, 4.

51. A. C. Young, "Some Functions of Academic Library Service for Multicultural Students," in *Multicultural Academic Library Service in Predominantly Black Institutions of Higher Learning Conference*, Greensboro, N.C., 1976, 24.

52. J. C. Smith, "The Four Cultures" in *What Black Librarians Are Saying*, ed. E. J. Josey. (Metuchen, NJ: The Scarecrow Press, 1970), 201.

53. C. L. Jordan, 1975, 149.

54. Josey, 1971, 440.

55. Stoffle, Guskin and Boisse, 1984, 5-6.

56. Libraries and a Learning Society, 1984, iii.

57. Newman, 1985, 98.

58. J. Naisbitt, "The Major National and International Societal Problems and

Issues Whose Resolutions Require Information Service in the Year 2000," in *Strategies for Meeting the Information Needs of Society in the Year 2000,* ed. M. Boaz. (Littleton, CO: Libraries Unlimited, Inc., 1981), 33.

Libraries and the Humanities:
The Case for Scholarly Activism
by Charles T. Cullen

The study of the humanities seems to be an undertaking that would fit hand in glove with libraries whether they be public, university related (academic), or independent. It could be argued that inasmuch as our libraries house the memory of mankind one can assume that they foster an appreciation for humanistic learning. Unfortunately, it may be true that many libraries have been taken for granted during most of their history. Those that could play an important role in the humanities and education are primarily research libraries, most of which are connected with a college or university. Important differences between that kind of library and independent libraries make generalizations difficult, but this paper will attempt to suggest that programs being developed at some independent libraries without the traditional student users could be adapted for use at other, non-independent libraries, and if that were to happen it would contribute greatly to excellence in education in the humanities.

During the past several decades – perhaps longer – faculty members and administrators have debated the proper position of university libraries within the academic program. The issue is whether the university library exists on campus as an integral part of the "instructional" program or as part of the "administration." Most often in budgeting and planning the library is regarded more as part of the latter. During times of too little money, the question most often asked has been how to spend the least amount on the library without harming the instructional mission of the university and the research needs of students and faculty.

Those postures have produced obvious results. Some librarians take their jobs for granted, viewing themselves more as administrators than as teachers or researchers, and they more likely than not play their expected role in helping answer the financial question. They begrudgingly look for ways to cut costs while still buying books and journals and special collections, and they have little time and decreasing inclination to think of the scholarly side of their profession. And they most often lack the clout that is possessed automatically by faculty members, making it difficult to maintain a leadership role of any kind in academic programs on campus. It then falls to faculty members who want to use the library as an active part of their instructional program to initiate suitable programs in the library. This is the least efficient method of making effective use of the research resources of most libraries.

Independent libraries are no exception to this history. Most of them have been regarded as repositories of books and manuscripts that sometimes cannot be found elsewhere, but they are taken for granted nonetheless: they exist to be used if one discerns a need for their materials. These kinds of libraries have been like file cabinets which are unlocked during working hours, and some of which are used more heavily than others. But the point is most have been content to be visited on an "as needed" basis.

Most librarians know that their libraries hold far more useful material than their audiences – or their potential audiences – generally recognize. This is especially true in special collections, the kind of library or the part of most libraries I know most about. I should like to share some thoughts on the kinds of activities occurring in some of the libraries I have worked in that suggest ways our institutions can play a more active role in scholarly activity, particularly in the area of the humanities. The primary purpose of this activity to be sure is the pursuit of excellence in education. If one answers in the positive the question whether our materials ought to be used by as large an audience as possible, then one has to search for ways to make our resources known to a wider audience. We are centers of learning, to be used by all who possess a desire to learn. And it should not be forgotten that the desire to learn is often awakened in the well educated as well as in the general public. Libraries must become aggressively involved in education. It is no longer sufficient for them to be passive parts of college campuses or of cities where their audiences need to know more about what they have to offer in order to further an appreciation of the humanities. Most libraries have taken at least some steps in this direction.

About ten years ago the Newberry Library of Chicago embarked on a campaign to raise funds to add a book stack building and to renovate its 100-year-old facility – in short to turn its original building into a "people" building by moving its books and other research materials into an area that would be a state of the art storage facility. While those in charge of the library recognized that its holdings were being used by scholars from around the world, their recognition that it should be used by more people coincided with their discovery that potential contributors in its own neighborhood knew very little about the place. Not only had many of these people never thought of taking advantage of the library, but they also regarded it as a scholarly fortress open only to those who held advanced degrees. This had to change if sufficient funds were to be collected, but also if the library were to be something more than a highly specialized library with a relatively small audience.

When the Newberry Library began its expansion program, the original building contained inadequate exhibit space. The renovation added two large exhibit rooms in recognition of the potential this kind of activity has for making known what kinds of materials are in these institutions. But exhibits can educate as well. Most libraries now exhibit materials, and most often in their manuscript or rare books rooms – in the area of special collections. It is too easy to exhibit treasures for the sake of admiration (or discovery) alone. Libraries are beginning to pay more attention to the pedagogical aspects of exhibits. While the Newberry recently closed a three-month-long exhibit on a special collection of books and manuscripts given to the Library, plans are underway for one that will illustrate the kind of work that goes on in this special research library. The curator of the cartography collection plans an exhibit entitled "What's in a Name?" It will contain several rare maps and will deal with the question of why America is not called Columbus. Another exhibit will use manuscripts from the Renaissance to answer questions about the role of women in that age. The overall theme of this rather large exhibit attempts to explain how one goes about doing research in history and the humanities, how one searches for answers to questions among the extensive holdings of the Library. This kind of exhibit is meant to be educational, but at the same time it intends to suggest that questions about our past can be answered in this kind of place, and in this suggestion lies an invitation to all curious people. At some point the Newberry will no doubt mount another exhibit that merely shows off some more of its treasures without trying to be pedagogical. This has to be done periodically in order to call attention to the fact that this library is still acquiring materials and to help attract them to this particular institution.

Exhibit work is the most obvious and the most prevalent form of "public" activism found in academic and research libraries today. But there is more that can and should be done to call attention to the valuable resources at these places. Developing what has become the largest residential fellowship program in an independent library, the Newberry organized "centers" around the various parts of its collections that are strongest. Thus we have a Renaissance Center, one on the history of cartography, another on the American Indian, and a fourth on Family and Community History that is based on very large genealogical collections. Through the use of fellowships and conferences or seminars the Library calls attention to some of the special features in these areas. Last year saw the beginning of a four year program in cartography called "Transatlantic Encounters," summer institutes concentrating each year on a different European country's exploration of America.

This year the Renaissance Center is sponsoring a spring seminar on Milton, and with Northern Illinois University a series of lectures on the seven liberal arts in the period, all of which may be studied by using the books in the Library's stacks. The Indian Center offers annual seminars on a theme in Indian history. This year, for example, three Indians who are scholars of Indian history will give lectures on cultural persistence in modern Indian history, focusing on music, Indian-run museums, and bilingual education. In the past, the center has offered summer institutes for high school teachers built around seminars and curriculum workshops. The success of these led to regional conferences and workshops which the Library helped sponsor.

The center concept is particularly well-suited for libraries, especially research libraries. Even academic libraries are relatively free from the institutional structure of the university. They have no disciplinary confines like departments, and are concerned with learning in the broadest sense. All the members of the economics department, for example, focus on that discipline most of the time. While the library contains much information and many materials in that area, it normally devotes only a small portion of its time to that subject. Moreover, libraries and librarians are free of the daily academic schedule, consumed by occasional classes and papers and exams. Finally, they provide common ground where scholars from all disciplines can come together to share and acquire new learning. At some academic institutions, the anthropologists will not talk with the sociologists, and the political scientists will not talk with anyone. The library provides the obvious meeting place for the consideration and exchange of ideas among all disciplines.

The concept of a center built around a topic that is perhaps interdisciplinary seems also a logical consideration for most libraries. Some universities have established centers for study in various fields. Some of these have been based institutionally (not just physically) in libraries, but often they are not. The University of Nebraska has a Center for Great Plains Studies that brings together those interested in the history and literature of the Plains people. Brandeis University once had a Center for the Study of Violence, a fashionable topic in the 60s and 70s. Libraries are in a better position to sponsor "fashionable" centers than are departments or whole universities; in fact, they are where they should be found. Women's studies programs would fit well into a library program, for example: if the library had no special materials on the topic why would the program fit better in the history or any other department? Waiting until a department starts a new program that ought to cross disciplines is passivity at its most pronounced.

Many academic or non-independent libraries could sponsor confer-ences on subjects directly related to their holdings. Papers presented at such conferences might then be published in book form. Thematic studies in book form might even be put together without convening a conference. The Darcy McNickle Indian Center at the Newberry, for example, recently negoti-ated a book to be written by 14 scholars and edited by a historian outside the Library. It is to be called *America in 1492* and is intended to present a com-plete and accurate picture of what the continent was like when Columbus arrived. Much of the detail work on the book will be done by the Library staff, and the Library will join in the publishing of the finished manuscript. Some argue that this kind of undertaking would be very difficult to organize outside a scholarly institution like a library.

The Family and Community History Center at the Newberry Library is currently working with the Ellis Island-Statue of Liberty Commission on a project to collect and publish translations of documents written by immi-grants to the United States, reflecting their experience in a variety of areas and arranged into separate volumes on such subjects as religion, labor, and education.

Editorial projects growing out of a library's special collections some-times fit best into the library's program itself, rather than trying to find a home in an academic department. Some documentary projects might be in better shape today were they more closely identified with the scholarly activity of libraries. The Melville edition being sponsored by Northwestern Univer-sity and the Newberry Library is one example of a kind of cooperative effort that does not have to be restricted to independent libraries; were the Melville collection housed in Northwestern's library it could have sponsored the proj-ect alone, taking its editor from the English department there or bringing in someone to oversee the work as a member of the library staff. The Carl H. Pforzheimer Library, now housed in the New York Public Library, is another example with its magnificent edition of *Shelley and His Circle*, and the great Adams Family Papers project in the library of the Massachusetts Historical Society and the Benjamin Henry Latrobe project at the American Philosophi-cal Society follow the pattern of the Melville edition at the Newberry (or vice versa). In fact, many if not most editorial projects are housed in libraries, but very few are actually sponsored by libraries. Some are loosely identified with history departments (Franklin at Yale and Madison at Virginia) and others are projects of specific foundations (U.S. Grant at Southern Illinois, spon-sored by the U.S. Grant Association). Various literary editions are situated similarly (Henry Adams at Virginia, Twain at Berkeley) with some ties to academic departments. Considering the kind of work required of these editions, they all seem fitting projects for libraries, and certainly offer an opportunity for a library to call attention to its strengths in a unique scholarly manner. This kind of project would help dispel the idea that librarians are often the agents of scholars. It is revealing that documentary editors who work out of library offices often attempt to separate themselves from the library staff, arguing that they are scholars rather than librarians, as if the two were mutually exclusive. Librarians need more staff members who are scholars engaged in scholarly research of some kind. Libraries house the raw materials of scholarship, after all, and librarians have a special opportunity to mine this material in order to call attention to what might be there.

In addition to the kinds of scholarly activity found in conferences, seminars, and publication projects, libraries can present their materials in ways that can involve an audience not limited to scholars. The Newberry's music collection is now being used to select pieces for four or five annual public lecture-concerts that have filled the house for the past two years they have been presented. A performance by a dance troupe and a talk by Agnes DeMille called attention to the growing dance collection that is now among the Library's holdings. The staff is helping the Illinois Secretary of State's office prepare a traveling version of a popular exhibit mounted in the Library last year showing the history of the growth of the state through original maps preserved in the Newberry. Moreover, the director of the cartography center prepared a booklet for classroom use showing the development of a Chicago area community through maps. (He was motivated primarily by his school-age children's "complete lack of knowledge" about elementary geography, he tells me.) These kinds of materials have been effective in educating students in such subjects as geography and cartography, and many young students have become interested in history in its broadest sense after doing some minor genealogical research. Observe what *Roots* did for genealogy. A special grant to the Newberry is now being used to collect materials especially on black family history to supplement the Library's vast genealogical holdings, and these materials are being used as rapidly as they are obtained. The next logical step is what some call "outreach." A proposal is being drafted to obtain funds to take aspects of this special material into the Chicago schools and to offer programs for teachers that can be useful to them in teaching black history and encouraging research into the subject.

Such activities traditionally have been developed by institutions or organizations other than libraries, most often by museums or cultural institutions focusing on one or two subjects – music, Indian lore, state and local history, etc. Given adequate support, it is worth pondering how much better libraries are equipped to do these things and to do them well. University libraries need to play an active role in their universities' efforts to teach; opening the doors and preserving primary and secondary materials is not sufficient because it falls short of teaching people what is available to them at these places. It is not my primary intention to hold up the Newberry Library as a model, but it is one that bears study. As a newcomer to that institution, I can say complimentary things about my predecessor's program and the staff he assembled. They are professional people, some of them trained librarians and some of them trained in academic subjects who are quite conscious of the need to share the treasures under their care and to be of the greatest possible assistance to those who embark on a quest for knowledge in some area of history or the humanities. This requires them to conduct research into their special areas of interest just as the classroom teacher must do to remain an effective scholar. Librarians need to reflect the skills of their audience in order to be most effective.

The definition of a library's audience is not as obvious as it may seem, even on a university campus. Each library needs to grapple with the question. Some members of the audience are students and faculty, but some may be the entire educated public in the geographical area surrounding the institution. Some will be those who, librarians hope, will support its development with money or books and manuscripts. Research libraries become regional or national or global centers for research in some fields, and this places a responsibility on that kind of library that cannot be ignored. As an urban, independent library, the Newberry has attempted to address the educated public by offering a regular series of lyceums. Lectures are given at night and on weekends and are open to anyone who is interested in the subjects offered. Specialists in the Library or in the Chicago area are asked to give the lectures, and they are paid by the fees charged those who register for the series. Often, these bear little relationship to the collections; their primary purpose is to offer adults an opportunity to explore in four or five lectures some topic of interest to them. The Library provides the common ground for the enrichment of learning and scholarship in its broadest sense.

Research libraries can form regional associations that might be patterned on the Newberry's program with the Associated Colleges of the Midwest and the Great Lakes College Association. More than 20 colleges participate in this program to help support the Library's Renaissance Center and to enable their faculties and students to use these materials effectively. This includes fellowships and travel grants, and in fact sometimes a college's full contribution (about $3,000 annually) is returned to its faculty and students in this form. The collective effort makes possible seminars on Renaissance topics that would not be possible at any one or two of the member college campuses, and it offers a way for these small colleges to strengthen their own programs without having to acquire Renaissance materials. I recognize that most research libraries are not accustomed to thinking about bringing in more people to increase demands on their staffs, but we should be thinking about making our resources more widely known to the scholarly public; and this can be done in ways that combine the skills of library scholars and those who are traditional teachers.

If librarians are to have a proper influence on excellence in education, they must think of themselves as active rather than passive parts of the learning process. The key, not surprisingly, is scholarship and a commitment by librarians to scholarly activity of their own design. This is the posture being taken increasingly by independent librarians, and it is being successful. Independent libraries may develop collections and programs without having to consider the specific needs of their constituencies, unlike academic libraries which must be guided by the special interests of faculty and students. Independent libraries are faced with the interesting challenge of cultivating a constituency for their collections, and in this situation they perhaps have given more thought to the need to do so, and to ways in which libraries of all types may be more effectively engaged in creative education. Every library, after all, is a source of valuable information, and in our increasingly complex society it is incumbent upon us to shine light on this material in order to help prevent its loss through neglect. In no area is this more true than in the humanities.

Academic Libraries and Teacher Education Reform: The Education of the Professional Teacher

by Jo Ann Carr and Kenneth Zeichner

In April, 1983, the report that initiated the "academic excellence" movement was issued. *A Nation at Risk,* prepared by the National Commission on Excellence in Education, focused on the "strengths and weaknesses of American education" with particular emphasis on elementary and secondary education.[1] In their examination of pre-collegiate education, the Commission also looked at the qualifications of those individuals who have the most direct impact on the quality of America's schools – teachers.

The Commission found that "not enough of the academically able students are being attracted to teaching; that teacher preparation programs need substantial improvement; that the professional working life of teachers is on the whole unacceptable; and that a serious shortage of teachers exists in key fields."[2] Criticism of teacher preparation programs cited the emphasis on educational methods at the expense of subject-oriented instruction. The pending teacher shortage will be compounded by the lack of teachers qualified in specific subject areas such as mathematics and science.

In addition to publishing its findings regarding the teacher quality problem, the Commission also made seven recommendations "intended to improve the preparation of teachers or to make teaching a more rewarding and respected profession."[3] Many of these recommendations involved the improvement of the working life of teachers and included recommendations to increase salaries, provide time for curriculum and professional development and develop career ladders for teachers. The anticipated shortage was partially addressed by a recommendation to provide incentives such as grants and loans to attract outstanding students to the teaching professions. The Commission's emphasis on subject knowledge over educational methods was evidenced by its second recommendation regarding the projected shortage – "recent graduates with mathematics and science degrees, graduate students, and industrial and retired scientists could, with appropriate preparation, immediately begin teaching in these fields."[4] Other recommendations regarding teacher education included the need for prospective teachers to meet high academic standards, to possess an aptitude for teaching and to display subject area competence. The role of master teachers in the preparation of teachers was also cited.

Just as *A Nation at Risk* spawned myriad reports on the reform of elementary and secondary schools, the Commission's recommendations regarding teacher preparation impelled many groups and individuals to write their own manifestos on the reform of teacher education. In the continuing debate on the reform of teacher education only one publication, *Education's Smoking Gun*, mentioned the role of libraries or resource centers in teacher education. In his indictment of the role of teachers college in the destruction of American education, Reginald G. Damerall decries the transformation of libraries into resource centers and the emergence of media materials over books.[5]

Three of the reports on teacher education have received the greatest amount of attention in both the popular and educational press. These reports are: *A Call for Change in Teacher Education* prepared by the National Commission for Excellence in Teacher Education; *A Nation Prepared: Teachers for the Twenty-First Century* authored by the Carnegie Forum on Education and the Economy's Task Force on Teaching as a Profession; and *Tomorrow's Teachers*, a report of the Holmes Group. It is interesting to note that, despite differences in the composition of these groups, their recommendations regarding the reform of teacher education are similar in many respects.

The National Commission for Excellence in Teacher Education (hereinafter referred to as National Commission) was composed of seventeen individuals of diverse professional backgrounds, including education deans, leaders in higher education, elementary and secondary school personnel, and political representatives. The National Commission report made sixteen recommendations in five areas:

1. Supply and demand for quality teachers.
2. Programs for teacher education.
3. Accountability for teacher education.
4. Resources for teacher education.
5. Conditions necessary to support highest quality teaching.[6]

The fourteen member Task Force of the Carnegie Forum was chaired by the vice-president of IBM, Lewis S. Branscomb, and was composed of political leaders, educators and concerned civic leaders. The Holmes Group, initially convened in 1983 by seventeen education deans from research universities, expanded its membership to twenty-three deans and several chief academic officers of research universities prior to issuing its report. The recommendations made by both of these groups focus on the same six areas:

1. Professional autonomy in school affairs.

2. Teacher education as a graduate program.
3. Academic and field experience components.
4. Minorities in the teaching task force.
5. Certification of teachers.
6. Career opportunities and salaries.[7]

The underlying theme of many of these recommendations is the creation of the professional teacher. As programs of teacher education revise their academic and field experience components, the teacher will be better equipped to serve as a curriculum developer. Miriam Ben Perez has stated that "teachers' involvement in curriculum development may be viewed as a means toward enhancement of professional autonomy, fostering the reflective stance that is important for participation in innovations and curriculum reform."[8]

Three areas of potential reform cited by these reports will have an immediate impact on libraries serving teacher education programs. The transformation of teacher education from an undergraduate to a graduate program would require that education libraries work with a substantially different student population. The National Commission's observation that teacher education programs "require special funding beyond that for traditional lecture courses" applies also to the libraries which serve those programs.[9] The increased professional autonomy of the teacher, discussed by the National Commission as part of the conditions necessary to support the highest quality teaching, and changes in academic and field experience components will require that the education librarian play a greater role in the teacher preparation process. The education librarian must work with the teaching and clinical faculty to assure that preservice teachers have the information access and instructional design skills required for the ideal teacher:

> The ideal teacher is a knowledgeable, well-organized and consistent classroom leader who interacts with students, colleagues and patrons purposefully and effectively. This individual sees teaching as more than working with students, and works with peers on identifying and acting on problems at classroom and school levels of the system.[10]

Teacher Education as a Graduate Program
In response to the recommendation in *A Nation at Risk* that greater attention

be given academic preparation, both the Carnegie Task Force and the Holmes Group have recommended the abolition of the undergraduate teaching degree. More years of schooling are needed to provide the necessary background in educational methods as well as academic content. The transformation of teacher education from an undergraduate to a graduate degree, if adopted, may change the characteristics, expectations and abilities of the education library user.

Those librarians who have worked with practicing teachers returning to the university for advanced degrees will recognize the characteristics that distinguish those users from the traditional age undergraduate. The multiple roles which these students are more likely to play (parent, spouse, worker and student) place greater demands upon their time and necessitate efficient use of library resources. This efficient use of information resources is further compounded by the rapid growth of knowledge – both academic and pedagogical. Differing perceptions of the technological changes which affect information access also leads to a relationship between the student and the education librarian that is more personal, ongoing, and detailed than that of the undergraduate user.

A model for providing library service for graduate or non-traditional age education students is provided by the National College of Education in Evanston, Illinois. Because many of its students are working adults, NCE has developed a Library Research and Computer Search Module that emphasizes the use of computer technology and a close working relationship with a professional librarian. This personalized outreach approach to the support of the education curriculum requires NCE library staff to serve as the guides to information in those libraries where the NCE students are located, in addition to in the NCE library. Thus NCE librarians play an integral role in the educative process.[11]

Strengthening Academic and Field Experience Components of Teacher Education

In their discussion of the need to strengthen the content area expertise of the teacher education students at the University of Wisconsin-Madison, a Dean's Study Group noted: "moreover, their understanding of the way that [a] body of knowledge is related to other significant bodies of knowledge is often even weaker."[12] The need for prospective teachers to recognize the structure of knowledge led to the 1982 publication of "Bibliographic Competencies for Education Students" by the Educational and Behavioral Sciences Section of the Association of College and Research Libraries.

These Bibliographic Competencies recognize the need for education students to gain knowledge of those resources which provide information for both their own work and in their work as teachers. The attainment of these competencies provides skills in resource identification, information evaluation, and information access – all essential skills in the development of an understanding of the interrelationships of bodies of knowledge.[13]

The recognition of the need for teachers to acquire bibliographic competencies predates the EBSS publication. In 1967, Jerry L. Walker surveyed students in Illinois and Oregon and determined that their library skills were inadequate in preparing them to use a modern library. A 1981 replication of this study at Idaho State University indicated that the ISU students were less adequately prepared than those in the Walker survey.[14]

Although research by Gengler, Harmer, McMillen, Yarling, Greve and Hale has shown that knowledge of library skills can be related to the improvement of student achievement, the integration of library skills training into teacher education programs has not been universally adopted.[15] The School Libraries Working Group of the International Federation of Library Associations and Institutions has examined the reasons for the reluctance of teachers to use the potential sources of information that surround them. Citing the role of information overload in teachers' rejection of problematic sources and a low priority assigned to the improvement of their own information handling skills, the Working Group notes that a general introduction to libraries and library resources may add to the concerns teachers have rather than reduce them. Information access skills must be an integral part of teacher education programs.

> It is crucial, therefore, for teacher education to provide opportunities for teachers to reflect on the concept of information; the decision making processes at work, and the sources on which they can draw to foster their continuing professional development.[16]

The integration of information access skills into both the academic and field experience components of teacher education can also serve as a model for the "school as a collegium" cited by the Carnegie Task Force.[17] In a report to the American Association for Teacher Education, Howsan said:

> College instructors must incorporate the same principles of instruc-

tion in their own teaching that they wish to engender in students...The complexity of teacher education makes the stereotype of the autonomous teacher working alone with a standard size class of students totally anachronistic.[18]

Pre-service teachers must receive preparation for their role as professionals collaborating with their colleagues in the creation of an institution where learning is valued and critical thinking is viewed as an integral part of the learning experience. Professional programs must place the same emphasis on learning how to learn and critical thinking skills as is required for the successful elementary or secondary classroom.

This collaborative model must extend beyond the academic librarian working with the teacher education faculty. Just as the Holmes Group has called for partnerships among university faculty, practicing teachers, and administrators, so must there be partnerships among academic librarians, school library media specialists and practicing teachers to ensure that pre-service teachers learn to apply those information access skills learned as a part of their education courses in a meaningful way in the classroom.[19]

Professional Autonomy of Teachers

The purpose of initial preparation is to prepare teacher candidates: (a) for the lifelong study of the world, the self, and academic knowledge; (b) for the lifelong study of teaching; (c) to participate in school renewal efforts, including the creation and implementation of innovations; and (d) to approach the generic problems of the workplace (the school and classroom).[20]

If the initial preparation of teachers does indeed meet the criteria cited above, the integration of information access skills must go beyond a mere exposure to sources of information. In order to develop a professional role, the teacher must be able "to grasp the full meaning of curriculum materials...for their professional use in classrooms."[21] Essential to an understanding of the meaning of curriculum materials is an awareness of theoretical "choice points." In developing instructional materials, deliberate choices are made regarding subject matter, learner, milieu, teacher and curriculum format.[22] Unless these choices and their impact are understood, the material cannot be used in the manner most appropriate to the learner. The successful use of the material may or may not be consistent with the intent of the developer. The teacher's ability to adapt or apply material to the needs of the learner is negated and these choice points and their impact are misunderstood.

This understanding for the meaning of curriculum materials requires abilities in materials evaluation and analysis and knowledge of the principles of instructional design. Librarians, who daily must evaluate and analyze the appropriateness of materials for their collections, can provide the introduction to models of materials analysis such as the *EPIE Profiles*.[23] Media specialists, involved in both selection and production of software, videotapes, slide tapes, audiotapes and other educational media, provide expertise in the practical applications of the instructional design process. Miriam Ben Perez has noted that "professors offer little help for daily planning and execution of teaching."[24] The library media specialist can provide the "missing link" among the theoretical aspects of teaching provided in methods courses, awareness of information sources and daily planning and execution of teaching.

Models of Integrated Instruction

The development of a model in information utilization was undertaken by Pauline Rothstein in her doctoral work at Fordham University. In describing this model at the 1980 annual conference of the American Educational Research Association, the ability of the Training System Model to meet the changing needs of students over time was emphasized.[25]

The Training System Model could be used with a number of existing publications to begin the development of an integrated program of information access and design skills in the teacher education curriculum. James R. Kennedy of Earlham College, an institution renowned for course integrated library skills instruction, has authored a *Library Research Guide to Education*.[26] Under the sponsorship of the Department of Education, Terrence Mech of King's College, Wilkes-Barre, Pennsylvania, has produced a self-paced workbook for *Library Skills for Teachers*.[27]

The need for analysis of curriculum materials prior to their use in the classroom is part of the course developed by the UNESCO Pilot Project on School Library Development. Designed to train primary and secondary teachers in the South Pacific region, the course includes modules on the evaluation of information resources and their integration into the curriculum.[28]

A description of the pilot project focusing on a faculty-centered library instruction program reveals that "students' skills in conducting library research and their attitudes toward such efforts were significantly improved."[29] The evaluation component of the model is especially appropriate to institutions initiating course-integrated instruction.

Conclusion

The reform of teacher education as envisioned by the Carnegie Task Force, Holmes Group, and National Commission reports will change the characteristics of those involved in teaching, the content of and balance between the academic and field experience components and the professional autonomy of the teacher. The academic library must be prepared to meet the demands of these new learners, provide a collaborative model in integrating information access skills into the curriculum, and contribute to the professional autonomy of the teacher by sharing their expertise in information access, materials evaluation and analysis and curriculum design.

Academic librarians serving teacher education programs must take a proactive position in the integration of information access, materials analysis and instructional design skills in the academic and clinical curriculum. They must work with faculty in strengthening resources for teacher education, and in providing a collegial model, in order to ensure the creation of the professional teacher.

References

1. United States Department of Education. National Commission on Excellence in Education. *A Nation at Risk: The Imperative for Educational Reform.* (April 1983), iii.
2. *Ibid.,* 22.
3. *Ibid.,* 30.
4. *Ibid.,* 31.
5. Reginald G. Damerall, *Education's Smoking Gun: How Teachers Colleges Have Destroyed Education in America.* (New York: Freundlich Books, 1985), 137-138.
6. National Commission for Excellence in Teacher Education. *A Call for Change in Teacher Education.* (Washington, D.C.: American Association of Colleges for Teacher Education, 1985), 8-9, 14-16, 18-20, 23-24, 26-29.
7. Sam P. Wiggins, "Revolution in the Teaching Profession: A Comparative Review of Two Reform Reports," *Educational Leadership,* October 1986, 56-59.
8. Miriam Ben Perez, "Curriculum Theory and Practice in Teacher Education Programs," in *Advances in Teacher Education,* ed. Lilian G. Katz and James D. Raths, vol. 1 (Norwood, N.J.: ABLEX Publishing, 1984), 21.
9. National Commission for Excellence in Teacher Education. 9.
10. G. Griffin, "Clinical Teacher Education," in *Reality and Reform in Clinical Teacher Education,* ed. J. Hoffman and S. Edwards (New York: Random House, 1986), 6.
11. National College of Education. Field Experience Programs. *Library Research and Computer Search Module,* rev. ed. (Evanston, IL: National College of Education, February 1984), 1.
12. University of Wisconsin-Madison. School of Education. Summer 1986 Dean's Study Group. *The Dean's Study Group on the Improvement of Teacher Preparation: Reflections and Recommendations* (September 1986), 3.
13. "Bibliographic Competencies for Education Students," *C&RL News* (May 1982), 209-210.
14. George K. Shepard, "Establishing Library Skills Proficiency in a Teacher Education Program," *C&RL News* (November 1982), 351.
15. Elaine K. Didier, "An Overview of Research on the Impact of School Library Media Programs on Student Achievement," *School Library Media Quarterly* (Fall 1985), 33.

16. Noelene Hall, *Teachers, Information and School Libraries.* A Report prepared for the IFLA Section on School Libraries Working Group (September, 1985), 7.

17. Carnegie Forum on Education and the Economy. Task Force on Teaching as a Profession. *A Nation Prepared: Teachers for the Twenty-First Century* (New York: Carnegie Forum on Education and the Economy, May 1986), 58.

18. American Association of Colleges for Teacher Education. Bicentennial Commission on Education for the Profession of Teaching. *Educating a Profession* (Washington, D.C.: American Association of Colleges for Teacher Education, 1976), 91, 107.

19. *Tomorrow's Teachers: A Report of the Holmes Group* (East Lansing, MI: The Holmes Group, 1986), 66.

20. Bruce Joyce and Renee Clift, "The Phoenix Agenda: Essential Reform in Teacher Education," *Educational Researcher* (April 1984), 8.

21. Ben Perez, 11.

22. *Ibid.*, 19.

23. *EPIE Pro/files.* (New York: EPIE Institute, 1980).

24. Ben Perez, 10.

25. Pauline Rothstein, *The Development of a Model in Information Utilization Skills for Education Students* (Bethesda, MD: ERIC Document Reproduction Service, ED 190 543).

26. James R. Kennedy, *Library Research Guide to Education* (Ann Arbor, MI: Pierian Press, 1979).

27. Terrence Mech, *Library Skills for Teachers: A Self-pace Workbook* (Bethesda, MD: ERIC Document Reproduction Service, ED 261 689).

28. Margaret Trask, *South Pacific Region Pilot Project on School Library Development Programmes for Teachers* (Bethesda, MD: ERIC Document Reproduction Service, ED 247 938).

29. Mark J. Tierno and Jo Ann H. Lee, "Developing and Evaluating Library Research Skill in Education: A Model for Course-Integrated Bibliographic Instruction," *Reference Quarterly* (Spring 1983), 284.

Fostering Research
by Herbert C. Morton and Sharon J. Rogers

The premise of this paper is that librarians are active partners with faculty members in fostering research on individual campuses and in national programs. We will explore dimensions of this research partnership by looking at the scholars, the academic library's role, characteristics of research activity, and the academic librarian's response to the scholar's needs.

The Scholar's Needs

Fostering research begins logically with fostering understanding among the participants in the research process, notably those two natural – or unnatural – though sometimes estranged – partners, scholars and librarians.

What do we know about scholars that ought to be useful for librarians to know? Nothing definitive – indeed, the question of how researchers use information resources is a neglected area – but let us suggest a few notions from the findings of a recent survey of several thousand scholars in the humanities and social services conducted by the Office of Scholarly Communication and Technology of the American Council of Learned Societies. The survey achieved a response rate of 71 percent, even though the 16-page questionnaire took 30 to 40 minutes to fill out, which suggests that scholars are willing to answer questions about their concerns and needs under the appropriate circumstances.

The survey confirms the impression that scholars are generally satisfied with their libraries, especially with the quality of library services – though as has been mentioned by some observers, we don't know the extent to which this reflects the modest expectations of scholars as well as it reflects good service from libraries. The survey also confirms the obvious – that scholars at research universities are more likely to be satisfied with their library collections than are scholars from colleges or comprehensive universities.

But more interesting is the fact that all college and university libraries appear alike in one respect. At research universities as well as colleges, scholars report that their teaching needs are much better served than their research needs. Compared to other library resources, book holdings for research purposes are the least satisfactory. Outside the research universities, more than 50 percent of the respondents say that *book holdings for their research needs* are only "fair" or "poor." At research universities, despite overwhelming satisfaction with libraries, nearly twice as many of the respondents gave low ratings to book holdings for *research* (26 percent) as gave inadequate ratings to book holdings for *teaching* (14 percent). Only 11 percent said journal holdings are inadequate for their teaching needs.

One obvious implication of this finding is that scholars must be helped to understand that the answer to their research needs is not going to come from a great increase in library acquisitions, but rather from effective resource-sharing. This is not a new theme for librarians, but a reaffirmation of a theme that they have been trying to get across to scholars for years: what counts is access, not holdings.

And access, of course, is something libraries can do something about – and are doing something about through conversion of card catalogs into online catalogs – through the organization of networks.

The survey also shows that more than a fourth of the respondents consider interlibrary borrowing to be very important to them for research, teaching and for keeping up with their fields. But nearly twice as many say they consider the college or university library itself very important. Thus it would appear that a large proportion of regular library users are still not taking full advantage of interlibrary lending possibilities. Since those who are using the interlibrary loans express strong satisfaction with them, one can speculate that it is not just the extra effort required that discourages such interlibrary borrowing but the simple awareness that it is a convenient and practical alternative. Whether reader awareness of this resource would lead to an increase in interlibrary borrowing and in user satisfaction is a question worth exploring. The relatively higher level of interlibrary lending and borrowing at the University of Illinois, where the library director (the late Hugh Atkinson) was an outspoken advocate of such exchanges, suggests that an active policy of encouragement can increase the use of this mode of access.

As for the newer technologies – online databases and computerized library catalogs – their effect was not yet being felt strongly up to a year ago. About 38 percent of the respondents report having used computerized database searches, and two thirds describe their results as mildly satisfactory or very satisfactory.

Less than half of the respondents report that their library catalog has been partly or fully computerized. (At research universities the figure is 63 percent.) About two thirds of those who say they have access have used the computerized catalog. About 40 percent of the users say that the computerized version has increased their access, and about the same percentage thinks it is more enjoyable to use. About one user in four reports that his or her productivity as a teacher or researcher has been enhanced at this stage in the transition to computerization. The impact of the computerized catalog appears still to be modest at this stage of the transition, as shown in the following chart:

*Percentage of academic respondents with access
to computerized catalog*

All academic respondents
N = 2,866

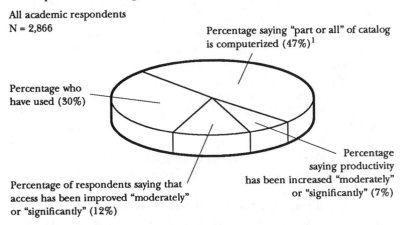

Percentage saying "part or all" of catalog
is computerized (47%)[1]

Percentage who
have used (30%)

Percentage of respondents saying that
access has been improved "moderately"
or "significantly" (12%)

Percentage
saying productivity
has been increased "moderately"
or "significantly" (7%)

---

[1] Includes 6% saying catalog "probably" is computerized

So far, librarians may be gaining more from computerization than schol-ars, since they need a managerial tool for coping with the publication over-load. Scholars, on the other hand, have been so used to the card catalog that they never considered it to be a major limitation, so that even if online service is better, the improvement is not likely to excite them. In any event, many scholars still would prefer to browse in the stacks.

It's also worth noting that a substantial fraction of survey respondents do not know whether the library catalog has been computerized, whether online searching is available, and whether instruction in library services is being pro-vided to incoming freshmen and established scholars. This is perhaps to be expected – though it is hardly to be ignored. If the service is available and scholars are not aware of it, the service may as well not be offered. Librarians are the ones who will probably have to see to it that the assistance is not only available but that scholars are aware that it is available and aware of its poten-tial benefits.

One of the great difficulties in assessing the meaning of survey data is deciding what are reasonable goals. Is it reasonable to expect, for example, that 75 percent of the scholars in humanities and social sciences should be relying heavily on library services (rather than half of them) or that half should be making use of interlibrary loans (instead of 28 percent)? Statistical data pertaining to library use are difficult to interpret as long as we lack good trend data as well as an agreement about what are appropriate goals.

As for their personal use of computer technology, scholars differ individually in their enthusiasm, but there is only a very small fraction who seem to be dead set against it. In addition to personal differences, there are also observable differences in computer use by discipline (with the sociologists and linguists making the most use and the historians the least). There are also differences by type of institution and the relative importance of different applications. Word processing is the most important, but for most survey respondents the computer is already more than just a superior typewriter. Of more than a dozen uses cited, the most important are compiling a bibliography or index (cited by 49 percent of the respondents), statistical analysis (37%), graphics (22%), and accessing online databases and other catalogs (18%).

It is also worth noting that the much maligned technology, microfiche, seems to have gained greater acceptance as the technology has improved. Two thirds of the respondents said they had made use of microfiche in the last three years and most reported that they were satisfied with access to machines and the readability of the fiche. But most of them reported dissatisfaction with the quality of the paper copies.

Turning to the other side of the communication process, what should librarians be saying that would help scholars understand the problems of access and how to cope with them? Generally, they need to say more effectively to the scholarly community what they have been saying to each other about resource-sharing, new technologies, and the range of services the library can provide. If an effective dialogue is to be developed that will lead to better collaboration in the research process, librarians will have to take the lead – both in providing information and in asking what scholars need, since scholars generally take library services for granted.

The Academic Library's Role

Frank Newman, in his important report for the Carnegie Foundation, *Higher Education and the American Resurgence*, takes a rather limited view of the research library. He states:

> Two major problems now face research libraries: the costs of providing for their users a huge and growing array of books, scholarly jour-

nals, government documents, and other works; and the confusion brought about by the advent of widespread electronic as opposed to printed information. Both demand fundamentally new ways of thinking about the function of the library.[2]

Newman does not identify just who is confused by the advent of electronic information, whether it is the librarians or the scholars, but he deserves high marks for mentioning libraries at all. Other such national studies, such as the National Institute of Education's *Involvement in Learning*, published in October 1984, and the National Commission on Excellence in Education's *A Nation at Risk*, ignored the contributions of libraries altogether.

Barbara B. Moran's *Academic Libraries: The Changing Knowledge Centers of Colleges and Universities* paints a somewhat different picture of academic libraries adapting to "a period of unprecedented change and adjustment." First, the problems are more complex, adding library management, role of librarians, preservation issues and the nature of a "library of tomorrow" to new technology and costs. The volume documents the ways in which librarians and their colleagues within academic institutions have, in fact, been thinking in fundamentally new ways about the function of the library.[3] Carrying discussion of the academic library's role to new arenas also is evident increasingly in the program content and attendance at higher education conferences such as the EDUCOM conference in Pittsburgh in the fall of 1986. The annual EDUCOM conference is becoming the meeting ground for librarians, computer center personnel and scholars, with joint and separate program tracks.

Understanding the Research Process

Librarians who want to encourage collaboration with scholars in the research process need to understand just what research is, and what kind of research is going on or might go on, with the librarian's help, in colleges and universities and how research patterns are changing. It is not our purpose here to argue the values of the various research methodologies. There is not much purpose in labeling one type of research more valuable than another or needing more or less support. But there is some purpose in reminding ourselves of the differences in research objectives. W.I.B. Beveridge discusses the various types of classifications of research in his *Seeds of Discovery*, stating that:

Research used to be classified simply as either pure or applied, with
the strong implication that pure research was concerned with fundamental aspects of science and led to new knowledge, whereas
applied research (or applied science as it was more often called) was
concerned with putting this knowledge to practical use.[4]

However, scientists have long pointed out that the distinction breaks
down because applied research may lead to new discoveries and pure or basic
research may turn up practical applications. Beveridge supplies different
classifications of research – "pure research" which is done for the pleasure of
exploring and discovery; "problem-oriented research" to be "directed at a
particular problem or just at a fairly broad field"; "goal-oriented research"
which is "planned to achieve a well-defined objective"; "developmental research" which "is concerned with the implementation of new knowledge under 'field conditions'"; and "operational research" which employs the methods, tools and techniques of the scientific method in solving problems involving the operations of a system. Operational research is interdisciplinary and
used mainly in industry or by military defense organizations.[5] Those of us
from all types of libraries may add another class of "research": that done by
students who have to have at least three sources "besides an encyclopedia" in
order to write a "research paper" before tomorrow morning. All of these traditional categories of research are legitimate, and all deserve our attention
to organization of collections and services.

Librarians also need to be sensitive to new patterns of research: the
trend toward collaborative research, the growing strength of informal information networks in the humanities and social sciences as well as the sciences,
and the growing importance of quantitative data generated, manipulated
and disseminated in response to immediate needs. As Francis Miksa pointed
out at a recent OCLC conference, it no longer makes sense to think of "a
universe of knowledge" from which new knowledge grows.[6] This early 20th
century concept of research, in which the library's role was viewed as one of
controlling and organizing the growth of knowledge, is outmoded. Research
today is problem-oriented, not disciplinary, and it is a pragmatic response to
practical needs, quite independent of the universe of knowledge. Thus it is
much more important today to be aware of research in process than what is in
the stacks. In many situations today, he noted, the researcher and the research librarian may be engaged in tasks that do not match.

Over the past twenty years leaders in the library field have been drawing on new technologies to improve their access not only to established collections but also to the new information in electronic formats. The question is, to what extent are librarians and researchers in tune with each other during this period of rapid change? To assist scholars in meeting their research needs, librarians are being required to move on two tracks – to provide help for traditional research and also to assist in the application of electronic technologies to the development and searching of electronic databases at remote as well as nearby locations.

Besides understanding the types and changing patterns of research, librarians are exploring the literature of how human beings think, how they learn, how they approach a problem. An understanding of this process is critical to knowing what to collect for our libraries and to knowing how to deliver the information in these resources and in what format. Many who studied for librarianship in a time when the book was the center of the library, may remember the classic phrase from Helen Haines concerning delivering "the right book to the right reader at the right time."[7] As quaint as some more technically infatuated colleagues may think that phrase, its sense is precisely what is practiced when librarians become involved in fostering research. Different workmen need different tools. Not everyone thinks alike. We mean that, literally, people think and learn differently. Beveridge discusses an "important development" in psychological research which recognizes "two distinctly different types of mind, using different ways of thinking: convergent and divergent."[8] He goes on to explain:

> Convergent thinking follows conventional ideas and it uses knowledge that has been taught in order to reach a goal that is accepted without question...In contrast, divergent thinkers are more imaginative, they see more possibilities...they tend to be unconventional and resourceful...Various tests have been devised to test creative ability and inventiveness, and divergent thinkers perform better in these than do convergent thinkers.[9]

Librarians who have taken or been exposed to those who have taken the very popular Meyers-Briggs Personality Type Inventory know that there are many ways in which individuals approach and deal with their world. The point in all this is to make us aware that while one professor or student may be exuberant over a computerized print-out of specific data, another will find inspiration and discovery through the serendipity of browsing the stacks.

Responding to Research Needs
Librarians have responded constructively to the various educational reports. "Libraries and a Learning Society," a year-long 1983-84 effort sponsored by the Department of Education's Center for Libraries and Education Improvement resulted in *Alliance for Excellence: Librarians respond to A Nation at Risk.*[10] Less widely publicized, JoAn Segal, Executive Director of the Association of College and Research Libraries, responded to the National Institute of Education's Involvement in Learning with a brief paper, "Involvement in Learning: Realizing the Potential of the American Library to American Higher Education."[11]

It is significant that the Involvement in Learning recommendations focus on exactly the areas where libraries can be of greatest use. Segal's point-by-point outline of the library implications of the NIE recommendations describes the current library programs for "fostering research." For example, increased service to undergraduates is recommended. Segal responds:

> Bibliographic instruction is a technique by which undergraduate students are encouraged to learn how to use the library resources in order to pursue their studies. It is a technique for getting students into the library, for increasing their interest in the subjects they are studying and for helping them to get more out of their courses.[12]

The NIE report recommends that "increased faculty/student contact is not hampered by learning technology." Segal responds:

> The library role in the networking of computers on the campus and among campuses is extremely important. Libraries have led the way in intercampus networking for many years. Faculty and administrators in institutions of higher education may not be aware that their libraries are involved in computer networks. Students need to be encouraged to take advantage of this opportunity to communicate with other campuses, to borrow items from other libraries, and to become aware of literature which exists outside but is accessible through the library on their campus.[13]

One more example: Institutions should match the content and delivery of the curriculum to the knowledge capacities and skills expected of students. The response:

The library should be expected to serve the faculty need to keep up with educational research and with other types of research activity. Through attention to the research needs of faculty, the librarians can also keep their own skills and knowledge at a level which will allow them to participate as peers with the faculty in assisting students to attain their learning goals.[14]

Involvement in Learning concludes that "our nation will require citizens who have learned how to learn – who can identify, organize, and use all of the learning resources at their disposal."[15] Academic librarians are convinced that information literacy is the one element among life-long learning skills that keeps the other skills renewable.

As an educational contribution to "fostering research," academic librarians have developed their own research programs and shared literature on linkages among faculty styles of research as they vary by discipline, translating variations in disciplinary research patterns into bibliographic instruction, and organizing collections and services to reflect research needs and preferences. The recent library and higher education literature reflects these commitments as a sampling of titles demonstrates: "Integrating Classroom Instruction and Library Research: the Cognitive Functions of Bibliographic Network Strucures," "Information Structure and Bibliographic Instruction," "Historians and Using Tomorrow's Research Library: Research, Teaching and Training," "The Information Needs of Historians," "Bibliographic Instruction in the Humanities: the Need to Stress Imagination," "Dissemination and Use of Information by Psychology Faculty and Graduate Students: Implications for Bibliographic Instruction."[16]

Recognizing the librarian's role in the research transaction may provide a "missing link" for enhancing the application of research findings. James Sundquist, Senior Fellow at the Brookings Institution, states that there is a "weak link" in the transmission of social knowledge. Sundquist laments the fact that there is a faulty connection between the "producers" of knowledge – the research – and a major "consumer" of knowledge – the policy maker.[17] He recommends the creation of a new discipline, that of research brokerage which will eventually be as well recognized and as "essential to effective administration as, say, budgeting, personnel administration or the procurement and distribution of supplies." He continues:

Universal acceptance would bring with it stability and continuity, which in turn would make possible a new self-conscious breed of re-

search brokers, men and women who would point their careers toward the development of that function, who would look upon research brokerage as a goal rather than a way station, who would stay
in the activity long enough to do it well, and who would devote
themselves to developing and standardizing the doctrines that need
to govern its performance. If career training could be devised, too,
the makings of identifiable discipline, profession or subdiscipline
would be at hand.[18]

Sundquist wrote this in 1978, some ninety-one years after Mr. Dewey first
opened his School of Library Economy at Columbia. It is ironic that librarians have been so invisible that an eminent scholar such as Sundquist has
failed to recognize them as the prototype of his "research broker." The over-
sight is especially ironic since it is not uncommon in institutions and organizations dedicated to learning. Scholars, students, teachers, critics of higher
education often do not understand who librarians are or what they do, not to
mention what librarians can do for them. Librarians have been aware of this
discrepancy and conflict in perspective. Richard H. Logsdon, former head of
the Columbia University Libraries, was dismayed to be told by history professor Austin Evans that "the librarian and the scholar are eternal enemies."[19]
Mary Biggs explored "Sources of Tension and Conflict Between Librarians
and Faculty" in a 1981 *Journal of Higher Education* article.[20] These sources
range from disputes over the nature and range of faculty involvement in library policy-making and procedure, the changing library needs of scholars,
fondly-held stereotypes of librarians, and the appropriate placement of librarians in the governance structure of the university. Our purpose is not to
detail this lack of congruity, but simply to recognize this historical context
underlying contemporary discussions. The failure of the various commission
reports to allocate active educational roles to libraries and librarians stems
from a persistent and pervasive myopia and bias. Changing this perception
may need to be addressed along with other substantive recommendations.

Conclusion
In summary, the academic librarian's commitment to "fostering research" is
demonstrated in all areas of libraries' activities: collection development and
preservation, organizational restructuring, professional development of librarians and delivery of new services. "Fostering research" is also the ultimate goal of the "about-to-be-invented" knowledge centers of the future and
the revolutionary change they represent.

References

1. Herbert C. Morton and Anne Jamieson Price, "The ACLS Survey of Scholars: Views on Publications, Computers, Libraries," *Scholarly Communication*, 5 (Summer, 1986). The survey sample was a random selection of 5,385 members of American Council societies in classics, history, linguistics, literature, philosophy, political science, and sociology.

2. Frank Newman, *Higher Education and the American Resurgence*, A Carnegie Foundation Special Report (Princeton, N.J.: The Carnegie Foundation for the Advancement of Teaching, 1985), 150.

3. Barbara B. Moran, *Academic Libraries: The Changing Knowledge Centers of Colleges and Universities*, ASHE-ERIC Higher Education Research Report No. 8 (Washington, D.C.: Association for the Study of Higher Education, 1984).

4. W.I.B. Beveridge, *Seeds of Discovery* (New York: W.W. Norton & Company, 1980), 54.

5. *Ibid.*, 78.

6. Francis Miksa, "Research Patterns and Research," paper delivered at the Fifth Annual Conference of Directors of Research Libraries in OCLC, March 30, 1987.

7. Helen Haines, *Living With Books: The Art of Book Selection* (New York: Columbia University Press, 1935), 35.

8. Beveridge, 92.

9. *Ibid.*

10. *Alliance for Excellence: Librarians Respond to A Nation at Risk* (Washington, D.C.: U.S. Department of Education, 1984).

11. JoAn Segal, Letter to Manual J. Justiz, National Institute of Education, January 21, 1985).

12. *Ibid.*

13. *Ibid.*

14. *Ibid.*

15. *Ibid.*

16. John MacGregor and Raymond G. McInnis, "Integrating Classroom Instruction and Library Research: the Cognitive Functions of Bibliographic Network Structures," *Journal of Higher Education* 48 (Jan./Feb., 1977) 17-38; Elizabeth Frick, "Information Structure and Bibliographic Instruction," *Journal of Academic Librarianship* 1 (Sept., 1975) 12-14; Melvin J. Rucker, Jane A. Rosenberg, Robert P. Swierenga and Charles

D'Aniello, "Historians and Using Tomorrow's Research Library: Research, Teaching and Training," *The History Teacher* 17 (May, 1984) 385-444; Margaret F. Stieg, "The Information Needs of Historians," *College & Research Libraries* 42 (November, 1981) 549-560; C. Paul Vincent, "Bibliographic Instruction in the Humanities: the Need to Stress Imagination," *Research Strategies* 2 (Fall, 1984) 179-184; Lyn Thaxton, "Dissemination and Use of Information by Psychology Faculty and Graduate Students Implications for Bibliographic Instruction." *Research Strategies* 3 (Summer, 1985) 116-124.

17. James L. Sundquist, "Research Brokerage: The Weak Link," in *Knowledge and Policy: The Uncertain Connection,* Study Project on Social Research and Development, 5, ed. Laurence E. Lyn (Washington, D.C.: National Academy of Sciences, 1978), 127.

18. *Ibid.,* 144.

19. R.H. Logsdon, "The Librarian and the Scholar: Eternal Enemies," *Library Journal,* 95 (September 15, 1970), 2871-74.

20. Mary Biggs, "Sources of Tension and Conflict Between Librarians and Faculty," *Journal of Higher Education* (March/April, 1981), 182.

The Jewel in the Temple: University Library Networks as Paradigms for Universities

by Louis Vagianos and Barry Lesser

General Introduction

We live in a complex technological society in which the only constant is the exponential rate of change and the explosion of new knowledge and its applications. As in the perverse world of Alice, we must now run as fast as we can in order to stay in place. Worse still, the explosion of new knowledge and its applications, coupled to the exponential rate of change, has introduced a level of complexity which has made it increasingly difficult to predict future needs or the range of effects a single event or innovation will have. At the same time, it is becoming increasingly apparent that human beings and institutions cannot adjust easily to change of the scale and speed the world is presently experiencing. The result is an unsettled society, undergoing a period of institutional instability and human uncertainty.

As we move towards the twenty-first century, the powerful forces of technology which are driving the changes within our institutions and our society show little sign of abating. In fact advances in computers, communications and micro-electronics are creating a new society, based on information services and built on a new style of commercial activity. What is obvious is that the information technology which supports the new information industry promises to change the manner in which we make decisions, govern, work, play, study, and transact our business.

Information-based or information-intensive services per se are not new. They have an existence which is thousands of years old. What is new stems from three factors:

- for the first time in human history, information-based industries have become the major source of economic growth;
- technology has altered fundamentally the amount, content, form and delivery of information services;
- the rate of technological change surpasses any previous period in human history.

In 1970 Stafford Beer encapsulated the problem neatly:

> Society has become a complex organism, and it needs a nervous system. Managing the development of informational science and technology is all about this task. There is no other message than this.

At the same time he advanced four fundamental propositions of information technology:

1. We can now automate whatever we can exactly specify.
2. Most (probably all) ostensibly human prerogatives for inferential, judgemental, learned, and adaptive behavior can be exactly specified – at least with respect to finite contexts.
3. Within specified frameworks, much ostensibly intuitional and creative behavior can be indistinguishably imitated by machine.
4. Distance is technically irrelevant.

For many of us in universities the doubts which may have been expressed about these propositions in 1970 have diminished in the face of 15 years worth of further technological advances. Instead, our attention has turned to harnessing information technology effectively within the university environment in order to cope with the challenges of the new technological order and to meet the increasing demands of our shareholder (society). To date, the goal has proven elusive.

This background paper takes as its fundamental premise two factors:

– The characteristics inherent in information (reproductivity, volatility, and value) combined with the technical capability provided by the new information technology (access, storage, communication, and control) have created the prospect of a new range of internal and external networking possibilities within universities that could provide a major impetus for constructive change in universities. In fact, creating electronic proximity can introduce the most transformative period of institutional renewal undertaken by universities in living memory, because electronic networking can provide a suitable mechanism for efficient linkage among designated teachers, students, researchers, librarians, administrators, and to both private and public local, state, and federal resources.

– As electronic networking develops, universities will have at their disposal the experience of an underutilized resource of great value – the university library. The understanding and implementation of systems which create effective electronic proximity are well into their second decade among university libraries, with many of the cooperative, resource sharing examples interesting and instructive.

The argument which supports our premise is developed within the following framework:

– some problems facing higher education which are emerging from the new order of things;

- some parallels which exist between the roles and activities of universities and university libraries;
- some specific lessons library networks offer which are worthy of consideration by universities;
- some further observations about the general problem of electronic proximity;
- a brief summation.

1. Some Problems Higher Education Must Confront

At a recent national conference on worldwide trends and their implications for higher education, nine trends were singled out for debate and discussion. Like all such lists, the trends selected are neither definitive nor exhaustive, but they do serve to illustrate the range of pressures involved:

1. issues of war and peace and freedom and survival;
2. exploding population growth with its concomitant pressure on world resources;
3. energy issues;
4. oceans and the whole question of ecology;
5. aging populations in development countries;
6. genetic engineering;
7. increased interest in how the mind works;
8. technological revolution;
9. the problem of change.

Obviously, any considered discussion about their implications for higher education is beyond the scope of this paper. No matter, even a cursory review of the literature dealing with higher education demonstrates a debate is raging and that there is plenty of material on the subject to go around. In any event our concern is more specific and centers on some of the immediate changes threatening the closed system model of the traditional university which emanate from information technology.

(An aside, before citing some obvious examples, one disquieting observation: the debate surrounding higher education has resulted in a mountain of commentary and a spate of suggestions for improvement, but there is conspicuous silence on the subject of the role of libraries and the lessons that might be learned by educators from the collective experience of librarians. This revelation is particularly upsetting when applied to universities, for, as will be argued, university libraries are central to the university's mission.)

The university is one of the leading traditional information industries in our society, but technology is creating challenges which are not being met. As a result, new forms of competition are emerging. They range from the in-house training programs of alternative institutions to corporate offerings of degree programs. Two examples of corporate offerings: Arthur D. Little offers an MBA program, while the Wang Computer Firm offers a master's degree in software engineering. These competitive pressures are likely to intensify in the years ahead as computer-communications network developments offer corporations and individuals a greater ability to supply educational offerings of all kinds.

The university's constituency is also changing. The 18-22 age cohort is declining in size, while the 30-50 age cohort is growing proportionately. At the same time technology is placing new demands on occupational mobility. The average worker today already is expected to undergo three distinct careers during his/her working life. Thus, not only is an adult audience now there in terms of numbers, but the need for adult education is also becoming more pressing.

Location is another area in which universities are under pressure. They are being asked to reach out to students, especially adult students, to bring program delivery to where those students work and live. The self-contained university campus is no longer adequate to society's needs.

Universities are also being asked to link with industry and government, to play a more constructive role in fostering research and development of general economic benefit. Technology has greatly shortened the time line between basic research, the traditional research field of the university, and applied research. But the institutional versus technological base currently available is not sufficient to accommodate this change. To solve the problem there has been a rise in private industry involvement in basic research as well as government laboratories. Thus, the university faces new competitive pressures on both its teaching and research functions.

Moreover, as is always the case with technology there have been unexpected side effects for universities which relate specifically to the phenomenon of creative destruction first identified by Joseph Schumpeter. As we have come to know, technology both regenerates and destroys. For example, as a major user the university is being directly affected by the impact of technology on a number of applications – research applications, library applications, administration applications, teaching applications. All are observable in the university, and all offer advantages in terms of increased efficiency/productivity (*e.g.*, more/better research). On the other hand these same applications are also a source of negative pressure, partly because they involve high start-up costs in a time of major financial constraint and partly because they evoke a resistance to the organizational change needed within the university community during this period of intense institutional insecurity.

In any event, the resultant institutional problems higher education faces argue for a different model of the university – one which will necessitate improved co-operative measures. From our vantage point the creation of networks for facilitating electronic proximity is one mechanism which should be seriously considered. It cannot solve all the problems higher education must overcome, but it *can* offer an environment in which useful educational reform can be effected.

2. Some Parallels Existing Between Libraries and Universities

The university library, like the university it serves, is also a major, traditional information-based institution in our society. It too is being buffeted by the forces of technology and changing attitudes within our society. What makes the university library's experience a valuable guide for university administrators is the fact that the university library has much in common with the university as a leading information-based institution. Consider:

The task of the university is to create an environment which permits reflection, research and specialized training. It is here that scholars, researchers, and students are encouraged to seek knowledge, to examine it, question it, and to learn to transmit it. And it is here that they are taught how to explore society's "collective" mind through the medium of ideas, to understand that everything vital to one's life reduces itself ultimately to ideas.

The raison d'être of the university library is equally clear: to collect, organize, disseminate, and preserve the "collective" mind. In short, to provide the information which underpins the university's mission. Librarians, like educators, have long understood man is what he thinks and so ideas are the motive forces which shape history.

Universities and university libraries thus share a common heritage and mission:

- Each, as it has evolved over time, has become an instrument for promoting equity, equality of opportunity, in our society.
- Each draws some part of its support from outside its direct user constituency, whether from government or private sector support.
- Each, in its essence, is a communication system, providing the connective tissue which joins different constitutencies, activities and resources.

- Each is critically dependent on public (voluntary and government) financial support which is declining in real dollar terms.
- Each has experienced sharply rising resource prices (the university for professors, equipment and physical plant; the library for staff, books/periodicals, and computer/communications equipment), both absolutely and relative to the economy as a whole.
- Each faces increased competition from external institutions – the university from private sector research and schooling, and the university library from private industry databases/information services. In both cases there is a distinct danger that "cream skimming" will have general effects which are permanently deleterious.
- Each must cope with intense public stresses as a result of the increased complexity of their social environments and the importance of intellectual property in the information age – for the university the issue is one of "core curriculum," for the library the issue is one of "fair use."
- Each has traditionally operated as a closed system in both spatial terms and in membership aspects, but the impacts of information technology are making this traditional, stand-alone model less desirable, less appropriate, and less possible.

Within these general similarities, there are of course differences. Take two obvious ones:

- The university is concerned with the generation of new knowledge, where the university library is concerned with the dissemination of existing knowledge;
- the university is concerned with the transmission of culture, while the university library is concerned with the preservation of culture.

These differences are, however, subtle, particularly if we define the university as an institution for the acquisition and communication of knowledge of the human condition. Within such a definition the symbiotic relationship between the university and the university library is obvious. Equally obvious is the fact that for reasons of quality, preservation of mission, maintenance of public support, and meeting the demands of constituents, the traditional closed system model cannot survive and must be supplanted by an open system model. In the context of today's communication environment this means adaptation to and acceptance of electronic proximity. And thanks to an extraordinary range of experience, it is in this context that university libraries have much to share with their "keepers."

3. What Lessons Involving Electronic Proximity Do Libraries Offer to Universities?

The impetus behind the development of co-operative networks among university libraries was originally an imperative for better service and more value for the limited monies available to them. Financial pressures on university libraries have always been continuous, unrelenting, and potentially erosive. They never had sufficient funds to meet user demands. Moreover, over the years the volume and variety of material has been growing almost exponentially, so that the collection, preservation, coding and retrieval problems inherent in this situation have made the self-contained comprehensive collection an impossibility.

In addition, libraries faced external competition as well. Many traditional library functions were externalized by information technology: private data base vendors offering search services, bibliographic services, index services, etc. became competitors to the library. This competition was stiff and remains in those areas with the greatest value-added for the consumer. And unless libraries can meet with the competition, they are faced with the prospect of being left with the residue of services which have the lowest value-added appeal, a base insufficient for the library to continue to command adequate public support. More importantly, further innovations such as CD-ROM's and full-text data bases will give a new flexibility and mobility to the materials traditionally held on deposit by the library, transforming fundamentally the notion of a library "collection." The advent of the PC will give the centralized vendors real power for the diffusion of their products through networking. And the ease and inexpensiveness of photocopying or other forms of duplication (*e.g.*, database downloading) will bring libraries into conflict with authors and publishers over what constitutes "fair use" of copyright material. In the face of such pressures, basic institutional survival could well be put into question.

The traditional network concept embodied in the library is one defined in terms of physical space and physical artifacts (*e.g.*, in-house or interlibrary loan). The world of micro-electronics, computers, and electronic communications has changed this permanently. The library of the future, if it is to remain a social institution true to its original mission, can no longer be defined by a building or a local collection. Rather, it will be defined by the value-added service contribution it offers to its user constituency. For this reason, libraries have worked, and will continue to do so, to create networks which allow remote access to appropriate resources for designated users, a service that will eventually be extended to all users and suppliers as well.

Briefly, then, university libraries are institutions with an extensive heritage and an entrenched organizational culture, which were strongly challenged by both users and potential competitors. While there remained a continuing need for the library as an archival depository within its primary setting, librarians recognized that the traditional role of university libraries as information collectors and information storage providers had to be enhanced, and where appropriate supplanted, by the new role of information processor. The initial response to the demands of a changed environment was to attempt to become *external* networking agents. The host of networking applications devised to fulfill this new mandate introduced three levels of lessons which are especially noteworthy for consideration by other university administrators:

1. the library as a role model of both an educational and a social institution;

2. the networking systems already provided for/by libraries, on which the universities may be able to "piggyback" for extended pedagogical reasons; and

3. the recognition that university libraries have an educational role to play, not only in terms of their role in providing support materials for courses and other educational offerings, but also in the important task of educating users in the tasks of information seeking and information use. These tasks will become increasingly integral to learning and to pedagogical technique as well as to research in the information age and will create a new internal role for the librarian as a member of the teaching/ research faculty team.

Put another way, during the past two decades, despite their relative insularity, financial constraints, and staff shortages, university libraries have succeeded in doing some interesting and pioneering work in the design and implementation of networks facilitating electronic proximity:

- common cataloging systems (one of the earliest examples of such networking);

- interlibrary loan networks;

- bibliographic/indexing services;

- electronic bulletin boards;

- electronic message systems;

- a systematic, comprehensive, across the board system for interaction with commercial vendors, etc.

In general, libraries have been ahead of universities as a whole in their participation in and use of electronic networks. Unfortunately, for a variety of reasons, most of these networks have not been directly accessible by users. (A partial description of some of those electronic network developments is attached as Appendix I.)

Among the more important lessons learned by librarians during the process which can be studied with profit by others within the university community are:

- the establishment of standards and protocols;
- experience with alternative electronic communication options;
- staff training requirements;
- equipment needs;
- database building;
- interaction with vendors and commercial suppliers;
- user interface requirements;
- inter-institutional resource sharing;
- inter-institutional cost sharing;
- usage pricing alternatives.

Some specific observations involving insights gained while developing university library networks may also be useful. Here are a few:

- the utility of local regional networks will be reduced or eliminated as random access to remote resources is improved and will lead to the requirement of individual workstations at which the scholar, student, businessman, and librarian transact their business directly;
- the important issue of centralization (desire to build large resource bases for national resources exchange, improved standards, inexpensive telecommunications) vs. decentralization (fear of loss of autonomy/control, increased telecommunications costs, technological advances in mini and micro-computers, increasing costs of network services) will require resolution but, given the changing technology, may have to resolved on an *individual* basis;
- economic realities constitute the largest problem in networking, with a particular issue being transaction-related pricing (OCLC) vs. resource unit use pricing (UTLAS);
- the focus of university library networking is shifting from applications systems (catalog card production, automated circulation control, bibliographic services) to creating real-time links with university library collec-

tions throughout the world, with the "linking" of disparate systems showing promise of becoming the major university library automation topic;
- a major problem in library resource-sharing networks, even after more
  than a decade of operational activity , is a chronic shortage of staff, resulting from the number of institutions involved, the size of staffs, and
  the variety of services. Accredited schools, in-service training, continuing education, and certification have all failed to solve the problem. One
  reason may be that competition from the private sector for skilled staff is
  increasing;
- electronic proximity involves the critical, and as yet unresolved issue, of
  intellectual property because a) the technology makes downloading and
  copying so much easier, and b) network systems require sophisticated
  software development and distribution, raising software copyright issues;
- while the adoption of micro-computers as the standard tool for network
  access is the result of unquestionable technical advantages (ubiquity, an
  established operating system, low cost, high reliability, and easy linkage),
  it also involves costs and complexity in training, follow-up, and liaison,
  and increases individual institutions' propensity to believe that they can
  go it alone;
- university library networking must cope with a hostile information and
  communications environment which is not likely to change and an un-
  stable internal control structure (contracts, ethics, consultation, and
  governance);
- networks represent new social structures in the academic world crossing
  geographical and political boundaries and rising above the established
  patterns of discourse in professional associations and among institutions
  and will require more imaginative legal and organizational arrangements.
Some other lessons gleaned from the experience of the OCLC Consortium, which has been in operation for some 15 years are also interesting:
- the final development of a network may not be imaginable at its inception (and if it were, might be successfully resisted on "political"
  grounds);
- the implication of electronic proximity may be the creation of an emer-
  gent institution which is invested with disproportionate power in relation to any individual network member;
- as a network becomes a value-added entity, new and important legal and

political issues will arise;

- standardization for communication and standardization for interfacing are not always congruent, and communication tends to set the pace for other network activities.

4. Some Further Observations About the General Problem of Electronic Proximity
As noted earlier, the lessons cited from the experience of university libraries as worthwhile or applicable for consideration by university administrators have all emerged as a result of the relentless push of technology towards an information society. Yet this technological push should not be permitted to cause us to lose sight of primary institutional goals. Constructive adjustment is one thing, pernicious compromise another. Again, it is instructive to quote Beer:

> We might as well say that it is a problem
>   not so much of data acquisition as of right storage,
>   not so much of storage as of fast retrieval,
>   not so much of retrieval as of proper selection,
>   not so much of selection as of identifying wants,
>   not so much of knowing wants as recognizing needs.

Beer was not speaking of universities or university libraries specifically, but his summary of the problem is equally applicable to both. Providing for *appropriate* user needs is what drives both institutions. Universities and university libraries must, therefore, not be pushed by a technological imperative. Rather, they must be pulled by the power of our mission.

Within this context the application of Beer's argument in university terms is obvious. As a closed system, the traditional university has been site specific; it has worked by bringing students, faculty, and support services all together in one place. University reputations have been built on such foundations as the number and quality of faculty, or the number and quality of students, or such supporting infrastructures as the size of the library collection. Part-time students have been regarded at best as peripheral and at worst as a disruption and a nuisance; full-time students count most because they are full members of the closed sytem. External influences exist but, as much as possible, they are internalized whenever the opportunity arises. Thus, faculty, programs, and students are seldom shared by universities even when they are located in the same community. In the past, universities have thrived on competition with one another for faculty, research grants, students, and other scarce resources, but such competition is now an expenditure of resources few can afford.

There is little doubt now that the closed model of the university will be changed by the forces resulting directly or indirectly from technological change. Already these forces have created the new constituency identified earlier – adult or life-long learners. They are also creating a greater demand for part-time studies, for time-of-day flexibility in course offerings, and for new mechanisms to bring courses to people rather than bringing people to courses.

Yet this is only a beginning of the changes. As full-text data bases become more prevalent, as CAI/CAL programs become more common and of better quality, as expert systems come to provide a real interactive machine learning capability, and as electronic networking makes the academic information entrepreneur a reality, the teaching function of the university will be under increasing competitive pressure.

And as R&D becomes quintessential to the technological world and its economic well-being, the basic research function of the university will be changed drastically.

If there is a major policy lesson universities can learn from libraries it is this: don't be negative or defensive. An active stance fostering progressive change and enlightened experimentation is the only way to ensure positive benefits. Higher education, like many of its libraries, must embrace the challenge of technology and its impact on society as a means of enhancing its unique contributions, reaching out to new audiences and new places through new programs and new associations. Universities, like their university libraries, can broaden their bases by developing the sorts of electronic proximity their new environment demands.

True, the university is but one piece of the complex fabric modern society has become; but, as a primary agent for the acquisition of information, it has a vital role to play in maintaining the durability of the social fabric. It cannot do without adaptation and modification; and, it cannot do it alone! The university library has already realized this, seeking out new networking arrangements which will help it survive as the public institution of social record. The university, of necessity, will follow in many of the library's paths and can benefit from lessons already well established.

Earlier in this paper, it was noted that the university library had to adapt and modify its traditional role as information collector and information storage provider to that of information processor. Such a change would lead to some interesting and innovative consequences but would require some major organizational adjustments within the university environment. What is noteworthy is that the change was not possible twenty years ago. Consider:

Technology, and the changing role of the university library it prescribes, implies a convergence within the university of the library and the computer center – a convergence which can be replicated on a larger scale in the university's relationships with society. In its traditional role, the library has acted as repository of pre-packaged information and as an information lender. The computer center, as it has been evolving, has provided for information input, storage, retrieval, and manipulation. It processes information, albeit not primarily that of a pre-packaged variety. As the technology improves, the computer center increasingly becomes the hardware link for faculty/student access to all types of information products. At this point, the evolutionary trends between the university library and the computer center will reflect an almost complete convergence at the technological level. More important, the skills of the university library staff, together with the necessity of the university library becoming an information processor, converge with the need and ability of the computer center to develop and provide such services. What should emerge is a single university information center, a fact not yet recognized at the organizational level in most universities.

This notion of a university information center formed out of the existing library and computing center units has been advanced by several commentators, including Vagianos, Battin and Neff and was, in fact, implemented at Dalhousie University in 1975. As noted, there are administrative and technical arguments to recommend this organizational change, but the most important is that such a move embodies the essence of the case set out for the university and the library to adopt new roles. Orienting their major focus to recognizing and meeting a set of user needs as information processors is a necessary and useful first step. In the information age this will mean accepting machines and electronic networks as the physical artifacts of a renewed educational system.

Put in these terms, the lessons drawn from the university library case can be generalized to the situation of the university as a social institution. Major parts of the networking functions libraries now operate in support of their own services may be extended within the university. For users and suppliers, the evolution of links may be transparent, that is not readily noticed as an element in the operational delivery of services, but in terms of recognizing and responding to users' needs the results will be very apparent. The symbiotic relationship of the university library and the university, complementing and reinforcing each other, can then be extended among other institutions as well.

This discussion does not imply that university libraries already have the answers. Far from it. But since a number of rivers have been crossed, often painfully, there is much experience to be shared. Part of the value for universities will be in learning what to try and what not to try; what to do and what not to do; what worked as well as what didn't. University libraries, though, still have an extensive future agenda of their own:

1. they must come to grips with networks as a primary service offering, not a peripheral undertaking;
2. they must extend network applications, creating electronic proximity at the user level;
3. they must see themselves as part of a larger community, with the primary purpose of serving the needs of that community while co-existing with other parts providing service.

Facing these issues implies solving such problems as the legal implications of sharing resources and of accepting and meeting obligations to external donors (government, private business, and the general public), sometimes at the expense of local service. Make no mistake, university libraries still have a lot to learn and a long way to go!

The transition of both the university and the university library from closed systems, defined by geographic boundaries and material and human resource collections, to open systems connected through networks for electronic proximity (i.e., location independent, distance insensitive) will necessitate extraordinary effort. Both universities and university libraries have been, to a large degree, passive observers of their larger environment. This passivity must change. What is needed is a leadership role in developing the networks which are called for while defining their place in the new order. The alternative may be to discover, too late, that the potential of the new technology has by-passed them and has been exploited by other, as yet undetermined, institutions.

The active stance of leadership in handling information issues which is called for requires a variety of institutional reponses from universities which will be difficult to initiate and sustain within the context of existing organization and charters:

— the adoption of a planning framework (something remarkably absent in universities and most university libraries);

- attitudinal changes at both the institutional level and staff level regarding the institutional mission, its relationship with, and its reponsibilities to, the internal university community and to other communities that must be involved;
- a new dynamism, meaning two things: the speed "with which messages are promulgated, overtake each other, and combine to form new patterns"; and the speed with which universities can respond to market pressures and opportunities.

Legal and institutional reform will also be needed to ensure inertia does not remain as an excuse for inaction.

The transition will involve substantial financial costs too. In the long run, the changes in operation will produce economies which more than pay for the investment, even in narrow financial terms. But in the short run, there will be major outlays for equipment, planning, promotion, and a host of unforeseen contingencies. In a time of major financial pressure on both universities and libraries, this is not a trivial concern and will call for resourcefulness and courage on the part of the players.

A Brief Summation

In the light of the problems of transition and costs described, is the prescription for change which has been made reasonable? The answer, we would suggest, is *not* whether the university or the university library, organizationally and financially, can afford the change. Rather, we would suggest that the answer is in fact another question – can either afford not to make the change?

In 1982, the U.S. Office of Technology Assessment, in a study of the impact of information technology on American education, stated:

Modern society is undergoing profound technological and social changes brought about by what has been called the information revolution. This revolution is characterized by explosive developments in electronic technologies and by their integration into complex information systems that span the globe. The impact of this revolution affects individuals, institutions, and governments – altering what they do, how they do it, and how they relate to one another. If individuals are to thrive economically and socially in a world that will be shaped to a large degree by these technological developments, they must adapt through education and training.

We have not advocated that universities embrace the changes recommended for defensive, self-serving reasons. We recommend them because the technological imperative is forcing us to think anew. To paraphrase Marshal McLuhan, a prophet of the new order: old ways of thinking and old formulations will not permit us to fit the embryonic world of tomorrow into yesterday's conventional cubby holes.

Part of what is unique about the university and the university library is that they are both educational institutions and social institutions. The information age is marked, amongst other things, by an increasing commoditization of information. Both the production and the dissemination of information are being increasingly commercialized for a profitseeking motive. But it is neither efficient nor equitable, at the societal level, to allow the educational function, as a primary information activity, to fall victim to this trend.

As social institutions, both the university and the library play major roles in "the acquisition and communication of knowledge of the human condition." In the new information order, it is important that these roles not be lost. We must be concerned with more than what is commercially viable; the human condition is more than just profits. It is this role of the university and the university library in serving those needs as an end that sets them apart from commercial information undertakings. From a perspective of universities and libraries as generic institutions, there is no more important lesson to learn. Universities and university libraries must be concerned with equity; welfare is not consonant with ability to pay. They must also recognize that networks are not just machines or wires or digital bit streams, they are people. Serving people must remain the essence of the university and the university library. That is what creating electronic proximity as a response to the changing information needs of society is about.

Finally, we should bear in mind that the information technology which is pushing us into a new age is a means and not an end, an aid and not a cure. It *is* ushering in an era of hitherto unimaginable potential and opportunity, but it is also fraught with danger and possible pitfalls. How prescient Goethe's remarks in 1810:

> The modern age has a false sense of superiority because of the great mass of data at its disposal. But the valid criterion of distinction is rather the extent to which man knows how to form and master the material at hand.

Appendix 1
Some Sources of Relevant Experience in Creating Electronic Proximity
The following appendix briefly outlines some major institutions in the library/information arena which have been major participants in the formation and operation of networks. It is not intended to be exhaustive, nor does the exclusion of any particular operation from this appendix mean that it has no lessons to teach. In particular, the rather large proliferation of small, regional networks may have specific lessons relating to getting started and overcoming institutional autonomy which will be of great value. The very specific nature of the lessons and the regions involved makes their inclusion in this general conspectus inappropriate.

Each entry covers the institution and its major operations, and provides a selection of recent literature. More attention to topics of universal concern can be found *inter alia* in the following:

Annual Review of Information Science and Technology 16, 18, 20 (White Plains, NY: Knowledge Industry Press).

Robert Axelrod, *The Evolution of Cooperation* (New York: Basic Books, 1984).

Bowker Annual of Library and Book Trade Information (New York: Bowker, various years).

Key Issues in the Networking Field Today.

Papers based on the Symposium, Networking: Where From Here? *Library Networking: Current Problems and Future Prospects*, ed. Walter Luquire. (New York: Neal-Schuman Publishers, 1980).

Susan K. Martin, "The New Technologies and Library Networks," *Library Journal* 109 (June 15, 1984): 1194-1196.

JoAnn V. Rogers, "Networking: Selected Research Studies, 1979-83." *Library and Information Science Research* 6 (1984): 111-132.

A. OCLC, Inc.
One of the major bibliographic utilities in the world, OCLC (the oldest and largest of the automated library networks) is a valuable object lesson in several important aspects of electronic proximity creation. Not the least of these is that a utility can take on forms which are a complete surprise to its original creators (OCLC was originally the Ohio Co-operative for Library Cataloging). OCLC represents the experience of a continental system which has had to resolve questions of resource use, the nature of the consortium "management" and its relationship both to member institutions and the networks through which access to OCLC resources is gained, the autonomy of net-

works, the role of network directors in OCLC governanace, and coping with the tendency of networks (which serve as OCLC conduits) to offer competitive services. The sheer size of OCLC operations makes it a good source of information about growth and complex management problems.

Some appreciation for the scale of OCLC activities can result from considering the following 1985 statistics:

6,082 member libraries

6,584 dedicated terminals on-line

25,500,000 items cataloged on-line

131,000,000 catalog cards ordered

2,200,000 inter-library loan transactions

1,140,000 cataloging records

756,768 titles ordered on-line

64 on-line union lists of serials supported for 2,065 libraries

200,900,000 location listings

43 computer service agreements serving 108 libraries

$69,069,000 in service revenues

$37,500,000 net worth

The financial statistics alone give a dollar quantification of the costs involved in creating networks at the international level.

In addition to the production of library cataloging, OCLC is involved in a number of projects and services for network application:

- the CONSER (Conversion of Serials) Project, the development of a national serials data base;
- collaborative development of non-roman alphabet capabilities;
- EASI Reference Service, subject access to a subset of the OCLC data base;
- retrospective cataloging production in machine-readable format;
- an automated serials check-in system;
- an automated acquisitions system available on-line;
- development of a Gateway Service, allowing the user to access different networks through the same terminal in the same session;
- sponsorship of research and development in areas outside "pure" library automation (e.g., teletex/viewdata).

Information sources:
Rowland C. W. Brown, *OCLC: Present Issues, Future Directions* (Dublin, Ohio: OCLC, 1985).
"OCLC at ALA," *Library Systems Newsletter* 5 (September 1985): 70-71.

"OCLC in 1985: At the Crossroads," *Library Journal* 110 (July 1985): 12-13.

"OCLC to Set Standards for Network Performance," Library Journal 110 (December 1985): 24.

Susan K. Martin, *Library Networks, 1981-82* (White Plains, NY: Knowledge Industry Press, 1981), Chapter IV.

OCLC: *Annual Report,* various years (Dublin, Ohio: OCLC, 1985).

OCLC Newsletter, various years.

Norman D. Stevens, "Copyright of the OCLC Database," *Library Issues: Briefings for Faculty and Administrators,* 4, (July 1984).

Address: 6565 Frantz Road, Dublin, OH 43017, U.S.A.

B. *Research Libraries Information Network (RLIN)*

RLIN is a program of the Research Libraries Group (RLG), representing an outgrowth of the Bibliographic Automation of Large Libraries using an On-line Timesharing System (BALLOTS) project. Originally designed to serve the Stanford University Libraries, the system was extended to academic and public libraries for cataloging, searching, and inter-library loan functions. RLIN has placed considerable emphasis on educating scholars about the current and future developments in research libraries, including interconnection of networks for electronic mail, computational resource access, scholarly information, mediated access to information resources, full-test retrieval online, digitally encoded image data, and international data retrieval. RLIN is developing the Linked Systems Project, which will not only provide interactive facilities for large centralized library data base systems, but will also interact with local systems at individual member institutions. The emphasis RLIN has given to electronic connections makes it a valuable source for lessons on both the organization and economics of electronic proximity.

In addition to RLIN bibliographic activities, the RLG is also active in a number of projects of wider scope:

- the sharing of collection information via the RLG Conspectus On-Line;
- development of expert systems software to aid users in formulating search queries and interpreting results;
- development of the Patron Access Project, allowing direct user search of networked library catalogs;
- harnessing optical disk technology;
- on-line implementation of non-roman alphabet capabilities (with OCLC);
- establishment of a real-time transatlantic telecommunications link with

the British Library for co-operative programs of research and development.

Information sources:
"British Library Transatlantic Computer Link," *Library Hi Tech News,* no. 18 (July-August 1985), 6.
Susan K. Martin, *Library Networks,* 1981-82 (White Plains, NY: Knowledge Industry Press, 1981), Chapter IV.
Richard W. McCoy, "The Electronic Library: Essential Tasks for the Scholarly Community," *Library Journal* 110 (October 1985): 39-42.
Wayne E. Davidson, "Building Networks for Scholarly Communication," *EDUCOM Bulletin* 20 (Spring 1985): 2-5.
The Research Libraries Group News, various issues.
Address: Jordan Quadrangle, Stanford University, Stanford, CA 94305, U.S.A.

C. University of Toronto Library Automation System (UTLAS)
UTLAS developed as a Canadian equivalent of BALLOTS: the computerized system of a major university library which developed into a utility network, with initial emphasis on Canada, and later extension to the U.S.A. The services offered by UTLAS include cataloging, retrospective conversion, data-base searching, on-line ordering, and catalog/circulation control systems. UTLAS is a good source of information for operations in a national context which differs from that prevailing in the United States, and for lessons relating to transborder data flows to and from the U.S.A.

Additional UTLAS developments include:
– integration of the REMARC data base (which allows for retrospective machine-readable cataloging) with the UTLAS data base;
– availability of MARC records for Japanese imprints.

Information sources:
"UTLAS in Westchester: Reconversion and Cataloguing," *Library Journal* 110 (July 1985): 20.
"UTLAS Expanded U.S. Activities," *Library Hi Tech News* 18 (July-August 1985): 7.
"UTLAS at ALA," *Library Systems Newsletter* 5 (September 1985): 71.
"Utlas [sic] Moves Into US Market with New Systems, Huge Database," *Library Journal* 109 (June 15, 1984), 1168.

Susan K. Martin, *Library Networks, 1981-82* (White Plains, NY: Knowledge Industry Press, 1981), Chapter IV.
Address: 130 George Street, Toronto, Ontario, Canada M5S 1A5.

D. *Regional Networks*

The following list of regional networks highlights only a major subset of such organizations. The systems and services available vary, as do the network topologies and environment, but each well may have important lessons to teach in relation to their specific region.

1. AMIGOS - a Southwestern U.S. consortium (with extensions into Mexico) primarily comprising academic libraries. See - "Micro Support from AMIGOS: Training, Consulting, Technical," *Library Journal* 110 (June 1, 1985) : 72; *Que Pasa?* Newsletter of the Amigos Bibliographic Network, various issues. Address: 11300 North Central Expressway, Suite 321, Dallas, TX 75243, U.S.A.;

2. Bibliographic Center for Research (BCR) - a Rocky Mountain/Midwest broker of automated library services. See - "50th Birthday Marked by BCR-Rocky Mountain," *Library Journal* 110 (June 15, 1985): 60. Address: 245 Columbine, Suite 212, Denver, CO 80206, U.S.A.;

3. Cooperative Library Agency for Systems and Services (CLASS) - formerly the California Library Authority for Systems and Services, a statewide data base and support services marketing agency which has since extended beyond state borders. See - Michael J. Bruer, "Lessons from CLASS," *Library Journal* 109 (November 15, 1984): 2119-2124; "CLASS to Work with UC on Conservation," *Library Journal* 110 (June 1, 1985): 60. Address: 1415 Knoll Circle, Suite 101, San Jose, CA 95112, U.S.A.

4. New England Library Information Network (NELINET) - a large regional network of diverse membership, supplying OCLC access and regional computing services. See - Betsy Kruger, "NELINET: A Case Study of Regional Library Network Development," *Information Technology and Libraries*, 4 (June 1985): 112-121. Address: 385 Elliot Street, Newton, MA 02164, U.S.A.

5. Southeastern Library Network (SOLINET) - one of the largest regional network organizations, with diverse membership, providing training for and access to OCLC and major information services. See - Ron Chepesiuk and Shirley Tariton, "SOLINET: What's In It For Us," *Wilson Library Bulletin* 58 (November 1983): 185-189; "AMIGOS and SOLINET Discuss Closer Linkage," *Library Journal* 110 (February 1, 1985): 19;

"SOLINET's New Program Will Support Networks," *Library Journal* 110 (April 15, 1985). Address: Suite 410, 615 Peachtree Street NE, Atlanta, GA 30308, U.S.A.

6. Western Library Network (WLN) - formerly the Washington Library Network, this regional organization provides computer and cataloging services for the Northwest U.S.A. with extensions internationally (especially towards Pacific Rim nations). See - "WLN Network Changes Name"/ "WLN New Software Product"/"WLN Software Installed," *Library Hi Tech News*, 18 (July-August 1985): 6/14/7; "Worldwide Licences of WLN System at Australia Meet," *Library Hotline* 14 (November 11, 1985): 11. Address: Washington State Library, Olympia, WA 98504, U.S.A.

Academic Libraries and Regional Economic Development

by Joan B. Fiscella and Joan D. Ringel

Public policy discussions which affect higher education in the 1980's are increasingly interwoven with threads of political reality. A case can be made that the sobering political truths of scarce resources have triggered a sequence of events which have caused public institutions of higher learning in Colorado to behave differently both within the political arena and the business community. And, if recent history augurs the future, this new sensitivity to the effect of alliances between academia and business bodes well, too, for academic libraries.

Scarce financial resources and internecine competition for public support for higher education in Colorado created an atmosphere of political competition second in intensity only to the maneuvering of the defense establishment in Washington, D.C. The political bickering, the proliferation of duplicative programs and the lack of accountability in higher education caused legislators in the late 1970's to move away from traditional line item budgeting to an innovative memorandum of understanding between the General Assembly's Joint Budget Committee and the governing boards and presidents of Colorado's various institutions of higher learning.

Under the new scheme, institutional leaders were to have broad authority in allocating public money as well as the ability to carry over year-end surpluses which was more in keeping with academia's need to make longer term investments beyond election year budgetary pressures. The flexibility and the longer planning view have been beneficial to Colorado's public institutions.

Yet, from the elected official's perspective, questions of duplication within the state's system of higher education, as well as concerns of accountability and quality, continued to nag. The new allocation system still depended on the legislature's deciding the magnitude of funding for each institution; and that decision was still largely dependent upon funding formulae sensitive to an institution's enrollment figures. Innovative and aggressive institutional leaders, therefore, became astute marketing experts. Degree programs became magnets for students; the limits of imagination and even whimsy became parameters for program development. Not surprisingly engineering, computer science, teaching and business programs sprang up throughout the state; even a lawn-mowing course briefly saw the light of day. Weekend and evening degree programs became readily available for the increasingly traditional, "non-traditional" student.

Yet, as marketing intensified, pressure on legislators also intensified: more students meant more competition for decreasing resources. The political realities of district lines, the location of institutions of higher learning, the number of jobs created by those institutions all created pressure on elected officials to sustain a public system of higher education established over time in a way that no longer reflected the state's needs, market place forces, enrollment potential or sound educational philosophy.

Enter Representative Paul D. Schauer, Chairman of the House Finance Committee and major architect of Colorado's tax policy. Motivated in some part by an astute awareness of the limits of Colorado's revenue picture, in some part by the courage of educational conviction and in some part by the reality that no major research institution was located in his own district, Representative Schauer shepherded HB 1187 through a political mine field in 1985 and, to the surprise of many, succeeded in abolishing and re-establishing the Colorado Commission on Higher Education.

Under the newly reconstituted Commission, legislators are to be assured of greater quality, less duplication, more accountability and funding based on a formula which reflects an institution's role and mission. And much to elected officials' relief, the forum for competition for decreasing financial resources shifts away from Colorado's General Assembly to the Commission. Time will certainly tell about the best laid plans...But to date the Commission has functioned according to design.

Throughout this political evolution, academic libraries have not fared well overall in Colorado. While acquisitions budgets have increased 2% and operations and salary budgets increased 6%, libraries generally have not been able to keep pace with inflation, and community college libraries have seen a 20% decrease in their acquisition budgets.[1] According to a formula developed by the Library Financing Formula Sub-committee of the Association of Public College and University Presidents, Colorado libraries were being funded at between 55% and 60% of the formula. According to Patricia Senn Breivik in "Colorado Funding of Academic Libraries":

> With the increasing need to access online databases and the expanding publication output, the ability of academic libraries to support existing programs has been further curtailed. In addition, there are no guarantees that new acquisition dollars will be provided when new programs are approved and it is even less likely that retrospective purchasing funds will be available. A frequent ap-

proach for a campus seeking approval for a new program from the Colorado Commission on Higher Education, is to claim that 'no new library resources are required.' To say otherwise might well jeopardize program approval. Thus, the already insufficient funds must be stretched even thinner.[2]

Given this situation libraries are poorly equipped to support Colleges and Universities that are attempting to further high-quality programs.

During this same period of evolution, academic institutions have begun to learn the importance of ties to the business community. Ways to encourage corporate giving, entrepreneurial potential between research activities and for-profit spin-offs, the formation of centers of excellence and the establishment of research parks have all become new tools in the armamentarium of academic leadership. Sluggish economies have caused elected officials as well as academic leaders to see economic development as the new magnet for public funding opportunities. Academic libraries could do well to learn from this new partnership.

Such a partnership could provide genuine benefits for members of the business community, elected officials, and academia. Businesses – particularly small businesses – stand to gain a resource they cannot afford to miss. Academic libraries have the potential of providing resources in marketing, personnel management and basic research that the average business cannot afford on its own; yet, business decisions made in an information vacuum often lead to failure.

One example of a program of relationships between business and academic libraries is the Business Partner Program at Auraria Library in Denver, Colorado. The Auraria Library serves three institutions at a combined downtown campus – Community College of Denver, Metropolitan State College and the University of Colorado at Denver. Among the three institutions academic programs cover vocational and technical, undergraduate and graduate education. The combined student bodies of approximately 30,000 (20,000 FTE) include traditional age students, 18-22 years, as well as older ones, with an average age of 28. Almost all the students work at least part time; and many take classes evenings and weekends while working full time. A large number of students are enrolled in the business programs of all three schools or take some business classes along with liberal arts, sciences or professional courses of studies. The location of the campus, the character of the student body, and the strength of the professional programs provided the

context in which to begin the Library's Business Partner program, in 1983.
A firm participates in the Business Partner program by donating a specified amount of money to the library and in turn receives library cards in the business name as well as discounts on certain fee-based services; the level of donation determines the extent of discounts. A librarian is named liaison to members of the firm. In brief the business gets access to the collection, reduced fees for services such as interlibrary loan, consultant services for database searching, labor costs for photoduplicating articles and the delivery of materials. In addition the librarian will design seminars for employees of the firm, introducing them to information resources and strategies relevant to their company and industry.

Interactions with a number of firms (some Business Partners, some not) provide examples of the ways in which business can benefit by using information resources. These examples are not meant to be conclusions of a full scale empirical study; on the other hand they are not simply descriptions of individual experiences. Rather they typify a number of situations in which businesses use information that can be provided by libraries. These selected examples provide models of service rather than recipes for relations between libraries and businesses.

The businesses using Auraria Library are involved in both service and manufacturing industries, with a broad spectrum of information needs. Three specific areas indicate the possibilities of economic development and the range of information required by companies to further that development: attracting new clients or buyers, providing services to another company, and developing new products and services.

Some companies become more profitable by expanding the number of their clients in proportion to their ability to serve them. Advertising, informal contacts and systematic approaches to companies or individuals provide possible new clients. Systematic approaches can take the form of either direct mailing or telephone calls to business firms or individuals in order to reach as many potential clients as possible. Since only a certain percentage of contacts will result in new business the soliciting firms have to find a balance between developing a large enough group to contact, but not so large that the costs of such a project will outweigh the business developed. Screening a potential pool through telephone books, other directories, and purchased mailing lists are always ways to develop selected contact lists.

A fourth way of identifying possible new clients is through the use of online directory databases which allow the searcher to select companies according to several different parameters, including size, sales, geography, industry, and so on. By carefully selecting characteristics, a company can tailor the list of potential clients to fit within a budget. Each of the four methods has advantages and disadvantages, taking into consideration factors such as cost, completeness, accuracy, currency, and time involved. Thus the company contemplating such a project has to evaluate the methods, the chance of success, and the probable long range results to choose the most suitable method.

A successful company sells its products or services by showing how they meet specific client needs. Thus the providing company needs to know the client company's finances, its structure, and its line of business. While the client company itself may provide the information, getting supplementary information from outside sources can provide useful comparative data to raise questions or to put another perspective on what is already known. Since such information gives the provider an edge in marketing, obtaining it more effectively and efficiently is an important strategy.

Availability of key information about a company is directly related to its status as private or public and its size. Securities and Exchange Commission reports are useful for information about public companies. The larger and/ or more dynamic a company, the greater chance there will be that articles will appear in newspapers or magazines or that press releases are available. Some excellent articles, providing information about private as well as public companies and appearing in smaller local/regional or business community newspapers or newsletters are now indexed in national online databases.

Currency and accuracy of information are crucial. Daily newspapers are very current, but there can be quite a bit of lag time until newspapers are indexed so that specified articles can be found without browsing each day's issue. Computer access is quicker, usually, but there still is some lag time depending on the kind of information needed and the updating policies of database publishers.

Accuracy of information is in part a factor of currency, particularly when the status of a company or industry is changing from day to day. But whether a researcher can depend on the information is also a factor of the reliability of the source. Astute questioning of the information resource and comparing one source with another can help safeguard against some inaccuarcy.

Cost is also a factor. One online database producer which provides financial information on private companies charges $18-80 per online record for that information in contrast to another which may charge only a few dollars. Usually businesses require in-depth information only for a few companies; to attempt to get such information for all potential clients is too costly and time-consuming. *Some* time and money are worth the effort. A company which has done its homework on the client company is in a much better position to sell itself, all other things being equal.

A third area of economic development is through innovation.[3] New product or service development is an important process in highly competitive industries, with the possibility of either great financial gains or losses. Product or service expansion may involve inventing new technology, restructuring available resources, or acquiring a new company. At the same time, economic, technical, and social contexts contribute to the success or failure of such developments. For this reason, access to information about industry trends, social patterns, and marketing demographics is essential to innovation.

One example of how a company identifies, locates and uses information comes from a study done in the early 1980's.[4] The company, known here as A/TECH, researched the feasibility of diversifying into the area of robotic components manufacturing by looking at the technical processes available, trends in technology and market projections. The corporate development office of A/TECH used information culled from a literature review, a national robotics seminar, and telephone conferences with well-known researchers as well as from selected other companies already in the field.[5]

The literature search for this project utilized publicly available online databases, specifically, engineering, business news, business forecasting, market research report, company directory, annual report, and investment report databases. These searches led to articles and reports on the state of the art in robot components, identification of some key researchers and companies in the field, and projections of the market, which then became sources of other unpublished information.

The literature review, discussions with key people, and investigations of the market led these researchers to recommend that A/TECH not enter into development of robotic component manufacturing at that time, since many of the original high market projections which had instigated this study seemed unrealistic. The rapid obsolescence of products and the necessity of entering into agreements with outside companies would have meant a profitable return too many years later for A/TECH's plans. Although this example does not show information leading to great profits, it does provide an example of a company gathering relevant information to make an informed decision, which in this case they judged saved them from a costly and unproductive investment. Each of the above examples illustrates ways in which businesses use information available through, although not exclusively, libraries. The information that companies use comes out of a combination of personal experience and insight, talking to colleagues or competitors, and publicly available knowledge. It should be clear in these examples that the information is sorted and evaluated by the businesses who need it for their own purposes. The information means something different to different firms. What may not be clear is the contribution of the library to that sorting and evaluating process.

Where do libraries fit in? Specifically, what is the role of the academic library in economic development? Libraries provide a number of services: general and special collections, computer and print access to their own collections and those of other libraries, computer search services, interlibrary lending, document delivery, reference, education. Access is one key concept by which to discuss the role of academic libraries in economic development.

Access can be thought of in terms of either physical access or intellectual access. One function of a library is collecting or gathering materials. Since an academic library supports the teaching/learning and research needs of an academic community, its collection will reflect the curricular and research directions of the campus, thus providing the specialized resources not always found in smaller public libraries.

Nonetheless, a collection has little worth unless it is accessible. Physical access involves being able to get to the resources in a nearby library or to get those resources to the requestor. It also means being able to get at something not held by any nearby collecting group. Consequently, closely related to acquiring materials is procuring them from other libraries. Academic and public libraries belong to networks which permit them to find research or specialized materials, even from other countries, and get them for clients. Although not every business question calls for the kind of background that publicly available materials provide, major projects often do require a context which is found in research journals or government publications, found in academic libraries.

Intellectual access takes the concept of access one step further.[6] Finding accurate information to answer a question sounds straightforward enough but it isn't, always. When it isn't, the ambiguity can be a function of the question, of the sources of information, or the information itself. Helping someone get at information is the role of a librarian or information specialist as consultant. Three aspects of this role are helping to formulate the question, getting the information, and interpreting the information.

Although formulating a question is not always an easy task, making its assumptions and purpose explicit enables the librarian to focus the direction of the search for information. This process is often an exercise in diplomacy since the librarian needs to probe without either implying that the question is unworthy or giving the impression of crossing the bounds of privacy. The consulting process is very important because by establishing the context and identifying the correct categories of the question, the librarian can more effectively connect the researcher with the correct information. The librarian often has to propose alternate ways of thinking about the issues since obvious sources of information do not always yield the answer. Not only are published and computerized resources at the librarian's disposal, but as part of the academic community she/he can also put the information seeker in contact with campus researchers who are working in areas of mutual concern.

Interpreting answers to questions is crucial. As indicated in the examples, individual patrons have to make sense out of information, but people new to the world of computerized information sources often place too much trust in what the computer provides. Working with the business person, a librarian can raise critical questions of the data and propose alternative perspectives.

Not only can librarians provide access to a variety of information sources, but they also have the potential of creating those sources. For instance, libraries in Oregon are developing the *Economic Information Network Index* and Denver's Auraria Library has begun its Colorado Information Resource Center.[7] Both of these projects are using technology to integrate regional business and economic resources and make them accessible through easy to use dial-up computer networks. Other possibilities include electronic bulletin boards and the integration of research done by chambers of commerce and other local research centers.[8]

In his work, *The Knowledge Executive*, Harlan Cleveland speaks about the attitudes of the generalist which include questioning assumptions, curiosity, and integration of people and ideas, among others.[9] A librarian consultant with those attitudes can contribute to a company's work through intelligent questioning, taking an imaginative perspective on the information, and critically evaluating sources of information. He or she may go further and work with companies to identify and help produce needed information resources to further economic development in a region.

In summary, what businesses can gain from relationships with academic libraries is physical access to research collections and intellectual access to people with expertise in the structure of information sources. Given the need for such access it makes economic as well as philanthropic sense for companies to help fund academic centers which can provide the resources and services that they need.

Given the scarce funding available for academic libraries, they too have to ask how such arrangements will benefit them. One answer is the potential political leverage for funding. Another is that direct contact with businesses provides libraries with insight into the kinds of information structures needed by business, which in turn makes them more effective partners in the education process. Students whose learning takes place in such institutions bring greater sophistication in integrating information resources into their work.

Two issues today, however, question the validity of the role of the academic library vis-a-vis the business world. One issue raises the question of relevancy; the other of legality. Neil Eurich's examination of education programs within the corporate context indicates that higher education is being challenged in its ability to educate students in communication and mathematical skills as well as state of the art research.[10] If corporations must provide needed education, are college and university programs, along with support structures such as academic libraries, simply irrelevant? Eurich does not recommend abolishing higher education, but reexamining its role in society today.

The legal question has recently been raised by small business leaders who are suggesting that the sale of consumer goods on college/university campuses is taking unfair advantage of non-profit status to raise money.[11] Libraries which provide services for fees to individuals and companies not affiliated with the academic institutions are part of this issue.

Neither question is easily answered. Ultimately, however, the issues must be analyzed by looking to the broader one of the relationship of higher education institutions to economic communities of which they are a part. Higher education institutions which place their mission of educating students and developing new knowledge within not only professional communities, but within regional and economic contexts as well will see their libraries as contributing to those missions in their work with businesses.

References

1. Patricia Senn Breivik, "Colorado Funding of Academic Libraries," *Colorado Libraries* 11 (Summer 1984): 10-13.
2. *Ibid.*
3. Donald A. Marchand and Forest W. Horton, Jr., *Infotrends: Profiting from Your Information Resources* (New York: John Wiley & Sons, Inc., 1986), 106. Frank Newman, *Higher Education and the American Resurgence* (Princeton, N.J.: The Carnegie Foundation for the Advancement of Teaching, 1985), 52.
4. This research was not done at Auraria Library, but used many of the resources that a library could provide.
5. An interview with one of the researchers indicated that approximately 1/3 of her information came from library research, 1/3 from personal interviews, and 1/3 from all other sources.
6. Interviews with two corporate researchers, Christy Campbell and Pam Martin, indicated that one of the benefits of their work with Auraria Library was access to personnel with expertise in doing research in a variety of areas.
7. For more information about the Oregon network index, contact Wes Doak at 503-378-4376. Information here was taken from a press release. Auraria Library's Colorado Information Resource Center was encouraged by Lucy Creighton, economist at First Interstate Bank, Denver. For more information about it, contact Louise Stwalley at 303-556-3532.
8. On February 5, 1987, the Denver Chamber of Commerce hosted 75 representatives from Denver metropolitan area businesses and governments to begin a collaborative network of economic development agencies. The Metro Denver Network (MDN) will coordinate economic development activities and provide consistent data to support activities that will bring new business and industry to Colorado. The members of the Network will use a computer system developed in cooperation with the Colorado Alliance of Research Libraries (CARL) to share data and enhance their communication.
9. Harlan Cleveland, *The Knowledge Executive* (New York: E.P. Dutton, 1985), 4-5.
10. Neil P. Eurich, *Corporate Classrooms: the Learning Business* (Princeton, NJ: The Carnegie Foundation for the Advancement of Teaching, 1985).
11. Scott Jaschik, "Small-Business Leaders Launch Campaign to Curb Campus Sales of Consumer Goods," *The Chronicle of Higher Education*, February 11, 1987, 21-22.

Technology and Transformation in Academic Libraries

by Ward Shaw

This background paper is intended to provide a brief overview of the use of computer technology in academic libraries, a sample of some of the directions in which the use of technology is moving, and a description of a few of the emerging issues and opportunities these activities create. The subject is both large and complex, and this paper intends neither depth nor comprehensiveness. Rather, it is meant to provide a point of reference and departure for the discussions of the Symposium.

One immediate problem with such a "broad brush" view is that it is necessarily an amalgamation. Some (not many) academic libraries make no direct use of computer technology at all. Others are involved in leading edge research and development far beyond what is discussed here. Either group may find the discussion irrelevant. However, the former should know what it has missed (or avoided), and the latter should know how far out they are. More importantly, to develop a common sense of direction and progression we need to know more about the forest than any individual tree.

At the outset, we should observe that library computing is quite different from most other kinds of computing. First, it is characterized by literally enormous files, and the files are seldom used as a whole; rather an individual record within a several million record file is retrieved, a few characters modified, and the record replaced in the typical transaction. Second, there is much more reading of files than writing them, by perhaps 30 or 40 to 1. Third, there is very little numeric computation involved; in fact, we have been unable to identify any library "numbers" that are really numbers in a computation sense – instead, words and concepts are the entities of interest. Fourth, the use of library systems is almost always transaction oriented and in real time as compared to batch oriented with users prepared to wait. Fifth, library computing is almost always performed by people with little or no computer expertise, and often little interest in learning it. Sixth, library data structures are among the most complex ever encountered with typically dozens of fields and hundreds of subfields in a single record, all variable in length, format and content. The document which describes the MARC standard for the construction of bibliographic records is more than 1000 pages long. Finally, users of library systems often approach the system with only a vague idea of what they want to do.

Successful library systems, therefore, are grossly optimized for moving information around, incorporate highly sophisticated file management techniques, are radically transaction oriented, require vast amounts of data storage and very advanced user interface technology. They do not fit well in general purpose computers used for a wide range of applications, both because their consumption of specific kinds of resource is voracious, and because their design usually requires exploiting the characteristics of the hardware and operating systems at a fairly intimate level, which often has disastrous effects on other applications sharing the same computer. This explains why most library systems development has been on "stand alone" rather than shared machines. It also explains why library systems are among the most complex found in academic environments.

The use of computing technology in academic libraries divides into two basic areas – the use by libraries of external systems for access to external information and the operation by libraries of internal systems for control and support of internal operations. External systems are those owned and operated by organizations outside the control of the library from which the library purchases systems; conversely, internal systems are those owned and operated by the library. There is a third category in which systems are operated by the university and used by the library, which creates a special set of issues beyond the scope of this discussion. For convenience, these latter are considered internal systems here.

There are two main categories of external systems in widespread use. First, most academic libraries have accounts with and use one or more of the large online commercial search systems such as Dialog, BRS, Mead Data, and the like. These systems, run by private companies for profit, acquire numbers of large files of mostly bibliographic abstract information from various sources, and make them accessible to trained searchers through powerful retrieval software. Examples of such files are Chemical Abstracts, ERIC, Psychological Abstracts, and so on. Only occasionally do the end users of the information actually perform searches, as the software is powerful, complex, and expensive. Accordingly, libraries have trained specialists expert in search negotiation and execution who work with researchers, formulating and refining information requests, and operating the system to extract the appropriate data most efficiently. Costs are transaction sensitive, and usually include a basic subscription fee, hourly connect time charges, and a fee for each record retrieved. Typical costs for a given search can range from $10 to $15 up to several hundred dollars for the most complex and broad ranging requests. Few libraries can bear the costs of unlimited searching, and so usually ask the user to pay some or all of the expense. Although no research project is complete without such a comprehensive review of the current literature as these systems provide, cost and complexity have tended to limit their broad use. The other category of widespread use of external systems is for the support of the library's operations. Most academic libraries are members and users of one of the nationwide networks – OCLC, RLIN, and WLN, for example – created by libraries to provide shared services. The basic idea behind these networks is resource sharing, and they have been most successful in two areas – first, as a source of catalog records, and second, as a location and messaging mechanism for interlibrary loan. The basic idea is that when any one library catalogs a book or other item, the record is stored in a large database accessible to all the members, who can use that record as the basis of their own cataloging. As the records are used, they are updated to indicate who owns the item described, and the files thus function as location tools. The scope of these nationwide networks is extraordinary. OCLC, for example, supports 7000 terminals in more than 5000 institutions. The data file contains 15,000,000 records. The system has been used to process more than 12,000,000 interlibrary loans. Individual institutions can, through access to such systems, enormously extend the resource they offer their clientele. And properly administered, they can save money over time by reducing the rate of increase of processing costs. Like the commercial search systems, they are for the most part used by librarians either in their technical activities or on behalf of users, and only rarely by users themselves.

In the last decade, many academic libraries have begun to use local systems to support internal operations. Major advances in both hardware and software technology, and in the creation and promulgation of standards relating to hardware interoperability and data structures, have made it economically realistic and politically possible for individual institutions to engage in local systems development, and for an industry providing turn-key local systems to the library marketplace to emerge. Until the last three or four years, these systems were almost exclusively designed to support and manage internal housekeeping operations, such as circulation control, accounting, acquisitions, serials check in, and the like. These operations, when manual, consume surprising amounts of clerical effort, and even then don't work particularly well. First attempts at automating these functions did not work very well either, primarily because their complexity was underestimated. To the casual observer, circulation control looks very much like inventory control, and more systems than we care to admit failed because the designers did not understand the complex public services inherent in the special functions libraries have created over time. Reserves, holds, recalls, fines, multiple locations, multiple media types with special loan policies, and so on, are all critical public services that circulation control systems must support, and may not be appreciated by system designers unacquainted with library practices. They are, however, appreciated and demanded by library users. But as systems and their design came more under control of the libraries themselves, the installation of systems to support these areas has become relatively routine and unarguably beneficial in all but the smallest situations. They do, however, represent major shifts in the kinds of activities engaged in by libraries, from the traditional "marking and parking" of books to the operation of sophisticated systems. This shift has and continues to create a conceptual gap between how libraries and librarians perceive themselves and how they are perceived by their campuses.

This gap has widened dramatically in the most recent three or four years with the introduction in libraries of Online Public Access Catalogs. All of the applications we have described to this point are systems used by librarians to do better what they have traditionally done. They have not changed the basic paradigm of librarianship, or the basic relationships of the library to its clientele and campus. Recently, however, that paradigm and those relationships have begun to change rapidly and inevitably.

As the computer industry and its market have recognized that computers are fundamentally information machines and only incidentally computing machines, they have begun to design machines oriented towards real time transaction processing and huge file management and manipulations. At the same time, the idea of microcomputers has raised the possibility and to some extent the reality of extending to the general public access to information processing capacity not previously realistic. Librarians, who have always operated large transaction oriented dissemination and control systems, albeit manual, and who are professionally familiar with how people seek and use information, have not surprisingly been pioneers in creating systems to deliver useful interactive computer based services directly to end users.

Online Public Access Catalogs, replacing and extending manual card catalogs, have met with enormous user success, even in their infancy. The use of these systems is truly phenomenal. For example, 25,000 people each day use the CARL System, generating 1.6 million transactions as they interrogate and manipulate the various files we have available. We have nowhere near satisfied the demand. The only other kind of application with anything like that level of penetration to the general public is automatic teller machines

operated by banks, and those systems have little or no intellectual or pedagogical content. There are four characteristics of Online Public Access Catalogs (OPACs) which, taken together, radically change the paradigm or model
of libraries and their relationship to their clientele.

First, one does not have to go to the online catalog to use it. In a manual
environment, in order to use a library and its catalog, the user has to go to the
library. This is inconvenient, takes time and therefore must be planned in
advance, and for almost all purposes restricts the library's utility to those
users located in reasonable physical proximity to its facilities. In an automated environment, anyone anywhere with access to a telephone and a terminal or personal computer can use the system as effectively as someone in
the library building. This single characteristic provides the institution with
the potential capability of delivering one of its most important services anywhere, not just on campus. As telecommunications, telefacsimile, and storage capabilities advance, it will become possible to provide access to the
source data and documents themselves as well as to index records describing
those data. At CARL and in other places a number of experiments are already
under way leading to this capability. This will create all kinds of opportunities, and problems, for academic libraries and their parent institutions that
we are just beginning to think about how to address. The most obvious opportunity is that just identified above – that is, the ability to deliver research
information in real time to wherever it is needed or wanted, including, of
course, off campus to business, industry, and homes. The most obvious problem is that of designing appropriate models to handle the proper compensa-
tions involved – users, universities, systems, libraries, publishers, authors, and
so on – of which copyright is just the tip of the iceberg.

The second characteristic of OPACs important to note here is analogous
to their first. Just as, at the user end, one does not have to go to the system to
use it, likewise at the data end the systems can be used to access databases not
necessarily resident on the campus, or on the local system. Several local systems, such as those at CARL, the University of California, and the University
of Illinois, already contain data describing the resources of groups of institutions rather than only one, and make it very simple for users to examine the
contents of multiple collections. And, considerable research and experimentation is occurring in the area of system interconnection. Again, the convergence of telecommunications and computer technology is the driving force
here. A great deal of work is being done now in the development of standards
and protocols for the interconnection and interoperability of computer sys-

tems, and much of the pioneering work is going on in the library context. Research universities have for several years had access to Arpanet, connecting their academic computing centers, but most of the traffic on that network has been oriented toward access for advanced research to large computing capability. As the newer standards such as the Open Systems Interconnection Reference Model (OSI) are defined, promulgated, and implemented, it will become commonplace for all users of public access systems to routinely examine collections of institutions across the country for research information, and such interconnections will not be restricted to library databases, but will extend to all kinds of research information files. At CARL, for example, we support interconnections with several other library systems, and with several of the local campus computers so that anyone connected with those systems has access to us. We are also currently perfecting a link to the University of California Division of Library Automation's system, which will soon enable both groups of users to routinely access each other's files. Again, both the opportunities and problems are legion, and again, most of the opportunities relate to extended capabilities and most of the problems relate to economics.

The third characteristic is more of a "sleeper." Manual catalogs of any size are necessarily linear, organized usually by alphabet and according to headings or entries assigned by catalogers. Typically, five or six access points are provided for any given bibliographic record. In computerized systems, however, the number of access points is limited only by the contents of the record itself, and those paths can be endlessly combined and related by users according to their individual requirements. Further, the system's messages, responses, and next choices can be based on the context of the given user interaction rather than predefined. The notion that computer systems are inherently de-humanizing is, therefore, exactly wrong. The best of them enable the transfer of control to the individual user, and encourage him to construct his own interaction with the research environment. The educational possibilities of this characteristic are just beginning to be explored, and we are just starting to take advantage of the feedback and heuristic capabilities inherent in the technology. Considerable research is in progress attempting to better understand the research process, and the mechanisms by which new information is created and enters the research infrastructure. When the interaction of personal computers and large search systems is considered, the design of enormously productive research work stations capable of supporting the collection and manipulation of large and diverse amounts of information, from many sources unconstrained by geography or time, toward the preparation of a variety of products ranging from publications to new learning, becomes a real and attainable goal. As this area is better understood, its extension to all users is likely, and will clearly change the way almost all academic activities on campus (or off) proceed. What is critical to understand is that the process of informing becomes as much an element of design as is the database and its manipulation, and that the two are inextricably interrelated. The shift in the model here is dramatic – the library and its systems are suddenly active participants or even leaders in the educational process, rather than reactive service bureaus. Here also, there are opportunities and problems. The opportunity is nothing short of improving the quality of both learning and research both locally and broadly. One obvious problem is conceptual – that is, we do not yet understand either learning or research well enough to know much about how to approach the task. Another is ultimately political – as libraries become active rather than reactive, the transformation will be resisted and misunderstood.

The fourth characteristic is less esoteric, and is that we are discovering that other kinds of data files work well in the structures we have invented for our bibliographic files. Again using CARL as an example, we have several kinds of non-bibliographic information accessible to users of the system now, and are exploring a wide range of others. An almanac and digest of current esoteric facts are currently available and generating considerable use. We are exploring files as diverse as a Bible, complete with a concordance, a general purpose encyclopedia, the official airline guide, a dynamic file of incoming airline passengers and flights at Denver's airport, commercial and residential real estate advertising, regional statistical data, classified advertising and more. This is not a wish list – in fact, we are not sure that we really want all of those – but each represents a real proposal before us right now. The point is that our user community perceives us as a general purpose information utility, and proposes to us that we do things that are considerably beyond our traditional conception of who we are and what we do. Once again, both opportunities and problems are present. One opportunity is that we might actually make money instead of consume it; and one problem is that we have no idea where we should draw a line to ensure that we are appropriately serving our primary purpose of bringing the best resources to the research and educational process.

It is clear that the application of technology in libraries has been and continues to be extraordinarily robust. Contrary to popular myth, libraries have collectively and enthusiastically embraced new technology when its use is appropriate, and created the research projects and experiments necessary to lead the transitions. It is also clear that the same process is causing a radical redefinition of the academic library, its role in the educational process, and its relationship to the rest of the institution. These changes are inexorable – the benefits are too great and the economics too compelling to resist. But they create confusion in various institutional perceptions that must soon begin to be addressed. Academic libraries have traditionally been the arena in which the leaders of our profession have created techniques and mechanisms to develop, teach, and support the relationship of information and ideas. It is my observation that, for whatever reason, that leadership has shifted to public libraries, which seem to have much more flexibly redefined their roles and activities, and are more and more frequently conducting the forward looking experiments. It is important that academic institutions begin to recognize that there is a profound set of changes under way, and quickly direct attention and resource to ensure that the changes are designed and implemented for maximum benefit to libraries, students, and to education and research.

It's Academic: The Politics of the Curriculum in American Higher Education

by Irving J. Spitzberg, Jr.

Never have so many said so much to achieve so little. This could be the judgment history will render about curriculum reform in American higher education in the 1980s. To understand this judgement, one will need to appreciate the structure of American higher education, the nature of academic decision-making, and the social and technological environment in which academic change takes place. This essay will provide an analysis of the politics of the curriculum. It will focus on the campus-based political system as it affects academic matters and the complex inter-relationship between the campus and its larger social context.

The Historical Context

A thumbnail sketch of the 20th-century history of the university and college curriculum will provide the foundation of my subsequent analysis.[1]

In the late 19th century, a group of small colleges and rudimentary land grant universities began the process of professionalization. They separated the professional and the practical from the arts and sciences. At the same time the arts and sciences themselves were becoming professionalized through the development of graduate faculties at a few institutions. On the eve of the 20th century, the scholars plowing the fields of the disciplines planted the seeds that would produce the husks of disciplinary dominance. As often happens with Harvard's role in the history of American higher education, Harvard's construction of the elective system directed the professionalization into the undergraduate curriculum.

After the world fell apart with the First World War, there was a temporary reaction to the fragmentation and destruction in the world order in a search for an understanding of the cataclysm which had occurred. This search for an understanding of the whole led to the reconstruction of a core in the undergraduate curriculum – *e.g.*, the Contemporary Civilization sequence at Columbia and the Hutchins era at Chicago.[2] It provided a new interest in the relationship among the arts, sciences, and social studies at the graduate level. Throughout American higher education, Western Civ courses tempered electives and various Chinese menus of distribution requirements.

Just after the Second World War, the Harvard Redbook provided a justification for the distribution requirements that would characterize American higher education through the mid-1960s. Here the Chinese menu would charge its ideological dues and the 20th-century enlightenment of the 1950s,

with its faith in and fear of technology, would define undergraduate education as a sequence of exposures very much like the achievement of the per-
fect suntan.

In the context of the turmoil of the 1960s and 1970s, with the civil rights
movement of the '60s evolving into the war protests of the '70s, one also observed the campus revolutions. The appeal of the authority of the curriculum eroded with all the other features of authority. This third moment of
societal disruption and campus change differed from the earlier ones in that
it destroyed the existing structure of the curriculum and left only a market
basket full of products. The most anti-market social and political movement
of the 20th century had left the American curriculum at the direct mercy of
the academic market. The faculty producers of the products essentially threw
up their hands and said, "Let them eat cake." They then were quite surprised
when the consumers only wanted cake, even while the faculty producers were
still producing the same pork and beans that had been their staple for years.

The American undergraduate curriculum had become a supermarket
where each department offered its wares and the institution was only a sum
of its parts. As in most economic markets where the structure is really oli-
gopolistic, the big and elite departmental winners got bigger and at the same
time more selective, and the small departments that accepted all comers and
were not presently in demand lost on a large scale. The irony was that many
of those departments most active in the revolution were the biggest losers –
e.g., sociology and philosophy.

The political agenda of active participation in decision-making succeeded in only one part of college life in decisions about the curriculum,
where the decision-making process in theory governed by faculty essentially
abdicated to a market of student consumers without adequate advising and
information disseminating systems to inform decisions. The faculty in their
corporate and collegial guises viewed the risks of campus political system
judgements about value priorities as too great for the parts; yet the reward of
leaving the decisions to the individual students was great for some, nonexist-
ent for others. By the end of the 1970s, the impact of laissez-faire on the undergraduate curriculum was clear in the redistribution of enrollments to
professional and preprofessional courses from the arts and sciences. The
change was not only in selection of majors, where everyone either became
preprofessional or a business major; it was also in choices of electives that
served similar vocational ends. These changes had serious implications for
many faculty and for the graduate schools. The surplus of Ph.Ds in many arts

and sciences disciplines in the 1970s in response to high expectations but in spite of larger market forces illustrates the impact of these changes. The subsequent real decline in faculty salaries and general social support for higher education were equally traumatic legacies of the abdication of curricular responsibility in higher education. Faculty could tolerate market decision-making when it did not risk the very existence of parts of the campus; when the market put at risk the core disciplines of the university and faculty in them, the need to reassert campus judgment about the curriculum became clear.

This account of the 20th-century history of the curriculum suggests that major changes have correlated with – though not necessarily followed from – important social changes, often political disruptions, in the larger society. Even when there was a clear and landmark event or sequence of events such as a war or the civil rights movement, the campus changes always emerged from campus politics, never directly from external intervention. The most recent changes, to which we now turn our attention, have flowed even more from the university rather than the larger society.

The National Politics of the Curriculum in the 1980s

The 1980s version of the politics of the curriculum actually began in the mid-1970s with the appointment of Henry Rosovsky as Dean of Faculty at Harvard. He and President Derek Bok, along with a cadre of senior faculty, decided to begin a long process of reconsideration of the Harvard curriculum that culminated in 1979 when the Harvard faculty reintroduced a form of distribution requirements that focused on the skills they wished Harvard students to have at graduation. The jury is still out on the impact of that change at Harvard; its impact on the larger universe of American higher education is clear.

In the early 1980s, while the Federal goverment, the states and individual households were cutting budgets and coping with inflation, American higher education had already begun its own reconstruction. It resurrected distribution requirements on many campuses as a way of regulating the free market that had concentrated enrollments in management, engineering, and computer science. Campuses also restored a faculty role in decision-making, although that had eroded so that only the curriculum was an arena where the faculty could exercise authority. Serious financial pressures imposed by Federal budget cutting and weak state budgets severely constrained this decision-making process. These discussions even more reflected the territorial imperative of the departmental structure of the university, where faculty control reigned supreme.

In this setting, Secretary of Education Terrell Bell appointed a distinguished panel of citizens to assess the state of elementary and secondary education. David Gardner, then president of the University of Utah – later to become the president of the University of California – chaired the group. This panel reported in 1983 in the now famous document *A Nation at Risk*.[3] This report characterized the public school system as so weak as to threaten the security of the United States. Its hyperbole generated a national reconsideration of quality in public education, in part because of its clever and catchy conclusionary statements and in part because President Reagan decided that it offered an agenda that he could adopt that would not cost the Federal Government money.

A Nation at Risk became a bible for educational reform at the local and state level. A number of governors – *e.g.* Republican Governor Lamar Alexander of Tennessee and Democratic Governor Bill Clinton of Arkansas – made substantial educational reform focusing on quality major political issues in their states. They also became interested in the quality of university education and made improvement of universities part of their overall educational plans. In both Arkansas and Tennessee, as well as many other states, the reform of teacher education became a state political issue. In Florida and Georgia, the state initiated testing programs for students mid-way in their college careers as well as for teachers. It is important to understand that these higher education initiatives flowed from *A Nation at Risk* and not from any higher education reports.

A Nation at Risk had profound impact on the public educational system because of the overt connection between all public school systems and local and state politics. The bully pulpit of the Federal Government had in fact ignited strong interest in the decentralized political system of public education. The role of this report in mobilizing public opinion was not unique in the history of public education – *e.g.*, the Conant reports in the 1950s after Sputnik had a comparable impact – but the fact that *A Nation at Risk* had its impact without Federal money yet because of Federal politics offers an idiosyncratic lesson about the politics of reports. If a report serves a larger political purpose, its impact can be great. Indeed, the power of a report generated outside of the educational system – higher or elementary or secondary – is completely dependent on the political investment in it. And in some ways it is easier for a report on public education to have substantial effect than one addressing its message to colleges and universities, because the non-partisan politics of elementary and secondary education is still quite public and accountable, whereas the tradition of autonomy of universities through boards of trustees and the standard of shared governance make the impact of external reports much more indirect than in the public schools.

A Nation at Risk had a threefold impact on campus. First, in a few states it led to the imposition from outside of testing programs (*e.g.*, Florida and Georgia, generally, and many other states in regard to teacher education). Next, in many states the increases in funding for public schools also occasioned increases in state funding for higher education. Finally, this report seemed to spawn a number of reports focusing specifically on higher education, although many of these subsequent efforts were already in process when *Risk* was publicly presented. *A Nation at Risk* is of such importance because it concentrated American attention on educational questions for the first time in two decades and because the interest that it mobilized focused on an agenda that also included universities and colleges through the impact of the subsequent reports. It is to these latter reports that we now turn.

Three general reports targeting undergraduate education followed within months after *A Nation at Risk*. First, then National Endowment for the Humanities Chairman William Bennett and a study group of advisors looked at the teaching of the humanities. Bennett wrote his report, *To Reclaim a Legacy*, that asserted the importance of revitalizing the humanities by strengthening the understanding of Western Civilization.[4] Bennett asked that institutions should agree on a core of texts that every student should read. He had his own list that became the touchstone for his report and the center of controversy in selection. Bennett's "great books of Western Civ" became the catch phrase that characterized his arguments in campus discussions about the undergraduate curriculum. The high visibility of *Legacy* helped catapult Chairman Bennett into the position of Secretary of Education when Terrell Bell resigned.

After *A Nation at Risk*, Secretary Bell appointed a small group to review higher education and the implications of the earlier report for higher education. This group, chaired by Dr. Kenneth Mortimer of Penn State, published *Involvement in Learning*.[5] This report considered not only the curriculum but also the pedagogy and priority (or lack thereof) of teaching as well as the curricular environment for learning in universities and colleges. *Involvement* came to be known as the report that prescribed greater student engagement with the learning process. It called for more writing, speaking and creativity and fewer large lectures and impersonal learning settings. The higher education community identified *Involvement* with pedagogical method more than recommendations for curricular structure.

The third report following *A Nation at Risk* was from the Association of American Colleges. Professor Frederick Rudolph, the distiguished historian of the undergraduate curriculum, drafted *Integrity in the Undergraduate Curriculum.*[6] It listed six skill areas that set the standards for high-quality undergraduate education and found that faculty had not given priority to these necessary skills in the structure of the undergraduate curriculum. The AAC report abjured text-centered recommendations or the use of Chinese menus, although the most probable outcome of the skills and knowledge areas approach is in fact a modified Chinese menu. *Integrity* emphasized the importance of planned course sequence in undergraduate education as a tactic to offer greater coherence to the market-driven reality in colleges across the country. The AAC report came to represent the importance of agreement about the skills needed by college graduates and a strong critique of the abdication of the faculty role in and responsibility for decisions about the curriculum as a whole.

These three reports provided the canon for the debate about the undergraduate curriculum as it evolved in the mid-1980s. Their impact was twofold: first, together they created momentum for campus discussion of the undergraduate curriculum at a level of visibility unseen since the late 1950s; second, they provided the footnotes for the particular discussions on individual campuses, although they did not – either one or all – dominate the reconstruction of the undergraduate curriculum that continues to proceed at this writing. Since all three were conclusionary and rhetorical rather than based upon substantial research and analysis about current campus reality, the actual debates focused on parochial realities of given campuses.

The three reports together framed the poles of the debates and offered appropriate justifications for just about any argument mounted on behalf of new curricular structure, although they all ruled out the recent approach of institutional abdication of judgment. Their rhetoric was their strength in that there was an aphorism for all seasons; it was also their weakness. Martin Trow, the distinguished Berkeley sociologist, concluded that these reports did more harm than good, "...because these reports, by substituting prescription for analysis, mislead our supporters and the general public into believing that these difficult problems are simpler than they are."[7]

An important distinction between the impact of these reports and *A Nation at Risk* was that no consensus about the details of reform emerged in higher education. The policy debate about public schools quickly focused on the nexus between better teacher salaries and improved teacher competence through minimum skills testing for both teachers and students. The poles of the higher education curriculum debate in recent months are summarized in arguments between Secretary William Bennett and Harvard President Derek Bok about the competing visions of a core built around the great books or competencies in assorted skill areas. The substance and potential resource implications of this debate have meant that on most campuses the systemic inertia has limited change to the reintroduction of the Chinese menu as it emerged on most campuses after the Second World War. The campus-based politics of the curriculum have been characterized by negotiations among departments about the hours devoted to general education and hours devoted to the major. These deliberations have resulted in a balance of power not unlike the treaties negotiated by Metternich or Kissinger.

One area of the curriculum that has been quite sensitive to outside intervention has been the arena of teacher education. Because of the political power of *A Nation at Risk*, teacher education has become the focus of the public school reform movement. Through the efforts of governors, legislators, unions, and foundations, a set of proposals for national examinations and more arts and sciences academic work has generated a degree of policy consensus about the future of teacher education, although there is great debate about the details.

The major campus response to this outside intervention in teacher education has been a coalition of elite private and large land-grant institutions known as the Holmes Group, which has recommended that teacher preparation culminate in a five year masters' degree certification for teaching. This response does not represent a consensus, since many public institutions – particularly the former teachers colleges – and small private campuses are strongly committed to baccalaureate certification. The example of the debate about the nature of teacher education suggests that even when there is a substantial consensus in the larger society for a need to change the substance of a particular part of the curriculum – either undergraduate or graduate – the tradition of institutional autonomy makes the politics of change very much a campus process. Each campus establishes its own curriculum and that curriculum is very much the sum of decisions taken in a decentralized departmental system on the campus. Even a weak school or department within the university – and departments and schools of education are the weakest in terms of campus political clout – still has great autonomy as it responds to external pressures.

Two national associations of states published reports on the state role in higher education. The Education Commission of the States published *Transforming the State Role in Undergraduate Education*, which counseled state interest but restraint in improving colleges.[8] The National Governors Association Task Force on College Quality published *Time for Results: the Governors' 1991 Report on Education*, which commented not only on the schools but also on the state interest in higher education.[9] Although these reports focused on state initiatives to monitor quality in higher education, they both distinguished between the more direct intervention possible in public elementary and secondary education and the need to respect campus autonomy in higher education.

A new and different report is stirring the waters in the American higher educational pond, although it is premature to assess its impact. Ernest Boyer, the President of the Carnegie Foundation, has written a book, *College*, that, unlike the previous reports, is a research-based critique of the undergraduate experience.[10] Boyer published an earlier report, *High School*,[11] that provided a research-based analysis and set of recommendations that complemented *A Nation at Risk* and contributed to the debate about public education. *College*, in addition to its research base, is distinctive in two other ways: like *A Nation at Risk*, and unlike most of the other higher educational reports, it is written for a general audience of parents, students, and policy makers as well as and even more than the academic community itself. Boyer considers not only the curriculum but also emphasizes the cocurricular components of the undergraduate experience and makes substantial recommendations about the need for improvement throughout undergraduate education. Since the Carnegie Foundation invests significant resources in the dissemination of its efforts, *College* is likely to invigorate the continuing debate about undergraduate education and become yet another text that provides the footnotes for arguments on each campus.

The debate about the curriculum in higher education in the 1980s has focused on undergraduate education, in part because the policy debate has ignored it and in part because the political economy and the disciplinary sociology have created a campus structure which made it difficult to look at the undergraduate curriculum as a whole. It took a political debate outside of the particular campus to force each institution to confront the institution-wide issues, although the confrontation itself necessarily takes place on each campus. Even though the debate has been enriched off campus, it is essential to see that the higher education system itself provided the brainpower for the enterprise. The panels that have fueled discussion have included faculty and administrators from higher education to a much greater degree than commissions reporting on the schools involved teachers and principals. The culture of campus autonomy has not been breached, insofar as campus insiders have actually written the outside reports.[12] The substantive focus on undergraduate education is part of a cycle of discussion about education that has arisen from the campus but has taken place in forums in the larger political system. It is only a matter of time until the focus will shift to the graduate and professional schools, particularly as the dominance of the elite research institutions and the sociology of knowledge become continuing themes in all of the reports. In all cases in regard to higher education, we will continue to need and will have the external political pressure.

All of these national reports and the politics of the curriculum that have evolved at the national level provide, at most, the environment within which the college and university citizens make the real decisons on campus. The politics of curriculum at the national level do not generate detailed debate in Congress or the executive branch, or even in the halls of many state legislatures. The national political discussion involves the campuses with the occasional interest of politicians. The legislatures, governors, and Federal officials are always interested in budgets but only rarely in curriculum. Their curricular interest usually flags when it encounters reports written by campus citizens. Because curricular decisions emerge in a culture which emphasizes campus autonomy, we must consider in greater detail the paradigm of curricular politics as campuses play the game in the 1980s; only then may we begin to turn our attention toward the 1990s and the 21st century.

The Politics of Change Making Curriculum Decisions on University Standard Time

Commentators have always correctly viewed campus politics as especially Byzantine. Woodrow Wilson could say that he went to Washington from Princeton to find a less complicated political system. Many wags have observed that political conflict on campuses is so petty and mean because so little is at stake. Wilson was right; the omnipresent wag is wrong. Since substantive academic decisons are the heart of the university, much is at stake in these decisions: principle, status, resources. The very fact that so much is at stake and that the culture of the university prizes consultation makes decisions about curriculum especially laborious and time consuming.

In many areas of university life and across the spectrum of institutions, the faculty no longer has an extensive and meaningful role in decision-making. Yet it is in the arena of curriculum that the faculty role is still primary and certainly meets the standard set by the AAUP in its 1966 Statement on University and College Government.[13] This reality means that even considering incremental decisions about the nature of departmental curriculum takes a long while to talk through. When an institution reviews its whole educational program for assessment and possible reform, one measures the consultative process in years, not months. This leads universities to be very conservative institutions.

Clark Kerr has observed that most of the changes in American higher education have come from creating new institutions, not from dramatically changing old ones.[14] The model of departmental dominance of research institutions has not changed significantly since the Second World War. Changes occur within institutions at the margin, seldom at the core, and they generally evolve over a long period of time. Even revolutions and *coups d'état* on campuses take a couple of years. This fact – that everything in universities takes so long to decide – leads to what I call university standard time. The irony of this fact is that the knowledge produced and disseminated in colleges and universities is on the cutting edge. This new understanding becomes immediately apparent to the research community around the world, as does the latest rumor about the love life of a distant colleague. We may explain this discontinuity in the distinction between research dissemination and agreement for action.

To clarify the reality of curriculum decision-making for the whole institution, I will offer a synthetic case of change drawn from a number of examples. This example draws from the case study database of the Carnegie Foundation study that led to *College* and from my own impressions drawn from over two hundred college visits.[15] It is enough to offer only one example, because, in spite of institutional diversity and differences in detail from campus to campus, the paradigm I am about to describe is typical across institutional types ranging from community colleges through elite private universities. I will describe the case and then indicate where the modest variation occurs.

The example is a review of the undergraduate curriculum with special attention to what is or ought to be common in the required work for all students. The usual initiative for such a review comes from either a dean or a provost/academic vice president. Once the proposal for such a review emerges, it becomes the enterprise of the faculty senate or the university senate. The campus creates a committee, sometimes appointed by the president or provost, other times selected by the faculty, often chosen by both. It includes senior faculty carefully balanced by discipline and by educational ideology – particularly designed not to have too many innovators – with a sprinkling of senior administrators and one or two figurehead students. The senior administrator(s) and the faculty charge the committee to review the undergraduate curriculum and the existing requirements or lack thereof and then to report to the faculty senate for first review no later than "next term."

During the first few months of deliberation, the committee will have a debate within itself which will invoke all of the national reports and which will generate as many as a dozen opposing plans for dramatic reform of the undergraduate curriculum. Impatience will quickly reduce twelve options to three or four, which will invariably include modest change in an existing Chinese menu, restoration of Western Civ and a great books core, abolition of all requirements, and/or a distinctive approach unique to the particular campus usually in the form of courses with "subject and..." titles, such as international affairs and physics, or the environment and economics, etc. "Next term" comes much too quickly, so the committee reports it has only begun its deliberations and will report next year.

Some enlightened committees initiate empirical studies of experiences of similarly situated institutions based on telephone surveys and also the actual longitudinal course patterns of students based upon samples of transcripts. These studies are often designed by a physical scientist on the committee and served by a part-time institutional researcher who spends most of his/her time doing budget and enrollment projections.

During the second year of deliberation, the committee spends some time reviewing the empirical studies. Often it finds a *de facto* core usually clustered in the required courses of the physical sciences and one or two spectacular lecturers who have been teaching for forty years. Everyone is suitably shocked by the lack of sequence experienced by most students outside their majors and the parochialism of the *de facto* core. The debates of the first year in the committee are repeated in complete detail, but at the end of the debate, there are two factions about equally balanced: those who wish a dramatic reform and those who wish only to modify the existing Chinese menu. The chair of the committee reports to the faculty senate the close division but assures his/her colleagues that the committee will report "next term" with a firm plan.

In the meantime the president has been fund-raising with the theme that the institution is in the midst of a major rethinking of its educational program with careful attention to quality. He/she assures alumni and foundations that the institution is carefully monitoring quality through a new testing program that will be part of the reform. The provost is busily modeling the alternative curriculum changes for their impact on the budget and quietly directing the budget process to support those who support the provost's view of the appropriate curricular changes. The provost and chair of the select committee on the curriculum are meeting regularly with senior faculty and deans to build coalitions to support the recommendations which they wish to be the heart of the report of the committee.

Between one and two years later than originally promised, the select committee reports a plan to the faculty senate which is heralded as a major change in the requirements for all undergraduates. The reform actually takes the existing Chinese menu and reduces the choices in each column and establishes another committee to evaluate proposed courses for inclusion in the general education program. There are two minority reports – one from a quarter of the committee that wanted a truly major restructuring with lots of required courses and one from a lone faculty member and the student representatives who wished to do away with requirements altogether.

The first minority report refers to Columbia, Chicago, and William Bennett; the latter invokes that "hot" university, Brown. The second minority report is an odd combination of student rhetoric about free choice and maturity and the faculty member's invocation of specialized accrediting agency requirements that supposedly limit campus flexibility in his discipline, usually either engineeering, computer science, chemistry, or management. The majority report is replete with references to Harvard, Derek Bok, and Ernest Boyer, selecting from each the most radical statements that then are used to justify even the most modest change.

When the committee reports to the faculty senate – or the whole faculty in a small college – the senate first repeats presentations which posit each of the dozen alternatives considered and reconsidered by the committee. This process exhausts the first scheduled meeting. The senate then schedules a special meeting to continue discussion. At this second meeting the majority report is the sole item on the agenda. The discussion moves item by item through the report. There are dozens of amendments from the floor. At the end of this meeting the original recommendations have been substantially amended to look more like the existing Chinese menu. The one recommendation which emerges with no change is the creation of a committee to oversee the implementation of the final plan.

At yet another meeting the senate completes the amendment process and sends an amended proposal back to the select committee for revision and editing for resubmission for an up-or-down vote at the next meeting. At that meeting the faculty senate approves the revised recommendations on a 55/45 vote. The senate then sends the program to the provost for comment and approval along with an assessment of the budgetary impact. The provost forwards the approved plan with a budgetary analysis to the president, who, with the provost, returns the plan to the senate with a request that its implementation be spread out over a three-year period for budgetary reasons. The senate complains but finally agrees. The new curriculum will begin in the next academic year: usually at least four years after the senate and president first appointed the select committee. For those four years the institution as a whole will have been reviewing its undergraduate curriculum as a political priority, an activity that seems to occur about every twenty years and that makes, for that short period of history, academic matters the center of campus politics.

Significant variations on this political process theme are relatively rare. In many community colleges, the academic dean – the equivalent of a provost – may take a much more active role and the faculty a more reactive role. In an historically black college, the campus president and the Title III Coordinator may be the only serious actors. An elite private university will have a council of elders composed of the most visible and senior professors and the dean of the undergraduate college as the main actors on stage, with subsequent decision-making a *fait accompli*.

There are some extraordinary exceptions. A large private university in the West, facing near bankruptcy and precipitously declining enrollment, saw its newly installed president – himself a long-term faculty member – and the Board of Trustees pass a core curriculum without substantive faculty consultation and impose it on the faculty, whose only leeway was in specifying the implementation. The legacy of this procedure was continuing faculty disaffection with the president and the board and lukewarm implementation. There is now general agreement that the core curriculum was a good idea and the fortunes of the institution seem to have improved significantly.[16]

The new president of a small private college in the East presented a general outline of the curriculum plan combining career preparation and a strong liberal arts program as part of his case for himself in the hiring process. Soon after his election, he presented a comprehensive plan to the faculty, which then massaged it and devised its own implementation strategy in the course of approving the sweeping curricular changes. One must distinguish this latter example from the former in that the administration did not impose the curriculum. The faculty, through traditional collegial consultation, approved the initiative of the president.[17]

Both of these examples anticipated the national reports; the reports influenced neither. The first case implemented a very traditional core curriculum; the latter case substantively tried to harness the student careerism of the 1970s and 1980s to the traditional values of liberal education. Neither offered a strikingly new approach to the nature of undergraduate education.

The central case and the variations on it document the institutional conservatism of universities and colleges. Even when there is political radicalism on the spectrum of national political views and dynamic discovery of new knowledge, the political process for deciding about the curriculum seems to guarantee an institutional entropy that tolerates little change. The power of departments that is central to the organization of knowledge by disciplines creates a number of decentralized power centers that seem to exercise veto more than contribute to shifting coalitions. Undoubtedly some are more equal than others in the university or college setting. Those who are most equal are the faculty with the most research, the most students, and the most to get out of the status quo.

We have now cataloged some of the complexity of the political process in curricular decisions on campus and the diffculty of substantial reform. None of the examples offer evidence to assess the connection between the political process and the quality of the educational experience. It is important to understand that the quality of the educational venture begins in the classroom but also depends upon the whole campus environment. In *College*, Ernest Boyer follows the precedent of *Involvement in Learning*, and correctly includes in his review and suggestions a critical assessment of cocurricular life, the role of libraries, and the admissions process. The campus political process seldom gives this complexity its due, because the professionals engaged in the correlative work are second-class citizens in the campus political community. They are middle and lower rank academic administrators. They do not have the collective authority of the faculty dealing with curriculum issues. They are not as well organized as a vocal student minority.

On campuses with university senates rather than faculty senates, one might expect the other constituencies to have more authority. But in fact, few

university senates have worked effectively, and most seem to leave all participants feeling impotent. No campus political system seems to have institution-
alized the capacity to make judgments in the interest of the long-term instead
of yesterday and today.

Strategies for Improving Quality and Reforming Curriculum
This account of the politics of the curriculum in higher education may dis-
courage those interested in improving the quality of teaching and learning.
Two *caveats* are in order: brevity has required an emphasis on one part of the
curriculum – the undergraduate experience taken as a whole, not graduate
and professional education or the departmental curricula constituting the
major as a significant part; second, Kerr's earlier point that substantively new
opportunities were provided in American higher education by the creation
of new institutions, not by the substantial reform of the old. Both of these
caveats should moderate the message of most of this essay that the politics of
the curriculum often precludes dramatic change. In particular programs on
every campus, quality is effectively monitored, and the substantive nature of
the programs often changes surprisingly quickly through the individual actions of faculty at the head of their disciplines and groups of faculty in departments committed to their students. As new organizational needs have sur-
faced at the system level, new institutions have emerged. The creation of a
national system of community colleges and the transformation of the teachers colleges into comprehensive universities testify to higher education's
flexibility.[18]

Let me offer a discount on the *caveats*: it is easier to be flexible in a
period of expanding rather than steady or contracting resources. The percentage of family income invested in higher education in the 1970s and
1980s has not changed significantly; inflation was about equal to increases in
federal aid. Federal budget deficits, and sluggish economic growth make it
unlikely that vast new resources will be available in the 1990s as we move into
the 21st century. So creating wholly new institutions will be a very difficult
goal to achieve. Therefore, we must think creatively about dealing with the
lethargy of existing campuses. We do have a silver lining to the current gray:
the retirement of faculty between 1995 and 2010. New blood might – but only
might – bring new curricular ideas.

The focus of the spate of reports and the efforts at curricular reform has
been revision of requirements and reallocation of current faculty efforts in
teaching and learning as well as the elevation of teaching and learning on the

priority agenda of campuses. This focus has been eminently reasonable for the 1980s. But the time has now come to begin careful reconsideration of the substance and the procedure of decisions about academic matters. We can expect a fifteen-year window for appointments – an opportunity unprecedented since the 1960s.[19] Decisions in the 1990s as to who will be appointed to faculty positions will set the course of higher education for the first half of the 21st century. To prepare for these judgements will require a political process quite different from that of the 1980s.

One lesson of the past few years has been that members of the university community – on particular campuses and nationally – are willing to enter into a serious discussion about the nature of teaching and learning, and debate quite vigorously the curriculum of a specific college or university. The problem has been that the deliberative institutions have been creaky, in part because of lack of exercise. Many sectors of the campus community have not even been effectively heard. Neither the middle-level administrators dealing with student life nor the alumni as a constituency prepared to take a more active role in the current life of the campus is considered an important factor in the contemporary campus political system. Presidents, provosts, and boards of trustees need to create deliberative bodies for all segments of the college community, delegating authority and power where appropriate and then resolving conflicts through small, representative cabinets that advise the whole institution and whose word decides most issues.

Faculty in particular have felt quite strongly that the campus has excluded them from university-wide decision-making. The work on the curriculum may go some distance to correct this view, but it will not change until faculty believe they are consulted on issues of overall direction and the allocation of resources. This observation leads me to the most important lesson of the politics of the curriculum of the 1980s for the 1990s and beyond.

The discussion of undergraduate curriculum or the reform of a professional school such as teacher education or medical training brings all of the members of the institution into a discussion about its heart and soul. If all of those with a stake in the outcome believe the "system" listens – even when their pet proposal does not gain institutional support – then a community evolves. The single most important contributor to quality in the educational experience is the belief that everyone is participating in a community that they have voluntarily joined.

The best American institutions, in the eyes of both faculty and students, according to the Carnegie Foundation surveys, are the selective liberal arts colleges.[20] In these institutions all members of the collegium believe they are important contributors to a community where they are respected and where the quality of life is high. The only other component of American higher education which has a similar self-image and probable reality is the handful of elite, private research institutions such as the Ivy League, Chicago, and Stanford.

Insofar as a governance structure seriously considering academic matters can build such a community, it can actually contribute to the quality of American higher education. Such a strategy is far more likely to improve the quality of American higher education than assessment, testing, and management by objectives.

This essay has been about the politics of curriculum and not the substance of the debate, but before concluding I wish to comment briefly on the substance, because it directly reinforces the importance of community to improving the quality of American colleges and universities. The three poles of the debate about undergraduate curriculum have been to do away with requirements, to impose a substantial core curriculum, or to restore a more rigorous Chinese menu. The last has won most arguments.

I believe the recreation of a modern version of the core curriculum offers the best hope of creating the academic community which cares enough to improve the quality of teaching and learning. I myself am a graduate of the core curriculum at Columbia that has served that institution well. It is highly unlikely that many institutions today can, through their consultative processes, create core curricula on such a scale. The decentralized power system with its mutual veto through consultation makes agreement about an extensive core almost impossible. But it is not too optimistic to believe that all campuses can agree on a minimal core – a handful of courses that all students take and many faculty teach so that there is a common language of debate. One cannot match in any other way the contribution of some common texts and many common questions to a community of scholars. The process of negotiating agreement for a minimalist core itself can create trust, the all-too-rare basis of real community.

To agree on core skills instead of core courses is to begin the construction of common though often competing goals. The real act of community building is to commit to a pattern of courses that require both students and faculty to share effort and make choices of priority among the skills and substantive areas. The community building through agreement about a minimal core of common courses can build school and departmental communities as well. Communities of research emerge without borders; communities of teaching and learning emerge only when we set new organizational and curricular borders and actively seek agreement from a majority of campus citizens acting in the interest of the community.

Regardless of what we do self-consciously, significant changes loom on the horizon of learning. In addition to the turnover of personnel with the turn of the century, we are already in the midst of the infiltration of new technologies that students and faculty will bring to the curriculum in a manner that could occasion profound change. Networks of microcomputers make possible patterns of study, interaction and research that can greatly improve learning. University standard time may become quite compressed insofar as networks of knowledge deliver participants from the need to resolve schedule conflicts as they make available original data and research on a real time basis.

The social revolution driven by technological forces will not occur by majority vote; it will occur by mass connection. Political action will likely confirm these changes, but they will have already become a reality. The knowledge revolution – and the access of individuals directly to networks of knowledge is the revolution of the inexpensive microcomputer and optical laser media and communications – will change the power relationships of the players of the academic games. Brilliant lecturers will lose to superb seminar leaders and insightful computer conferencing chairs. Research librarians and microcomputer hackers will be teaching traditional faculty. The norm will continue to be "publish or perish," but publication may be to be stored in a prestigious computer bulletin-board or to be listed as a central participant in a select computer conference.

No matter how extensively networked we all become, electronic connections will never guarantee either community or quality, though they can contribute to both. All curriculum change depends upon academic politics, which is unlikely to change unless there is as much campus political action as there is national educational talk. All academic change both begins and ends with writing and talking – what John Austin called "performative utterances," words that actually change things. Our task is to understand the realities of academic politics in an institution that is engaged in technological evolution on a new scale through market forces. Only then will talk and reports be about academics but not academic.

From *Higher Education in American Society* (revised edition), edited by Philip G. Altbach and Robert O. Berdahl (Buffalo, NY: Prometheus Books, 1987). Copyright 1987 by Philip G. Altbach and Robert O. Berdahl.

References

1. The following commentary on the modern history of the college curriculum has been informed by but should not be blamed on Frederick Rudolph, *Curriculum* (San Francisco: Jossey-Bass, 1977) *passim,* and Clifton Conrad, Ed., *ASHE Reader on Academic Programs in Colleges and Universities* (Lexington: Ginn Press, 1985), *passim.*
2. Daniel Bell, *Reforming General Education* (New York: Columbia, 1964).
3. United States Department of Education, *A Nation at Risk: The Imperative for Educational Reform* (Washington, D.C.: National Commission on Excellence in Education, April, 1983).
4. *To Reclaim a Legacy,* (Washington, D.C.: National Endowment for the Humanities, 1984). (ERIC Document Reproductions Service ED-247 7880).
5. Study Group on the Conditions of Excellence in American Higher Education (Washington D.C.: National Institute of Education, 1984). Southern Methodist University, Dallas, Texas, March 12, 1986: 19.
6. Frederick Rudolph, *Integrity in the Undergraduate Curriculum* (Denver: Educational Commission of the States, 1986).
7. Paper presented to the faculty seminar on "Ideas of the University," Southern Methodist University, Dallas, Texas, March 12, 1986: 19.
8. *Transforming the State Role in Undergraduate Education* (Denver: Education Commission of the States, 1986).
9. *Time for Results: the Governors' 1991 Report on Education* (Washington, D.C.: National Governors Association, 1986).
10. Ernest Boyer, *College* (New York: Harper and Row, 1987).
11. Ernest Boyer, *High School* (New York: Harper and Row, 1983).
12. For a comparison with other reports, see Janet R. Johnson and Laurence R. Marcus, *Blue Ribbon Commissions and Higher Education: Changing Academe from the Outside.* Washington, D.C.: ASHE-ERIC, 1986.
13. *AAUP Policy Documents* (The Redbook). Washington, D.C.: AAUP, 1984.
14. Clark Kerr, *The Uses of the University* (New York: Harper and Row, 1980): Introduction.
15. As a consultant to the Carnegie Foundation, I reviewed all of the survey data and also all of the 29 case studies prepared as background for the book. These data reinforce each other and proved the power of research that combines quantitative survey data with case studies, in this instance written by journalists who spent at least two weeks on the campuses about which they reported.

My review of these data has persuaded me of the general wisdom of the analysis and recommendations by Ernest Boyer in *College*, but my impression of the case study data suggests that the general quality of undergraduate education for the majority of students in American colleges is worse than one might conclude by Boyer's evenhanded reporting, since about twenty-five of the twenty-nine reports described harassed and/or disinterested faculty, teaching passive and unprepared students. Yet the best ranks with the most excellent in the world.

16. The evidence for this report emerged from a consulting mission when I visited the university.

17. The evidence for this report is drawn from conversations with the president and other staff as well as review of documents submitted to me by the college.

18. Kerr, *The Uses of the University*.

19. Howard Bowen and Jack Shuster, *The American Professor* (New York: Oxford University Press, 1986).

20. Boyer, *College*, and my review of both case and survey data.

This summary was abstracted from a panel discussion of library directors and from the discussion which followed.

From the papers and exhibits of the symposium it is clear that the library community anticipates the impact of a range of new information technologies and is prepared to adopt them. In the mid-60's an international machine-readable format was developed by the Library of Congress that could standardize the transfer of bibliographic information among libraries around the world. During the 1970's large bibliographic utilities with vast computer facilities were created in order to accommodate the need for libraries to store, retrieve, exchange and process information about their holdings or materials being acquired. Currently these cooperative systems host more than 10,000 terminals in libraries and information centers around North America.

Originally these systems were used to share the costs of cataloging and classifying the millions of items acquired by libraries each year. Organized into electronic card catalogs, these computer files were then used to support interlibrary lending of materials to supplement local holdings. The immediate acceptance of the online databases pioneered by the National Library of Medicine, which is still the largest vendor of databases in North America, was directly related to the existence of a substantial number of libraries with terminals already being used to process bibliographic information. Although commercial vendors of databases had the enormous task of creating networks of users who were knowledgeable about online retrieval of information in law firms and corporate offices, existing library networks found a new justification for the purchase of terminals. Libraries also had another advantage since the content of many early non-numeric databases was composed of references to materials already held in libraries. Demands that exceed the capabilities of libraries and the number of students and scholars who find alternatives to using academic libraries represent new opportunities for expansion and development. The decline of funding for higher education in general, and for libraries specifically, limits the capacity to meet the challenge posed by these new opportunities. Yet the need to finance rapidly escalating costs for journal subscriptions and other materials while investing in software and hardware that will allow more direct use by library clientele grows inexorably.

At MIT, where the library is open 24 hours a day, simply requesting more money from university administrations will never be a successful strategy.

...increasingly administrations are becoming more concerned about effectiveness and utilization of resources so when one asks for more money, the question is "what are you doing with what you've got?" – Jay Lucker

Money may be less of a problem than the need to change the way librarians operate. For Lucker the key elements in this process are cooperation, innovation, reallocation and transition. Established ways for libraries to cooperate date back to the early 1900's, when the first code governing the conduct of interlibrary lending was promulgated by the American Library Association. Prior to the development of computerized library networks there were cooperative microfilm libraries, microfilm projects, cooperative local and regional delivery systems as well as coordinated acquisition plans to reduce duplication of scarce and/or expensive materials. Innovation and reallocation go hand in hand for, if libraries are to find effective ways to handle increased demands on their services and to reach out to those who are not taking advantage of existing services, some creative new techniques will need to be employed. For example, making libraries accessible from dormitories, offices and homes via computer terminals requires hardware and software for which incremental funding is not available in current library budgets. Reallocation of funds within library budgets offers limited prospects while the politics of obtaining a substantial reallocation of institutional resources seems beyond the grasp of most library directors.

According to Ed Holley, there can be no reasonable effort by libraries to improve current practices or even to maintain the status quo without access to increased funding. The demands of reform agenda for higher education will inject some realism into the budgetary thinking related to libraries.

Those who believe that the current budgets of colleges or universities can somehow magically be reallocated to provide the technology, the sophisticated personnel and the new data bases and electronic interconnections are surely living in a dream world. – Edward G. Holley

The history of the modern library movement in North America is one of leading by example. How libraries address the reform agenda of education will be influenced less by an emphasis on technical and technological advances than by a focus on how libraries can help create a new environment so that "students can learn, researchers can advance knowledge, and we can live in a humane society." (Holley)

Librarians want to be involved and want to involve libraries more in the educational process. The literature of the field is full of experiments and model programs aimed at developing effective and appropriate roles for libraries and librarians as more effective participants in the educational process. Getting students and scholars to see librarians and libraries as sources of assistance and training in mobilizing information resources to support teaching and learning has not yet occurred.

> We've been doing pilot programs now for fifteen or twenty years and we haven't yet cracked the basic understanding that this needs to be part of what education is. – Sharon Hogan

New roles for libraries and librarians again beg the question of where the increased resources to support library program innovation will be obtained. Matheson cited the example of some health sciences libraries that are now mounting subsets of the MEDLINE database on local campus equipment and making them available without incurring the telecommunications charges for online access. The impact at Johns Hopkins has been over two hundred new MEDLINE database users each month plus increasing numbers of repeat users. The investment in an expanded capability to meet the immediate needs and interests of biomedical library users resulted in an immediate response.

> ...if libraries are going to change their role and become more involved in the educational process one of the barriers that is going to have to be broken down is the cost barrier to accessing information. People just won't learn about it from where they are now if they have to pay close to $100 to connect. – Nina Matheson

Identifying new roles and finding the funds to finance their implementation poses a classic dilemma for the U.S. library community. On the one hand there is the prominent example of the National Library of Medicine, which redefined biomedical information for students, researchers, librarians and health science practitioners by developing its computerized bibliography of medical literature which was made accessible through several databases distributed primarily through a network of health sciences libraries that provide the literature as well. Building the regional medical library system required a major infusion of funds.

One of the many important things the National Library of Medicine did was to engage its constituency in defining the vision of the system that was to serve them. – Nina Matheson

Congressman Owens noted that from the perspective of a legislator it is not clear what percentage of the institutional budget the library should command. The 5% used by Boyer in his study is not realized by many institutions. Yet, if major assistance is to be forthcoming from some source, what is the order of magnitude of funding necessary? How can we move to define the limits of the new institutional role for libraries in ways that are both flexible and feasible?

We're living in an environment in which the need for our services is changing, and we're ambivalent as to whether we're looking for more things to put on the railroad or whether we're in the transportation business. – Richard Rowe

We have an information crisis in this country in terms of access to information, the importance of information and restrictions on information. – Jay Lucker

The arguments seem compelling that future developments in the library field will require both innovation and substantial new funding. Stimulating innovation assumes a research base and a constant supply of bright and eager new practitioners. The excitement of participating in the redefinition of the mission of the academic library could possibly attract several more generations of students, researchers and practitioners to the field. But financing the process is likely to require more than an idea of what libraries can contribute to educational excellence.

G*rowing out of small group* discussion sessions, one of the key issues to emerge was the lack of a close working relationship among faculty and librarians that is required to respond effectively to the reform agenda of higher education.

There was clear consensus that faculty involvement is necessary to encourage student use of libraries and other information resources and that librarians need to involve faculty in the planning and design of library services. The unstated assumption was that such activities do not occur routinely.

Suggestions were raised that faculty have a different perspective on the teaching and learning process into which librarians do not easily fit.

> The faculty want different things from libraries than librarians want faculty to get from libraries.

Recognition was given also to a tendency for librarians to close ranks into a professional insularity that can be in confiict with their role as a linking agent.

> Having been characterized for the first time in my life as a *non-librarian*, it appears that the library mission is frequently distinct from the institutional mission.

Rather than attempt to assign blame for the tension the panel looked outward.

> To simply document that the antipathy and distance exist, I think, is problematic for us at this point. One of the things we might do is work on a model of shared responsibility among administrators, faculty and librarians around some key issues to try to break up the logjam. – Judith Eaton

While the question of how to get faculty and librarians a shared vision of how to respond to the reform agenda was a key issue, the more central questions addressed by the panel were how to empower students to be more effective learners and what role the library can and should play in this effort.

"To what extent do students leaving the institution, we hope with diploma...take with them the kinds of skills and attitudes regarding libraries and data sources that will serve them in the future? – E.K. Fretwell

Many students never use a library, and some others use it simply as a study hall or social gathering place. Implications of the nature of study habits learned prior to college suggest the need for involvement with school and community librarians and their programs. The need for higher education to pay closer attention to the non-traditional learner complicates this issue further. Many institutions in higher education, especially urban institutions and two-year colleges, enroll students with a wide diversity of learning abilities. These were among the first to redefine their libraries as teaching/learning centers in the 1960's. With limited information resources and a wide variation of student abilities, research-based efforts to strengthen student learning skills were centered in the learning resources center [library]. Experimentation with many new educational technologies paved the way for the extensive use of technology today to make available a vast array of information resources to students.

The library can be fully effective only if the students know how to find, evaluate and use information stored there. – Anne Mathews

Unfortunately, many institutions believe they cannot afford to underwrite the costs of access to databases and other resources and pass on some, if not all, of the costs to the student. Other institutions, as a matter of policy, have done more to underwrite completely the costs of certain database services resulting in spectacular growth in use. Either policy has consequences for institutions in terms of budget and educational policies. The gap between the "information rich" and "information poor" will inevitably widen if ways cannot be found to encourage use of new technologies with demonstrable learning benefits rather than discouraging use through the imposition of fees.

Co-opting institutional policy to treat issues related to libraries and librarians more visibly and more effectively excited the interest of the panel.

One of the things the library can do to take advantage of the politics of the institution and make itself more visible...is to deliberately design its mission statement to carry our parts of the mission statement of the institution. – Rebecca Kellogg

Focusing less on defining what the library is and more on developing its role in the teaching and learning process was one of the suggestions. Another was to influence accrediting bodies to adopt an evaluation standard based on learning skills acquired through use of the library.

Any enlargement of the responsibility of the library to be more actively involved with the faculty and to mount new programs that will help to achieve the educational goals of the institution implies libraries' having greater access to university resources or external funding. The only course of action recommended to acquire more resources was to gain the support of the CEO and the Trustees of the institution.

Indirectly, the way to the institutional agenda may lie in gaining a position on the national agenda for public policy on education. National recognition of the potential role of libraries at all levels of education, that would prominently include provision for student mastery of learning skills which would empower them to achieve higher levels of performance, would be a significant achievement.

In the discussion of courses of action to improve the use of libraries in support of educational excellence, there were no definitive conclusions reached and few precise explanations of how libraries can become more active forces for reform of higher education. What did emerge was a broader realization of untapped resources in the library that can be exploited by each institution.

I cannot leave here today not being more concerned about libraries than I was. – Judith Eaton

Academic Libraries and the American Resurgence

by Frank Newman

I would like to ask your help on something! It seems to me that there has been considerable discussion about the value of interactive processes. Most of the discussion went on in a non-interactive mode which is in keeping with the academic traditions. Would it be all right with you if this is an interactive mode, that is to say, that there will be discussion as I go through this, are you all in agreement? I need a little more vigorous response. Are you all in agreement?

I always feel compelled to remind people about the urgency of following the academic format. That is, when you really want to make a speech and not ask a question you disguise it as a question; add a little inflection toward the end of "don't you think?" or something like that.

This is, I would argue, obviously a period of high rates of change for libraries – high rates of change compared to their long history. Five or six times in the discussion it has been pointed out that this is a period roughly comparable to the introduction of the printed book and that the change is likely to be as significant. Ernest Boyer mentioned last night that the difference is that there wasn't a field of professionals then. I was kind of struck by that. I always thought there was a field. I had this vision of little monks with those tiny little paint brushes and so on. They must have felt that it was a field at that time. I can see the same kind of discussion: "We monks haven't been included in these discussion groups. How many gold letters can you put on a page?"

It's clear that there is an enormous amount of progress going on in the evolution of the library. Since I had the opportunity to meet with Pat Battin, Jim Haas and Dick Couper when we were writing *American Resurgence*, to talk about what's happening to libraries and, in particular, research libraries, one can see an inescapable array of things happening that are going to change profoundly how we deal, not just with libraries, but with the whole question of higher education. Still, in the best of traditions, I would like to argue that there are some things that we need to adjust, and I would like to put those questions in front of you. Before coming to those specific questions, there were three pointed concerns that I was fascinated with that came up over and over again in the notes of the different groups and in papers I had. The three concerns I noted were:

  1. Librarians should be more involved in campus discussions. That issue came up in the last discussion we had and the previous discussions –

equal voice, shared responsibility, involvement in the curriculum and involvement in teacher education; the profession needs to be redefined.

2. Libraries should be seen as part of the central mission of the institution. They ought to be seen as part of the whole mission of scholarship and learning. The campus reports, the campus mission statements and reports on higher education fail to acknowledge libraries and librarians adequately.

3. The issues being discussed here are ones that call for policy attention based on the substance of the issues at a national level, and there ought to be considerably more national policy attention to the subject.

Why is it that these three things have been such a strong theme here? More importantly, I suppose, is what can be done to bring about the kind of change addressed? Why do they keep recurring? First is the question about whether these are only efforts to bash the library. The point was made earlier that to some degree we spend so much of our time talking about the flaws and faults in the library that we fail to recognize adequately its virtues and the number of things going on. I would argue that to an important degree the American mode of progress involves a substantial degree of criticism. There is a widespread feeling in the higher education community that criticism is the kiss of death – that the worst thing that could happen to any part of our academic community is that it be criticized.

All of the objective information is on the other side of that argument. I have been having a sort of friendly disagreement with Martin Trow, from the University of California at Berkeley, over this point. Marty's argument is that criticism, particularly from within the academy, is extremely damaging and that people outside the academy seize upon it and say, "See, I told you that you people were rotten to the core. Therefore, we're cutting off all your funding for your library." The evidence goes the other way. The evidence is that in this country criticism precedes funding. I don't know what it is about the American mode, but I give you just a most recent example of this. The whole process of reform of the elementary and secondary community involved criticism which has been far, far more severe than it has ever been of higher education, even in the same mode. This criticism sprang from the idea that schools were a failure and the prime reason they were a failure was that teachers were incompetent, uninterested and poorly trained people who basically should not be in the schools. The result has been the largest growth in real dollar incomes in the states which were the most critical that we have had in a very long period of time. Now I'm not recommending that we go out and wear sack clothes and ashes; I'm saying that I think it's perfectly legitimate for us to address criticism.

Ask yourself how you feel about the legal system of this country and what you get is intense anger. Why? It is not because we don't think the legal system could be improved with a little effort. It is because lawyers have told us that the legal system is the way it is because God has ordained it and it cannot be touched. Think of the medical system and we say that costs are mounting too rapidly. The doctors do not say that God has ordained the system; they say God ordained the doctors, and our reaction again is one of intense anger. If we were to ask this group here to vote on the continuation of the medical profession's privileges it would be hard to get any kind of a vote of support. So the answer is not that we should be sensitive. The answer is that we should be concerned that the criticism be adequate and that it should bring forth a sense of positive response to the real problems.

We can look at the strategy to deal with the three points that I made. I would say that the strategy is one that was referred to earlier, but I would like to make it more explicit. The answer is action. I discovered a rule when I first went to Stanford about being involved in a university like Stanford. In the academic world no one can bestow upon you the right to have authority over a given area. It's not like the corporation or the military. In a corporation, if you were to pursue the public relations activity of General Motors and you were not in the public relations department there would be a voice very quickly in your ear, "Smathers, knock it off. That's been assigned to the public relations department." There is no such voice in the academic community; and, if you don't believe me, think of the people on your campus who are engaged in the public relations process, largely by themselves and often very successfully. No one ever says to them, "Look Smathers, I know that grant you got in microbiology is a terrific thing, but it's probably not going to revolutionize the world the way you think. Besides that, we've already got a guy over here who works in PR." The opposite is also true. No one can deny a determined person coming forward.

I would argue that the answer to these questions is to remember that presidents, faculties, deans, legislators and governors pay attention when someone proposes to solve *their* problems. They do not pay attention much when you propose to solve *your* problems. The need for libraries then can be couched in terms of solving the major problems on the desks of the president, faculty or others, and you will find a ready willingness to listen. On the contrary, I think almost no one interacts on the principle that interaction is good. There are a lot of principles we have like that about things being good. It's like that old cartoon, you remember, that came out of the 1930's *New Yorker*. I used to see it in those collections they had of old cartoons with the kid who is sitting there with the progressive parents, and the progressive parents are terribly concerned that he is not eating what's on his plate. He is looking at them saying, "I still say it's spinach and to hell with it" and that's how faculty, when you tell them it's time for interaction, respond.

I now want to go on to the three central questions, but I was hoping that someone would raise a point of disagreement with what I am suggesting in answer to the previous three points. I am going to pause here in the hope that someone will raise a penetrating comment disguised as a question. Now you must agree or disagree. I should tell you, if you don't disagree, I'm going to tell the world that you've all agreed with me and publish this somewhere. You're in agreement. OK, I move on to my three questions:

Question one: If libraries are to be considered the center of teaching in the information age, what is it that libraries should teach? We had a good deal of discussion about the importance of the library as teacher but not much about what it should be teaching. And I have a set of suggestions I want to put in front of you.

One thing they should be teaching is the ability to search for information and ideas. We've talked a lot about libraries as the centers of information. We haven't talked about the whole question of ideas; and ideas obviously are as important as information, perhaps more important. The library needs to think about its dual role as a center of these things and its role in teaching how to encourage students to search and think. The reason I put it in these terms is that largely what passes as higher education today is a tendency on our part as teachers to tell students what it is they should know and give them a carefully selected set of sources. We go further than that by telling them what those sources say and how they should be interpreted.

There are some grievous flaws in this process, not the least of which is that it becomes hard to function once one leaves the womb. Seldom on your job do you get the same kind of treatment. Now you do at this meeting because the organizers have been very nice and have sent us materials. They did not tell us what we should think, but it did certainly help us in pulling the information together. The fact is that the crucial element of scholarship is digging, finding, and being excited by that. That is absent in the very large percentage of all courses on the college campus. We tried a little while ago to estimate what percentage of college courses actually engaged students in a serious effort to hunt and dig and find and think about sources in a non-routine mode. I can't give you a good answer, but I know the number wasn't twenty percent of the courses in the college and university setting. So, if the library is to play a new role, certainly one of the things it ought to be is a center for teaching people how to do that exciting task.

Q: Do you want a challenge to that?

A: Absolutely!

Q: You tend to draw a distinction between ideas and information. I have not gathered from this process that libraries would be central to the teaching process. Rather, they would be central resources.

A: I would agree with that although I took the phrase right out of one of the prompt sheets.

Q: If the libraries are to be centers for teaching, what are they teaching?

A: I think a better way of putting it is that the library must assist the faculty in this process.

Q: The library should help the faculty solve their problems?

A: Yes, I would agree, and the other side is that the faculty doesn't even know it has that problem, and that makes this problem very difficult. But it certainly means that we have to think about the mode with which that interaction takes place so that it can be successful. How do we raise the issue in a way that the whole idea of active learning becomes an integral part of the campus discussion?

Q: How do you empower the students to be active, lifelong learners? We don't do that by teaching per se in either the library or the classroom.

A: I agree with that too. The fact is that students don't learn because we teach them, they learn because they become excited learners and get involved in the process. We can assist them in that process, but students don't learn because we teach. Students are not vessels; and we, who after a great deal of work have filled ourselves with knowledge, cannot pour a measured amount of our knowledge into students and fill them up. Of course, this is a very incorrect model.

Q: You said that, "If libraries are to teach, what do they teach?" Perhaps that means that librarians should be more involved on the campus. Perhaps your first question should be, "How do libraries and librarians help students to learn?"

A: Yes, but I really want to stay with the point of what libraries teach for just a moment. How can libraries assist in teaching? In addition, how do they assist students in searching for information and ideas. And there are a couple of other questions. One is how to think about knowledge, data, ideas, and information. One of the major problems for us at the moment is that we think poorly about these matters.

That's even true of the printed word. We convinced students to have a very high reverence for the printed word; if it is in a book, it's right. Yet we know that, since many of us write books, that's foolish. I had a marvelous experience when I was at Stanford. I was asked to teach a graduate seminar in the education school. They were talking about a book that I had written; I gave them an interpretation, and they disagreed with it. They kept arguing and finally I said, "I wrote that"; and they said, "It says right here..." Now that's a failure to think about information rationally. This is a particular danger in the electronic media. We have to think about it. For example, all information is not in an electronic database. If the limits become what is in the database, we've arbitrarily destroyed our access to true education. The same is true of electronic data. It comes out of a computer, it looks correct, but it may not be correct at all. There are limits, uncertainties about data and information and ideas that need to be brought across.

My other point is that we have to teach people how to think about and integrate ideas. There's a whole new opportunity to do this as a result of what we're talking about here. One of the constant failures that shows up in all measures of student learning – even at the very best institutions – is how little students learn to integrate what happens on campus into different types of ideas.

Q: First of all, libraries don't do anything. Only the people inside do things, and librarians don't teach. I think that if they want to be teachers, they should join the faculty. Librarians teach students to seek, find and evaluate ideas and information. Libraries should be repositories of knowledge and information.

A: I am in strong disagreement with almost everything you've said. Let me give you an example.

Librarians aren't teachers. Everybody on campus is a teacher, and unless you understand that you don't, if you'll pardon me saying so, understand a campus. I remember a marvelous session we once had with Warren Wilson. A member of the team was a chief electrician, and he was the hit of the show. What he said was, "My job is to teach people how to think about responsibility and to think about how to accomplish tasks." He was wonderful! I think everybody, the dean of students, the police officer, everybody is a teacher. And not

only that, they're role models. And all of you have students – particularly
people in the library have students – who work for you. Every bit of evidence
shows that those students learn more working for you than they ever do in
their courses. So I agree that each one of us has responsibilities. I think students can even learn from the president. Of course, your job is to catalog,
and, of course, a faculty member's job is to do research, and, of course, the
dean of students' job is to worry about discipline. But the campus is a teaching center because everybody there has taken on the peculiar responsibility
of mentoring young people through this particular stage in their lives. I appreciate your point, but I really do disagree with it. I really do believe the
library, the athletic department, the symphony orchestra have important
teaching roles. If they don't, I have to question why we spend so much money
on them.

Q: It would be fatuous to argue that a whole range of experiences occurs on
campuses. It would be equally fatuous to argue that all of these experiences should occur on campus. The risk of this line of discussion is that
it is a caricature of education.

A: First, I don't argue that all learning ought to be accredited. I made no
argument at all that, if the electrician does well in teaching students responsibility, students should get course credit. I don't make that argument at all. Nor do I argue that the electrician or the librarian should be
equated to the faculty. I think those are different roles. I don't see any of
those as addressing the central issue which is, "How do we view ourselves
on the campus?" Let me give you a few examples of this.

I once had a very disturbing experience which gave me a strong sense of
this. I was at a faculty senate meeting, and I was sitting with the student
officers. After the meeting the student president turned to me and said, "You
know, one of the most damaging things we ever do is bring students to these
meetings." "Why?" I asked. He said, "Because students believe faculty are
inherently interested in students, and it's only when you come to a faculty
senate meeting that you realize that's not true." Now I believe faculty overall,
are inherently interested in students. What the faculty in those circumstances
forget is the message they give in the classroom about integrity. The messages
they send students are extremely important. That is true for all of us.

What I am arguing is not that they are the same roles. I argue that in the
library and in every role on the campus we are teachers. We are teachers and
role models, whether we like it or not. When they watch us operate students
learn whether we believe in integrity and scholarliness; are we interested or

excited about information, and, do we care about other human beings? All those things are grist for the learning process. If that's true, then we ought to ask ourselves one of the questions that has come up here over and over again. How, then, does the library become a greater center of learning?

Q: Should the question be, "Can the library be a center of learning?"

A: I agree with that; in fact, I thought that's what I was saying. What I am saying is that all learning does not go on in the classroom, because the faculty member stands up in front. In fact, the best thing the faculty member can do is to empower the student to become a learner. It takes skill to empower a student to become a learner, to excite the student about wanting to learn, to draw on sources of information, knowledge and ideas. That is exactly what a good librarian does. In that sense they have a common function. That's not to say that the way they function is the same, because they are set in different points. But the ideal librarian, as far as students go, is someone who does all those things and engages students in a learning process.

Now I want to continue, as it is clear we agree on this point. I'd like now to ask: Are students being enabled to think about learning in the sense we are talking about? Do we know how to encourage students to think carefully about data and information and ideas, and question whether they are right or wrong? How do we balance it? Do we get them to think about the integration of ideas and methodologies and so on? How do we know if students are gaining these skills? If active learning is indeed the key – and I would argue that it is – as opposed to passive learning, can a library be a means of moving higher education more from passive to active? Really, that's the art of education. Can the library become the vehicle for helping faculty members move from what is currently an overly passive mode to an increasingly active mode? Can we encourage the students to become more like scholars, evaluators of information rather than simply absorbers? To do this I would argue that libraries have an added responsibility. They have to help students see that information exists outside the library: there are experts, reports, community resources, a host of additional resources. Otherwise students develop a dependence on libraries rather than a dependence on their own skill of finding, understanding and evaluating knowledge and ideas.

Well, if all of this is true, if the point that you all are making is true, what does all this imply for what should happen in the classroom with the faculty member? I would argue that one of the things it implies is that we need to find a way to encourage the classroom to be more of a centerpoint of the learning process that begins to share students' excitement about learning with other parts of the campus. We are a long way from that, and some thought needs to be done in that regard. But before that can happen I would argue we need to address why so few students use the library now. In a number of cases we do know something about this. I think we do know more, and I'll bet we could gain a lot of information from digging out the studies on different campuses. Yet knowing how much students use the library is only part of the problem. We must ask the question, "How can we make the library an exciting place for nontraditional as well as traditional students?" Those are questions that I think need to be raised about learning and students' relationships with libraries.

Before I go to the next point, I think it's time for people to make some comments.

Q: I am not comfortable with your use of the word library to suggest a piece of real estate. What I think we are talking about is how to use and take advantage of information systems or services. The information function goes well beyond the real estate.

A: I would normally agree strongly with that, but I think that your point is getting more irrelevant every day, because we're moving away from the idea of the library as a fixed piece of real estate and increasingly into the library as something else.

Q: The question is not, "Did you use the library today?" It ought to be, "Did you access information today?"

A: I was looking for a way to agree, because I felt that I had been a little arbitrary earlier, but I disagree. I think your point is right that students access information on a very broad basis, and there are some sources that aren't under the university's control, such as television, conversations with colleagues, hundreds of other things. It may well be that students talked to other students who went to the library and gained a good deal out of that conversation.

There certainly is a lot of evidence of that. What troubles me I guess, is that there is also a body of information showing that a significant percentage of students on every campus – less on the smaller liberal arts campuses, far more on the larger state institutions – for whom the capturing of minds and intellectual processes simply does not take place. Whatever sources of information they have are relatively limited. That doesn't mean that they don't pass courses. They pass their courses and go on about their work.

The phenomenon has also been noted by all serious scholars of the high school. You may remember Ted Sizer's argument in his study of the high school in which he says, "For a very significant group of students, they learn a lot more on the job than they do in the classroom and they know it." My point is not that under the best of circumstances lots of things aren't happening. I would argue that however accurate the statistics are, they point to a problem. The problem is that we want every student to become a learner and that only a fraction of the students are becoming learners. It may be that only ten percent or even 20 percent of students really do interact and appear in the figures Ernie Boyer was quoting and that other study shows. But even that's not good enough. I would argue that we have a problem in front of us, but I don't want to argue that we are failures. I don't think libraries, academic libraries in this country are failures. That's not my point. My point is that these are indicators of issues about which we should be concerned, because we are concerned fundamentally about the problem of excellence of American education. If it turns out that there are only ten percent of students that we could seriously influence to become more effective learners, that would be enough. That would be a very large number of people, but obviously, we can reach many more students; the number is probably closer to 50 percent. But whether it's ten percent or 50 percent, it is an issue that we should be deeply concerned about.

If information is exploding in volume and changing in form, how must the library change? Obviously the library is changing and changing in fairly drastic ways, but still it seems to be an important question.

A certain part of us deals with the question of timeliness. One of the groups had a very interesting sequence. They said that, as you move toward timeliness you move away from the book to the monograph series, to the periodical, to the newsletter, to the online bulletin board or database. Obviously, as always happens, technology comes in bits and parts. It doesn't come evenly. It rarely ever comes in cosmic revolutions. It tends to come a piece at a time. Change occurs, and we are clearly moving in the direction in our society in which the tail end of the list is becoming more and more important. In more and more disciplines the lack of timeliness makes books, monographs, periodicals less important. That's clearly true at the moment in many of the sciences, but it's also happening in a variety of other disciplines as well. But this is likely, if anything, to speed up, because we've now been through a very important revolution. We've been through the revolution of word processing, and the reason I say that is so important is that word processing was the thing that finally drove faculty members across the campus into the use of the

computer. It used to be a bifurcated faculty until all of a sudden word processing came along. And now faculty members who used to hate computers now
are deeply engaged in the search for more computing capacity. As a conse-
quence we are going to move rapidly into more wide-spread computing.

We were talking earlier about artificial intelligence as a field in which
one can't possibly keep up with by reading the journals, because the journals
are so out-of-date compared to what's going on in the newsletters, the bulletin boards and the other things that people in the field deal with. We talked
about this when we wrote the *American Resurgence* and met with a group of
people to discuss some of these issues. One of these people was Ken Wilson;
of course, deep into that issue his comment was that the journal article he
now writes is simply a memorandum to the record. It has nothing to do with
his daily life or scholarship. It couldn't possibly help him, because it's a year-
and-a-half behind and a year-and-a-half is everything. In fact, he uses a computer bulletin board. This, I think, is spreading across the different disciplines. Economics is moving in that direction; it's not quite there yet, but it's
moving rapidly in that direction.

This change has a terrific effect. I'll give you one personal example. I am
married to a faculty member, an anthropologist. On our anniversary late this
fall, I proposed that, since we had lost a pair of earrings in some lost luggage,
and since these were the kind of things I had given her early in our marriage,
we might go out shopping and find a new pair of pearl earrings. Thinking
that would bring a very warm response, I noticed a kind of puzzled look on
her face. I said, "Well, is that a bad thing?" "Oh no, no that would be wonderful," she said, "Could it be something else?" I said, "It's your anniversary; you
name it. I thought pearl earrings were kind of romantic." And she said, "Well
yes, but how would you feel about an external disc drive?" One sees in that a
transformation, and I'm sure you know how it turned out – we acquired an
external disc drive and a pair of pearl earrings.

There are a lot of unexpected side effects of this technology, and we're
beginning to see some of them. A question was asked about the major effects
of the development of the transistor. Shockley responded without batting an
eyelash, "The development of Radio Cairo." He said that the development of
the transistor radio allowed people in remote villages to have radios. At that
time the only radio broadcast in the Middle East was Radio Cairo. Radio
Cairo began to push transistor radios around the Arab world and push Radio
Cairo, and pretty soon the Pan Arab movement was begun. That's an unexpected by-product of technology. That happens to us all the time.

What does this mean in terms of what we're doing? Well, it means that we've got to think about this, I think, in a somewhat different way than we've been thinking – although I do think we've made enormous progress on this front. It's complicated by an added point, which is that the range of materials we're dealing with keeps proliferating, as you know all too well. It's not just government reports; it's state government reports, commission reports, campus reports, association materials. This seems to bring us to a point where we have to recognize that certain things are beginning to break down.

The advance of electronic information has led to at least three flaws in the system as it is evolving. One is that there is no quality control on much of the material. That is to say that a database, unlike a periodical, doesn't have built-in controls. The periodical is reviewed by a peer review system. If the article has flaws, if the data is inaccurate, or if something new has been done, all of that gets incorporated in the quality control process. If there is a database and you tie into it, there is not a way of knowing that it's been through the same kind of quality control. Second, there are no traces, and lots of things can happen. Artificial intelligence is a great example. Unless somebody sits down and takes the time to write a journal article which appears eighteen months later, we don't even have the traces that we used to have. Third, there are no cross-disciplinary means of access. There are on certain things, but large numbers of things are going on that the people in the field know all about that might be valuable to somebody else; and it's always possible, if there is a journal article, to find it through the indices. If I'm interested in something that has to do with artificial intelligence and it's all going on on bulletin boards, I don't have any way of knowing it's going on – let alone find anything. So we are losing, unless we think through this more carefully. We have, and we're losing at least some of the very valuable assets, that, if I use the term widely to encompass publishing, that the library process has done for the academic world. I think we need to think about that.

Now I want to add just one more point and then go to your criticisms and suggestions. We talked a lot about the flood of information. The trouble with access to too much information is its equivalent: access to no information. When I was at Stanford we argued about this. One of the librarians pointed out to me that in the days when there used to be four or five file drawers of books on Shakespeare, one could simply go over to the file drawers and read through them. But when you get eight file drawers on Shakespeare you can't leaf through them any more. Too much information can mean that you don't have any sort of information if you can't find it. How, then, can we devise ways to sort this growing flood?

We used to sort by some of the things we were talking about. Periodicals sorted information for us. They told us what was worthwhile. Now those modes are being overwhelmed, and we need to think about what it is out there that's valuable and how to sort by considering two things: the relevance and the quality. I would argue that all this calls for some major changes in the library. Changes are occurring, but they may not be occurring in the right directions. We've got to think about how we link all this together, how information gets sorted, how we provide quality controls, how we provide cross-disciplinary access. Someone suggested earlier that faculty are handling this overload by teaching themselves and by teaching their students to focus on an ever-narrowing set of disciplinary information in order to cope. In the long run that leads to losses, while in the short run it may lead to gains. At any rate, I would argue that it's time for a conscious effort at defining the future rather than evolving toward the future. Some things we don't have yet (and I realize that there's been a lot of discussion about this and what's happening in the library community and in other communities) is a plan that is adequate to the seriousness of the problem.

My last point is that if library costs are increasing, if the costs of printing are increasing and the costs of electronics are decreasing, if technology is evolving rampantly, if sharing has been steadily growing (which it is and which I think is very much to the libraries' credit) how, long can the traditional view of the library remain in place? Do we have to accelerate the questions of policy and organization to shift to a new view because the problems and burdens overwhelm the current view of the library? We have talked about that, and I will simply remind you here that we talked much about the question of fees as related to this area. How long, for example, is it logical to continue the current fee-based principle? Some libraries you mentioned earlier have already made some adjustments. The general rules still remain that current print material is acquired and given to those who need it free; electronic material is charged. How long can that rationally stay in a world in which electronics is becoming increasingly important?

I'd like to close by concluding that there is in front of us a considerable opportunity. Newspapers present a whole list of changes facing the world. There were two changes that I would argue that should be added to the list. First, is that the world has become increasingly competitive, not just economically (though that is certainly true) but monetarily and ideologically. It is a much more competitive world, and I think it is important we learn to be and remain skilled competitors. How do we deal with an increasingly competitive world where information is so important, and we're sitting on all that information? It's like being a banker in the rise of the city-state period, when you sat on all that money and people wanted access to it. Right now we are sitting on information, and people want access to it. Second, is that it's an increasingly complex world. We deal with things such as in-vitro fertilization and acid rain – terribly complex issues. How can you be a citizen unless you are much better informed?

Both of these questions require a couple of things: 1) the capacity to have access to information and 2) the capacity to find information and evaluate it, and to understand and integrate ideas. As a result, it seems to me, we could find entirely new opportunities for the library in the midst of this change.

The issue is not whether we are loyal to the concept of the library. What matters is not whether we can prove fidelity to the book, it's whether we can find ways to translate this discussion into hard action that will transform the library into a different mode within our society. The push is already on. The ice floe is clearly moving. The question is: can we, as a group of people, add to that and make it go not only faster but in a more thoughtful and intelligent way?

Thank you.

Discussion Outcomes and Action Recommendations

Background

The following is a synthesis of the action recommendations from the small discussion groups, the discussion of Tuesday morning and Frank Newman's summary comments. Emphasis was placed on capturing all of the recommendations brought forward through the small group as well as the total group discussions. As individuals and organizations commit further thought to ways of implementing the various suggestions, some will certainly emerge as being of more value and/or of being more practical for implementation than others. It is clear that the Association of College and Research Libraries has a pivotal leadership role to play in the accomplishment of many of the recommendations.

There was consensus – perhaps partially due to Ernie Boyer's presentation – that current concerns for better undergraduate education require better incorporation of libraries in the learning process. Other areas for desirable expanded use of libraries to meet institutional goals also emerged but not as strongly as in the area of undergraduate education.

What also emerged was a very strong picture of what will need to occur for libraries to be more active partners in the educational arenas both at the campus and the national levels. Inherent in these discussions was the belief that in many areas libraries did seem to have a unique contribution to make that was desirable toward the accomplishment of institutional goals. Bottomline to make those contributions possible was the need for academic leadership (including in some cases librarians themselves) to break through old images of libraries to a point where they can objectively explore with librarians the ways in which librarians can support their campus' goals, what needs to transpire to use fully and effectively library resources (including personnel) to achieve those goals, and finally how to align library objectives and support accordingly.

Libraries Facilitating Learning

If a library is to contribute to undergraduate education it must align its goals and objectives with the mission of the institution and must also inform and influence the institution's mission statement.

Reports on undergraduate education identify the need for more active learning whereby students become self-directed independent learners who are prepared for lifelong learning. To accomplish this, students need to be-

come information literate whereby they:
- understand the process and systems for acquiring current and retrospective information, *e.g.*, systems and services for information identification and delivery;
- are able to evaluate the effectiveness and reliability of various information channels and sources, including libraries, for various kinds of needs;
- master certain basic skills in acquiring and storing their own information, *e.g.*, database skills, spreadsheet skills, word and information processing skills, books, journals, and report literature;
- are articulate and responsible citizens in considering current and future public policy issues relating to information, *e.g.*, copyright, privacy, privatization of government information, and those issues yet to emerge.

To make possible the above, information gathering and evaluation skills need to be mastered at the undergraduate level, and learning opportunities should be integrated within the existing departments, analogous to "writing across the curriculum," rather than as stand-alone bibliographic instruction programs. Administrators, faculty and librarians should be engaged in creative new partnerships which transmit to students the value and reward of research in their lives as students and beyond. Information literacy should be a demonstrable outcome of undergraduate education.

Action Items
1. The American Association of University Professors and the Association of College and Research Libraries will sponsor a second symposium to bring together faculty and librarian leadership to further define the role of libraries in quality undergraduate education.
2. Information literacy assessment will be featured along with assessment of communications, critical thinking and computer literacy skills at the American Association of Higher Education conference on assessment in Denver in June 1988.
3. The Council on Postsecondary Accreditation should take a leadership role, working with the regional accrediting agencies, in developing more consistent accreditation standards in relation to libraries and their use. More emphasis should be placed on how libraries are contributing to the instructional, research, and service goals of their institutions.

Relating Campus Technologies to Libraries and Academic Programs
The convergence of information technology and information content is influencing (limiting) the degree to which planning for technology can be divorced from planning for instruction. Needed is broad-based research on who uses information resources in the academic setting and who does not use the available information resources and why.

Library expertise in database design, development and operations should be used to serve the information management needs of the institution overall, with librarians being in the forefront of the development of information studies and having a leading role in assessing, selecting, and managing information resources for the academic community. To ensure effective use of all campus information resources, librarians need to work as part of information access teams which include personnel from academic computing and telecommunication areas.

The governance of technology on campuses is a crucial issue. A high degree of centralization of decision-making will favor one purpose over another. Over-centralization will make coordination and compatibility difficult. The library must be one of the principal players, if not the principal player, in that game.

Faculty, students and administrators need encouragement and assistance in learning how to use the new information technologies to solve problems and to extend knowledge. Any fee system for access to new technology should be so designed as not to deter access and should be equitable.

Action Items
1. The Association of Governing Boards of Universities and Colleges will develop an information access checklist for trustees and publish it in one of its publications.
2. Based on the above, institutions should conduct periodic "information audits" to determine resources being allocated to instruction, research, and service; the access of students and faculty to these technologies; and their interrelations and the impact upon students. Where mechanisms do not already exist teams of the campus information experts should be established for ongoing planning and evaluation of issues and activities related to information access and use.

Libraries Facilitating Campus Linkages to Local and National Communities
Serious national information policy issues need to be addressed including

issues of:
- access
- ownership
- funding
- competence needed for access

Two Symposium participants are involved in a tripartite – U.S., U.K., and Canada – commission charged to develop a national agenda on information policy which will report this summer, and further U.S. efforts should build on outcomes from the commission. The conveners of the Symposium should take the initiative to ensure that a committee be established to develop a policy for endorsement by all relevant groups.

Leadership from academic libraries is needed to facilitate the online networking of scholars developing in the various disciplines for exchange of research information and particularly in providing access into such systems for scholars outside of the particular disciplines. Opportunities and options related to online publishing and other full text databases need to be developed and communicated to other higher education agencies for joint action.

If funded to do so, academic libraries have the capacity to offer important services to the business, public service, and health institutions of their communities through activities such as interlibrary loan, lending privileges, and online access. Moreover, academic libraries have an important role to play, in conjunction with school and public libraries:
- promoting the culture of the book
- stimulating adult literacy
- improving the literacy skills of K-12 students

Action Items
1. The Columbia University School of Library Service will monitor outcomes of the tripartite commission and initiate efforts to convene a follow-up U.S. group as appropriate.
2. As major information policy issues are identified, appropriate library representatives should gain forums within existing higher education organizations such as the American Council on Education and the Association of American Universities in which to exchange information, build consensus and support.
3. The President of the American Library Association will establish a presidential committee to address the role libraries can play in promoting information literacy for their communities. The effort will consider the

impact such efforts can have on problems of literacy and student retention as well as on promoting the culture of the book. It will also address
implications for teacher education. (Authorization for committee given
June 1987.)

Means to Promote More Effective Use of Libraries
While there was concern for the need to "fundamentally and expansively"
redefine the role of libraries and librarians in terms of teaching and research,
there seemed to be broader consensus that more action and dialogue with
higher education communities was needed before redefinition could occur
in any meaningful way. Staff and faculty development efforts are needed to
ensure the building of a sense of shared vision and responsibility among librarians, faculty and other professionals on campuses. Of particular concern
is the need to include libraries in discussions related to teacher education. To
facilitate progress in this area, the following should be pursued:
  – Libraries should be featured on state and national higher education
    programs and on the programs of other professional organizations, as
    well as being featured in the literature of these groups.

Action Items
  1. AAUP/ACRL national symposium.
  2. Summer 1987 issue of *Change* will feature academic libraries.
  3. AGB article.
  4. Publication of Symposium papers and outcomes by Scarecrow Press.
  5. Information literacy assessment workshop at June 1987 AAHE confer-
     ence on assessment.
  6. The Association of College and Research Libraries should provide na-
     tional leadership in providing clearer understanding of librarians' new
     and differentiated roles in the use of information for instruction and re-
     search. Besides reports, articles and case studies, it should develop and
     disseminate a TV documentary and/or other multimedia productions
     which explain the librarian's role in the Information Society.
  7. ACRL should consider the establishment of a Council of Presidents to act
     in an advisory capacity to its Executive Committee to ensure ongoing
     dialogue on policy issues and priority setting.
  – Campus administrative and faculty leadership and librarians should en-
    gage in more meaningful and ongoing dialogue. Opportunities avail-
    able through the co-opting of state or system agendas as a means of

influencing library use should be aggressively pursued by librarians.

Campus administrators should involve librarians in leadership roles on campus-wide committees and should incorporate libraries into institutional planning documents rather than treating them as separate entities. Mechanisms for effectively linking all campus information providers should be established. Academic leadership must also be committed to recruit effective leadership for their libraries and ensure salaries and benefits which are commensurate with responsibilities and performance.

Librarians should sponsor meetings, reports, papers and other activities that will create awareness of library and information issues, ensuring that campus personnel can relate these efforts to campus priorities and opportunities. Faculty should be directly involved in discussions of library and information issues, ensuring that faculty and key academic administrators are familiar with library resources and systems.

Action Items
No action items are suggested here, since these issues are campus specific. However, the information access checklist being developed by the Association of Governing Boards of Universities and Colleges could be a useful tool for campus administration in initiating such dialogues.

Research and Dissemination Needs
In many areas there is a need to better understand the difference that better use of libraries and increasing information literacy could make in areas of national concern such as student retention, creating independent self-directed learners and better teacher education. More research is needed in a number of areas, and the Association of College and Research Libraries should be encouraged through the efforts of the members of its Executive Board who attended the Symposium to encourage appropriate research. The following is a list of suggested ACRL actions related to the need for more research and research dissemination:

Work with other professional organizations to better define the type of research and data collection which is needed and change procedures accordingly.

Develop a research agenda that addresses the role of libraries in support of national higher education imperatives as well as on career patterns for library and information professionals.

Push for full funding of Title II-B of the Higher Education Act, and seek other funding sources to be made available for research.

Work with Major Owens to draft a bill proposing:
- prototype pilot programs of information management and transfer systems to be located in academic institutions throughout the U.S.
- prototype pilot program of the undergraduate educational process with special emphasis on the role of information in their academic affairs.

Patricia M. Battin, Columbia University Libraries
Ernest Benjamin, American Association of University Professors
Ernest L. Boyer, Carnegie Foundation for the Advancement of Teaching
Susan Brandenhoff, American Library Association
Donna S. Breed, California State University
Patricia Senn Breivik, Auraria Library
Rowland Brown, Online Computer Library Center
Jo Ann Carr, University of Wisconsin-Madison
Margaret E. Chisholm, University of Washington
Eileen D. Cooke, American Library Association
Charles Cullen, Newberry Library
Phyllis Dain, Columbia University
Richard De Gennaro, The New York Public Library
Jean DeLauche, Alverno College
Marva LaVerne DeLoach, Illinois State University
Gertrude Eaton, University of Maryland
Judith Eaton, Community College of Philadelphia
Shirley T. Echelman, Association of Research Libraries
Donald P. Ely, Syracuse University
Emily Epstein, Columbia University
Joanne R. Euster, Rutgers-The State University of New Jersey
Joan Fiscella, University of Houston
A. Thomas Flaherty, The Connecticut State University
E. K. Fretwell, The University of North Carolina at Charlotte
Robert L. Gale, Association of Governing Boards of Universities and Colleges
Elizabeth D. Gee, The Alexandria Institute
E. Gordon Gee, University of Colorado
E. Burr Gibson, Marts & Lundy, Inc.
Robert F. Goldberger, Columbia University
Warren Haas, Council on Library Resources
Edward Hays, Savannah State College
James A. Hefner, Jackson State University
David M. Henington, Houston Public Library
Sharon Anne Hogan, Louisiana State University
Edward G. Holley, University of North Carolina at Chapel Hill
Carole Huxley, New York State Education Department
Rebecca Kellogg, University of Arizona
Lisa Kinney, Wyoming State Senator

Augusta S. Kappner, Borough of Manhattan Community College
Dan Lacy, Publishing Consultant
Carol L. Learmont, Columbia University
Jay K. Lucker, Massachusetts Institute of Technology
Heidi L. Mahoney, New York State Education Department
Nina W. Matheson, The Johns Hopkins University
Anne Mathews, Office of Educational Research & Development,
    U.S. Department of Education
R. Kathleen Molz, Columbia University
Michael J. Mooney, Columbia University
Herbert C. Morton, Office of Scholarly Communication
Milo Nelson, *Wilson Library Bulletin*
Paula Newberg, Markle Foundation
Frank Newman, Education Commission of the States
Major R. Owens, U.S. House of Representatives
Hannelore B. Rader, University of Wisconsin-Parkside
Sister Joel Read, Alverno College
Lelia G. Rhodes, Jackson State University
Joan Ringel, Colorado Association of Commerce & Industry
Carlton Rochell, New York University
Sharon J. Rogers, George Washington University
Kenyon Rosenberg, Aide to Congressman Brown
Robert M. Rosenzweig, Association of American Universities
Richard Rowe, The Faxon Company
JoAn Segal, American Library Association
Ward Shaw, Colorado Alliance of Research Libraries
Hoke L. Smith, Towson State University
Irving J. Spitzberg, Jr., Association of American Colleges
George Sullivan, Academy for Educational Development
F. William Summers, Florida State University
William P. Timlake, The Research Libraries Group, Incorporated
Barbara Uehling, American Council on Education
Louis Vagianos, The Institute for Research on Public Policy
Colette Wagner, City University of New York
Clyde C. Walton, University of Colorado
Robert Wedgeworth, Columbia University
Kenneth M. Zeichner, University of Wisconsin-Madison

Academic libraries. *See also* Black academic libraries; Community college
    libraries; Education libraries
  accreditation standards, 188
  as archival depositories, 112, 116
  and the business community, 129-135
  changes in, through automation, 47
  and community relations, policy on, 189-190
  competitors of, 111
  computer use in, 137-144
  criticism of, 174-175
  and education, role in, 25-26, 33-34, 81, 82, 102, 112, 144, 191-192
  exhibits and programs in, 17-19, 23-24
  funding of, 20, 75, 111, 130-131, 135, 165-168, 171, 174
  and income earning potential, 143
  as information processor, 112, 116-117
  instructions in use of. *See* Library instruction programs
  and local library interaction, 22
  merging with computer center, 117
  and the non-traditional student, 43-55, 170
  parallels between university and, 109-110
  position of, in academic program, 75
  role in leadership development, 14, 15, 23-24
  and scholar's research, 93-102
  sponsoring editorial projects, 79-80
  as study place, 8, 15
  as teaching/learning centers, 9-10, 78, 81, 170, 171, 174, 176-180, 187
  technological innovation in, 137-144
  usage of, 7-8, 25, 31, 169-170, 181
Academic Libraries: The Changing Knowledge Centers of Colleges and Universities
    (B. B. Moran), 97
Accreditation standards, and libraries, 188
Active *vs.* passive learning, 180
Adult education, and universities, 108
Afro-American collections, 66, 80
The Afro-American Heritage: Viewing the Past from the Mississippi, 67
Alexander, Lamar, 148
Alliance for Excellence: Librarians Respond to A Nation at Risk (Center
    for Libraries and Education Improvement), 100

American Association of Higher Education, 188
American Association of University Presidents, 154
American Association of University Professors, 188
American Council of Learned Societies. Office of Scholarly
    Communication and Technology, 93
American Library Association, 166, 190
American Philosophical Society, 79
AMIGOS, 125
Arpanet, 142
Artificial intelligence, 183, 184
Ashby, Eric, 9
Asian-American students, 59, 62
Association of American Colleges, 29, 150
Association of College and Research Libraries, 187, 188, 191, 192
Association of Governing Boards of Universities and Colleges, 192
Association of Public College and University Presidents. Library Financing
    Formula Sub-committee, 128
Atlanta University School of Library and Information Studies, 65
Auraria Library, 134
    business community relations, 129-130
Austin, John, 162

Baldwin, James, 64
BCR (Bibliographic Center for Research), 125
Beer, Stafford, 105-106, 115
Bell, Terrell, 148, 149
Bennett, William, 149, 151
Beveridge, W. I. B., 97-99
Bibliographic Center for Research (BCR), 125
"Bibliographic Competencies for Education Students" (Association of
    College and Research Libraries), 86
Bibliographic instruction programs. *See* Library instruction programs
Biggs, Mary, 102
Black academic libraries, 62-63. *See also* H. T. Sampson Library
    instruction programs of, 63-68
Black colleges
    and curriculum reform, 157
    and open admissions policy, 62

Black colleges (continued)
vocationalization in, 60
Black public schools, 59-60
Black students
deficiencies in education of, 58-59, 61
and financial assistance, 60
motivation of, 61
Upward Bound Program for, 67
Bok, Derek, 147, 151
Book budgets
in colleges, 20
in public schools, 6
Book holdings, for research, 93
Boorstin, Daniel, 8
Boyer, Ernest L., 33, 173, 182, 187
Bradley, Ed, 65
Brandeis University, 78
Branscomb, Harvey, 8
Branscomb, Lewis S., 84
Breivik, Patricia Senn, 50, 53, 64, 128
Brooklyn College, 50, 53
Bulletin boards. *See* Electronic bulletin boards
Business community
and academic institutions, 129, 135
and academic libraries, 129-135
and in-house training programs, 108
Business Partner Program, 129-130

CAI/CAL programs, 116
California State University at Long Beach, 37
A Call for Change in Teacher Education (National Commission for Excellence in Teacher Education), 84
Card catalogs. *See* Online card catalogs; Teaching catalog
Carl H. Pforzheimer Library, 79
CARL System, 141-143
Carnegie Forum on Education and the Economy. Task Force on Teaching as a Profession, 86

Carnegie Foundation for the Advancement of Teaching, 3, 5-6, 8, 9, 14-24, 25, 33, 39, 152, 154

Cataloging, using electronic networks, 139

CD-ROM's effect on academic libraries, 111

Chicago University, 145

City University of New York, and the non-traditional student, 44

CLASS (Cooperative Library Agency for Systems and Services), 125

Cleveland, Harland, 134

Clinton, Bill, 148

Closed system, of universities, 115-116, 118

Collection development
 of Afro-American materials, 66, 80
 in foreign languages, 53
 for non-traditional students, 54
 for research, 93

College graduates, as leaders in society, 14

College libraries. *See* Academic libraries

College students. *See also* Asian-American students; Black students; Non-traditional college students
 academic quality of, 3-4, 35
 and information skills, 33
 and lecture recall, 26
 and library usage, 7-8, 25, 31, 169-170, 181
 and self-sufficient learning, 9-10, 187-188

College teachers
 appointment, 160
 and computer usage, 182-183
 and library relations, 36-37, 171, 177
 and library usage, 31-32
 role in curriculum decision-making, 147, 150, 154, 160
 and student use of libraries, 8, 169
 teaching methods, 8, 28-33

College: The Undergraduate Experience in America (Carnegie Foundation for the Advancement of Teaching), 5-6, 8, 9, 14-24, 25, 33, 39, 152, 154, 158

Colleges and universities. *See also* Black colleges; Community colleges
 and closed system, 115-116, 118
 and community relations, 22-23, 67
 competition from corporate training programs, 108

Colleges and universities (continued)
    information technology, effects on, 107-120
    parallels between libraries and, 109-110
    and public school relations, 7
    relations with business community, 108, 129, 135
Colorado, funding for higher education, 127-129
Colorado Commission on Higher Education, 128-129
Colorado Information Resource Center, 134
Columbia University, 145
    and the "Information Amphitheater", 22
    School of Library Service, 190
Community
    and college relations, 22-23, 67
    and library relations, 80
    policy on, 189-190
Community college libraries
    in Colorado, 128
    instruction programs of, 48
    and the non-traditional student, 46, 52
Community colleges
    and curriculum reform, 157
    and the non-traditional student, 48
Computer center, merging with library, 117
Computer conferencing, 162
Computers
    in library exhibits, 17
    library use of, 137-144
        for internal systems, 138-140
    and scholars' use of, 96
    and teachers' use of, 182-183
Conferences, sponsored by libraries, 78
Continuing education, and H. T. Sampson Library, 69
Cooperative Library Agency for Systems and Services (CLASS), 125
Coordination center. *See* Teaching/learning center, libraries as
Copyright issues, 111, 114, 141
Corporations, and in-house training programs, 108
Council on Postsecondary Accreditation, 188
Council on Library Resources, 65

Creative destruction, 108
Criticism, library, precedes funding, 174
Cross, K. Patricia, 44
Cross-disciplinary access, in online databases, 184, 185
Curriculum, college
    campus autonomy in, 151, 153
    changes in, slow moving, 154
    Chinese menus in, 145, 147, 150, 151, 155-156, 161
    history of, 145-147
    and information management learning, 36
    library as center of, 55
    reform in, and politics of, 145-162
    role of departments in, 151, 154, 158, 159

Damerall, Reginald G., 84
Dougherty, Richard M., 52
DuBois, W. E. B., 60

Earlham College, 37, 38, 48, 89
Eaton, Judith, 169, 171
Economic development, and academic libraries role in, 129-135
Economic Information Network index, 134
Editorial projects, sponsored by libraries, 79-80
Education, quality of, 25-26
Education libraries, 85, 86, 88, 90
Education reform, 148
    librarian's role in, 9, 58, 67, 167, 173-174, 187, 191-192
    recommendations for, 187-193
    reports of, 57-58
Educational philosophy, 32-33, 36
*Education's Smoking Gun: How Teachers Colleges Have Destroyed Education in
        America* (R. G. Damerall), 84
Electronic bulletin boards, 162, 183
Electronic networking, 100, 106-120, 139
    effect on curriculum, 162
    effect on universities, 116
    and centralization vs. decentralization, 113
    changing universities' closed system, 115-116

Electronic networking (continued)
    and information policies on, 190
    and intellectual property, 114
    of OCLC, 114
    origins of, 165-166
    participants in, 121-126
    pricing of, 113
    shift from applications to real time links, 113-114
    staff shortages in, 114
    standardization, 115
    transborder data flows, 114, 123
Electronic screens, in library exhibits, 18
English as a second language program, library materials for, 53
EPIE Profiles, 89
Eurich, Neil, 135
Evans, Austin, 102
Exhibits
    in academic libraries, 17-19, 23-24
    at Newberry Library, 76-77
Expert systems, 116

Faculty. *See* College teachers
Fax, Elton, 65
Fees, access, online databases. *See* Online databases: access cost
Formal and informal teachers, 10-11
Fretwell, E. K., 170
Full text databases, 116
    effect on university libraries, 111
Fund for the Improvement of Post-Secondary Education (FIPSE), 65
Funding
    of academic libraries, 20, 75, 111, 165-168, 171, 174
    through services to businesses, 130-131, 135
    of higher education, 165
    in Colorado, 127-129

Gardner, David, 148
General education
    and information literacy, 15
    vs. specialized education, 9, 23-24

Gowdy, Mississippi, 67
Great books of western civilization, 149, 151, 155
Great Books Reading Forum, 64-65

H. T. Sampson Library, 58
    Afro-American collection, 66
    and library instruction program, 63-69
    outreach program at, 67
Harvard University, 145, 147
Harvey, William H., 37
High school libraries, 6
    book budget of, 6
    training in use of, 7
High school students, 182
    and reading, 6
High Schools (Carnegie Foundation for the Advancement of Teaching),
        5,152
Higher education
    effects of technology on, 107-109
    funding for, 165
        in Colorado, 127-129
    and information literacy, 27
    reform in, 145-162
Higher Education and the American Resurgence (F. Newman), 67, 96-97, 173,
        183
Hogan, Sharon, 167
Holley, Edward G., 166-167
Holmes Group, 84, 86, 88, 151
Humanities, 75, 82, 149

Idaho State University, 87
Independent libraries, 75, 82
Informal and formal teachers, 10-11
Information
    access to, 186
    evaluation of, 134, 186
        by students, 180
"Information Amphitheatre", 19, 22-23

Information audits, 189
Information center, through merger, 117
Information flood, 63-64, 184
    and quality control, 185
Information literacy, 26-27, 35
    definition, 15, 27
    library's role in, 15
    for lifelong, 9-10, 35-37, 101, 170, 187-188
    of minority students, 70
    training for, 16, 36
Information management, and libraries role, 189
Information policy, 189-190
Information society, 115
Information technology
    effect on society, 105-106
    effect on universities, 106-120
    guidelines for use of, 189
    impact on libraries, 165-168
    influence of, on education, 119
    and research, 99
In-house corporate training programs, 108
Integrity in the Undergraduate Curriculum (F. Rudolf), 150
Interlibrary loans, 166
    and scholars, 94, 96
    through electronic networks, 139
Involvement in Learning (National Institute of Education), 97, 100-101,
    149-150, 158
"Involvement in Learning: Realizing the
    Potential of the American Library to American
    Higher Education" (J. Segal), 100-101

Jackson State University, 65, 67-68
    See also H. T. Sampson Library
Jones, Virginia Lacy, 65
Josey, E. J., 54, 63, 66

Kellogg, Rebecca, 171
Kennedy, James R., 89

Kerr, Clark, 154, 159
Knaub, Richard, 38

Lacey, Paul A., 30
LaGuardia Community College (CUNY), 52
Language skills, 4
  education in, 4-6
  related to library usage, 6
Lanning, John, 38
Leadership, education for, 13-24
Learning, 177, 182. *See also* Teaching/learning center, libraries as
  from campus' role models, 179
  in classroom *vs.* other resources, 7
  library based, 32, 169
  for lifelong, 187-188
  passive *vs.* active, 180
  role of librarians in, 100-101
  self-directed, 187-188
  the teaching of, 26
  through various styles, 35
Learning experience, 35, 37
Learning resource center. *See* Teaching/Learning center, libraries as
Lecture recall, 26
Lectures, at Newberry Library, 78, 81
Liberal arts colleges, 160-161
Liberal arts education, 9, 24, 33
  Dubois on blacks' education in, 60
  for information literacy, 15-16
Librarians
  as consultants, 133-134
  and education, role in, 9, 58, 67, 167, 173-174, 187, 191-192
  faculty status of, 15
  leadership, lack of, 75
  and scholar's research, 93-102
  as scholars, 80, 82
  as student mentor, 10
  and teacher relationship, 36-37, 169, 171, 177
  view of, 102

Libraries. *See also* Academic libraries; High school libraries;
      Independent libraries; Public libraries
   changes in, 173, 182, 185
   and community relationship, 80
   and education, role of, 76
   emphasis on acquisitions and preservation, 8
   funding of, 76
"Libraries and a Learning Society" (Center for Libraries and
      Education Improvement), 100
Library instruction programs, 15, 100
   classroom based, 49, 52, 53, 65
   credit for, 49-51
   at H. T. Sampson Library, 63-68
   for information literacy, 70
   for minority students, 64
   for non-traditional students, 47-54
Library of Congress, 165
Library programs, and invited speakers, 19
Library Research Guide to Education (J. R. Kennedy), 89
Library Skills for Teachers (T. Mech), 89
Literacy, adult, 4
Literature courses, required, 16
Little, Arthur D. (firm), 108
Local area networks, 113
Location, of university, and adult education, 108
Logsdon, Richard H., 102
Lucker, Jay, 166, 168

Malcolm X, 43, 45, 55
Massachusetts Historical Society, 79
Massachusetts Institute of Technology library, 165
Matheson, Nina, 167, 168
Mathews, Anne, 170
Mech, Terrence, 89
Media specialist, 89
MEDLINE database, 167
Microfiche, and scholars use of, 93
Microforms and readers, in library exhibits, 18

Miksa, Francis, 98
Minority students, 58-59, 64, 70
Mississippi, black public schools in, 60
Morgan, Barbara B., 97
Mortimer, Kenneth, 149

Naisbitt, J., 69
A Nation at Risk: The Imperative for Educational Reform
    (National Commission on Excellence in Education), 57, 58, 83-85,
    97, 148-149, 150-151, 152
National Assessment for Educational Progress, 4
National College of Education in Evanston, Illinois, 86
National Commission for Excellence in Teacher Education, 83-85, 97
National Endowment for the Humanities, 65
National Institute of Education, 97, 100
National Library of Medicine, 165, 167
NELINET (New England Library Information Network), 125
Networking, electronic. *See* Electronic networking
New England Library Information Network (NELINET), 125
New students. *See* Non-traditional college students
New York Public Library, 79
Newberry Library, 76-81
Newman, Frank, 25, 96-97, 187
Non-bibliographic information, on online databases, 143
Non-print materials, 20-21
Non-traditional college students, 43-55
    characteristics of, 44-45
    collection development for, 54
    fear of the library, 45-46, 48, 49
    library instruction programs for, 47-54
    and library usage, 170
    women as, 44
Northwestern University, 79

OCLC. *See* Online Computer Library Center, Inc.
Off campus usage, of online services, 141
Office of Scholarly Communication and Technology (American Council
    of Learned Societies), 93

Online card catalogs, 140-141. *See also* CARL System
    increased access points in, 142-143
    interconnection of, 142
    off campus usage, 141
    use of, 94
Online Computer Library Center, Inc. (OCLC), 114, 121-123
Online databases. *See also* Full text data bases
    access cost , 138, 167, 170, 185, 189
    information value of, 178
    and interconnection, 142
    lack of access across disciplines, 184, 185
    lack of quality control in, 184
    library use of, 138
    of non-bibliographic information, 143
    and scholars, 94
    training in use of, 189
       at H. T. Sampson Library, 68
Online Public Access Catalogs. *See* Online card catalogs
Open admissions policy, 62
Open admissions students. *See* Non-traditional college students
Open Systems Interconnection Reference Model (OSI), 142
Oral communication, 6
Oregon, and the *Economic Information Network* Index, 134
Outreach programs
    of H. T. Sampson Library, 67
    and libraries, 80

Paperback books *vs.* reserve books, 29
Passive *vs.* active learning, 180
Perez, Miriam Ben, 85, 89
Philosophy of education, 32-33, 36
Problem solving, and information base for, 27, 32-33
Professors. *See* College teachers
Project LAMP, 65
Public education, reform in, 148-151
Public libraries
    college graduate use of, 36
    and information literacy programs, 190-191
    and technological innovation, 144

Public schools. *See also* Black public schools
   and college relations, 7
   quality of education in, 148-149, 151
Publishing, around special library collections, 79-80

Reading, 4
   aloud to children, 6
   educational benefits of, 8
Reallocation of funds, 166
Recommendations, for reform in undergraduate education, 187-193
Reference interviews, 134
   as instruction in library usage, 48
   and student's library skills, 47
Remedial students. *See* Non-traditional college students
Research
   broker, 102
   classification of, 97-98
   emphasis on, by teachers, 30
   and libraries role in, 93-102
Research and development
   competitive pressure on universities, 116
   cooperative efforts, 108
Research libraries, 81. *See also* Academic libraries
Research Libraries Information Network (RLIN), 123-124
Research parks, 129
Research skills. *See* Information literacy; Library instruction programs
Reserve books, 8, 28-29
Reserves-lecture-textbook teaching method, 8, 28-33
Resource sharing. *See* Electronic networking
RLIN (Research Libraries Information Network), 123-124
Role models, on campuses, 179
Rosovsky, Henry, 147
Rothstein, Pauline, 89
Rowe, Richard, 168
Rudolph, Frederick, 150

Schauer, Paul D., 128

Scholars
   awareness of library services, 95
   and library usage, 96
   and online catalogs, 94
   and research needs, 93, 97
School Libraries Working Group of the International Federation of Library
      Associations and Institutions, 87
Schumpeter, Joseph, 108
Science and technology students, and library instruction programs, 64-66
Segal, JoAn, 100
Seminars, at Newberry Library, 77-78, 82
Senate (university), in curriculum reform, 154-159
Shores, Louis, 65
"Situation Room", 17-19, 23
Sizer, Ted, 182
SOLINET (Southeastern Library Network), 125-126
"Sources of Tension and Conflict Between Librarians" (M. Biggs), 102
Southeastern Library Network (SOLINET), 125-126
Specialized education
   and information literacy, 15
   vs. general education, 9, 23-24
Suarez, C. C., 64
Sundquist, James, 101-102
System interconnection, of online databases, 142

Teacher education programs, 83-90
   emphasis on education methods, 83
   graduate degrees from, 86
   library role in, 84, 191
   reform in, 83-85, 88, 148, 151
   testing of, 149, 151
Teachers. *See also* College teachers
   autonomy of, 85, 88-89, 90
   as curriculum developers, 85
   formal and informal, 10-11
   improvements in working life of, 83
   influence of, 11
   information access skills, 86-90
   instructional materials of, 88-89

Teaching. *See also* Teaching/learning center, libraries as
   technological aids in, 11
Teaching Catalog, 54
Teaching/learning center, libraries as, 9-10, 78, 81, 170, 171, 174,
      176-180, 187
   in community colleges, 48
Teaching library
   H. T. Sampson Library as, 63, 64, 67
Teaching methods
   improved by greater use of books, 30
   library based, 37-39
   reserves-lecture-textbook method, 8, 28-33
   of searching and thinking, 176-178
   for various learning styles, 35
Teaching with Books: A Study of College Libraries (Harvey Branscomb), 30
Technological change, effect on curriculum, 162
Technological innovation, of libraries, 137-144
Technology. *See also* Information technology
   effect on society, 183
   use of, as aid to teaching, 11
Television, as informal teacher, 10-11
Time for Results: the Governors' 1991 Report on Education, 152
To Reclaim a Legacy (National Endowment for the Humanities), 149
Tomorrow's Teachers: A Report of the Holmes Group, 84
Transborder data flows, 114, 123
Transforming the State Role in Undergraduate Education
      (Education Commission of the States), 152
Trow, Martin, 150, 174

UNESCO Pilot Project on School Library Development, 89
Universities. *See* Colleges and universities
University libraries. *See* Academic libraries
University of California, 141
   Division of Library Automation's system, 142
University of Colorado, 26, 38
University of Illinois, 94, 141
University of Nebraska, 78
University of Nebraska at Lincoln, 29

University of Toronto Library Automation System (UTLAS), 124-125
University of Wisconsin at Parkside, 36
University of Wisconsin-Madison, 86
Upward Bound Program, at Jackson State University, 67
U. S. Office of Technology Assessment, 119
UTLAS (University of Toronto Library Automation System), 124-125

Van Horn, Richard, 33
Vocationalism, in black colleges, 60

Walker, Jerry L., 87
Wang Computer Firm, 108
Washington, Booker T., 60
Wayne State University, 37
Wedgeworth, Robert, 64
Western Library Network (WLN), 126
Wilson, Ken, 183
Wilson, Woodrow, 153
WLN (Western Library Network), 126
Women, as non-traditional students, 44
Wonderful Wednesday, 65
Wriston, Henry, 28
Writing competency, 4, 36